North Londoner Matthew Bazell was born in Euston in 1977 and is a lifelong follower of Arsenal. His second team is the mighty Darlington and he also has a soft spot for Millwall. *Theatre of Silence* was originally published in 2008 and was his second title about football. His previous book, *Invasion & Deportation*, was published in 2000.

John Lydon first came to the attention of the world as the singer/songwriter of the Sex Pistols. Brought up in Finsbury Park North London, Lydon has been an Arsenal fan since the 1960s. He has made numerous TV appearances in Britain and America and still tours the world with Public Image Ltd who, like the Pistols, are regarded as one of the most influential bands of all time. His autobiography *Rotten: No Irish, No Blacks, No Dogs* was originally published in 1995. John currently lives in Los Angeles and still follows Arsenal.

Rodd Liddle was born in South London and is a lifelong fan of Millwall. He is a respected and controversial figure in British journalism. He has edited the *Today* programme on BBC Radio 4, presented documentaries on Channel 4, has had a column in *The Guardian* and edited *The Spectator*. He currently has a weekly column in the *Sunday Times*.

THEATRE OF SILENCE

The lost soul of football

Matthew Bazell

THEATRE OF SILENCE

The lost soul of football

Pegasus

PEGASUS PAPERBACK

© Copyright 2011
Matthew Bazell

The right of Matthew Bazell to be identified as author of
this work has been asserted by him in accordance with the
Copyright, Designs and Patents Act 1988.

A CIP catalogue record for this title is
available from the British Library.

ISBN 978 1 903490 57 0

Pegasus is an imprint of
Pegasus Elliot MacKenzie Publishers Ltd.
www.pegasuspublishers.com

First Published in 2008
This edition published 2011

Pegasus
Sheraton House Castle Park
Cambridge CB3 0AX England

Printed & Bound in Great Britain

Author's note

Major gratitude and appreciation to John Lydon, Rambo and Rodd Liddle. I asked them for something and they asked me for nothing, total respect.

I'd also like to say thanks to: Catherine Bazell, Danny Miller, Brendon Smyth, Tim Bazell, Katie Bazell, Ben Bazell, Jamie Mash, Stephen Pickup, Gerry Fagbemi, Dave Hooke, Marc Cohen, Henning Trolsen, Tom and Carol Youlden, Neil Marchant, Mel Prescott, Fanos Charalambous, Petros Petrou, Mick Dean, Tim Howarth, Ant McGinley, Paolo Vignali, Graham Liader, Stefano Galligani, Nils Hanover, Penny Bazell, Richard Bazell, Debbie Bazell, Violet Bazell, Max Lowe, Will Moss, Mike Slicker, Kevin Proctor, Cvetanka Cambell-Smith, Jon Ewart, Grant Jenkins, Andy Walsh, Warren James, Darryl Johanson, Kelvin 'Singer' Meadows, Derek Currie, Stephen Powell, Malcolm Clarke, Ivor Heller, Steve Bunce, Reggie and Elaine Calcagni, Kirsty Fuller, Lee Fernandes, Tim Watson, Kim Frost, Nikki Kenny, Mark and Tina Hannon, Marco Aleni, Luca Pugliese, Neg Dupree, Billy Potter, Gareth Howe, Dave Worthington, Sam Neave, Andrew Evangelou, Markos Evangelou, Mirjana Mihajlevic and Shakirah Mustapha.

I would like to dedicate this book to my grandmother, Margaretta Calcagni, who although greatly missed, is remembered with happiness.

Foreword by Rod Liddle

I first met Matt in the interminable queue for a drink at half time during one of Millwall's witless and desolating home defeats. Against Northampton, maybe, or Brighton. I'd been sitting in my usual seat in the west upper stand, enduring the usual misery, the ball lumped into the seats every fifteen seconds, our forward line as mobile and deft as a bunch of fucking Victorian wardrobes and me, freezing, all the while yearning for a drink. Should I leave my seat two minutes before half-time (or "the interval" as my Chelsea-supporting media friends call it), so that I can be served before full-time? But what if something happens, on the pitch? What if we score? So I sit there and wait until the bitter end, under a ludicrous, hopeless, delusion and finally get my pint of gassy piss just as the players come out for the second half. Nothing happened in that final two minutes. Maybe someone kicked someone else, or took a throw in, but that's about it. Stewards won't let me take the pint back to my seat in case I try to ram the plastic glass into the opposing full-back's eyeball. Can't drink alcohol in your seat, mate. Can't smoke any more. Can't call the ref a blind cunt. Nothing to alleviate the harrowing boredom. It was nil one at half time. Nil one is what it stayed. It's always nil one; nil one is a sort of given, at the Den.

I mention all this stuff, the, uh, downbeat side of watching Millwall so that you can appreciate how bizarre it was to meet Matt. You see, I have to go to Millwall: I've been supporting them for forty years or so and, as the Irishman sung, it's too late to stop now. Millwall are my team and it doesn't really make any difference if they're playing in the Premiership or the Southern Counties Doug and Dinsdale Pirhana Loan Shark League. I don't really have a choice in the issue: it's ingrained. But Matt came up and introduced himself to me as an Arsenal fan, a gooner – and the shock of hearing this, of meeting someone who *didn't have to be there but had chosen to come of his own free will* so disarmed me that I failed to do what Millwall supporters are meant to do when approached in their own ground by an oppo fan, and stab him or something. And as I listened to his story it struck me that I was pretty lucky, all things considered. I had it easy.

There's always someone worse off than you, isn't there?

Matt's story – which I had related to me first while we queued for a drink and later, at subsequent Millwall games where we lost nil-one to someone shit – was basically an explanation as to why he was there. Why he preferred the lumpen dross I have to watch every week to the gilded, bejewelled beauty of his own side, Arsenal. It began with a statement which made me think he was mentally ill: it's more fun at Millwall, he said. Where's the fucking fun, exactly, I wondered, a little mordantly? It's not much fun for me and still less for the players, to judge from the unfamiliarity and caution with which they address the ball. But it transpired that his point was that his team, Arsenal – and indeed the whole fabric of his chosen spectator sport, football – had changed beyond recognition. He had been left behind, somehow. It wasn't simply that he couldn't afford to go very often to the beautiful Emirates Stadium on account of the extortionate ticket prices. Nor simply that once there he would be sitting among people who remained silent throughout the game not because they were in awe of the football but because they went so irregularly – for the same reasons as Matt - that they didn't know the words to any of the songs. For Highbury Library, now read Emirates Morgue. It was something more atavistic and elemental; the remoteness of the players from the fans, for a start. Hired mercenaries possessed of no loyalty except to their careers and their bank balances. Possessed of no connectivity to the local area. Distant from the fans not merely financially, but not even speaking the same language – either metaphorically or indeed literally. (Remember the European Champions League tie between Arsenal and Bayern Munich a few seasons back? I remember cheering for Munich because, in Owen Hargreaves, they had the only British player on the pitch. And even Hargreaves only just sneaks below the bar.....) If you're cheering for Arsenal – or Chelsea, Spurs, Manchester United, Liverpool etc - under those circumstances, what exactly is it that you're cheering *for?* The successful accumulation of money? That your club, either through the dubious benevolence of some strange Russki, or through the sale of replica shirts in Thailand, has made enough money to buy some French speaking bloke from the Cote D'Ivoire, who'll stay and kiss the badge for a couple of seasons until a more propitious offer crops up somewhere else? What's to cheer, if you're an old North Banker, or a Holte Ender, or from the Shed; just a name, an old agglomeration of vowels and consonants. A franchise. Chelsea, Arsenal, Villa, Burger king, Starbucks, Halliburton. Or maybe you're cheering a distant memory, of how it used to be.

Of course, you may find it difficult to get tickets for your club even if you can occasionally afford to do so, because there are a lot of new fans around. These are the people who have swallowed whole the New Football concept; football as a sort of lifestyle choice; yeah, of course, I was at the game on Saturday, won again, think they'll do it this year. The careful and considered acquisition of vicarious success. These new people, converts perhaps from the 1996 European Championship when football, oddly enough, didn't quite come home, do not wish to buy into torment, longeurs and misery. Why should they? Possessing no real attachment to the clubs they now claim to support, they are instead buying the human right to be uplifted by victory every week. And only victory every week will do. Did you see how many people turned up to Chelsea's Champion's League game against Rosenborg following a "mediocre" start to the season (third place! Oh, the ignominy!) and a bruising draw against Blackburn Rovers? Some 25,000, that's all – round about what Notts Forest and Sheffield Wednesday get for games below the Premier League, week in week out. And that's the other point; these new converts to New Football have a commitment to their clubs which is as fragile and tenuous as the surface tension of water, a skin so thin that it will break at the slightest disturbing current. A fairly famous mate of mine in the media decided a few years ago that he "ought" to support a football team and alighted upon – hey, guess what, kids – Chelsea. It was rather like choosing between Conran and Heals for a sofa. I bet he wasn't there for the Rosenborg game. Even a hint at the withdrawal of success and these new fans will melt away into the night. Fair enough, I suppose, that's their choice; I don't hate these people, I don't want them *killed.* But they have wrought an enormous change on the game I love and it has not been for the better.

Chewing gum doesn't lose its flavour no matter how long you have it in your mouth. What happens is your taste buds become bored of the flavour and begin to ignore it, so it tastes of nothing even though really the same sugars are being released by the gum. So it is with winning football games. Begin every season expecting to lose two or three games and soon enough a home victory over Fulham or Wigan is so boring as to become unpalatable. A few seasons back, Millwall were relegated from the Championship in a season as dire and dispiriting as any I can remember in 40 years. Every game brought a new humiliation, another crushing of the soul. Then, one cold night in early winter, we played Norwich City, Darren Huckerby and all, and – quite unjustly – won the game one-nil. I'm not kidding: we were out all night in Bermondsey celebrating, me and my friends - utterly euphoric. If there is anything to be gained vicariously from football it is this sense of a shared ordeal, of a community suffering travails but still being there and, on those wonderful occasions, sharing the delight in an unlikely victory. Can you imagine the New Football converts buying into THAT sentimental rubbish?

Football has been tidied up, its edges smoothed down, its nastinesses outlawed. I suppose in many ways it is a more socially inclusive activity than it once was; women quite like it, these days, and gay people too, at Crystal Palace and Charlton. We see some magnificent football on our televisions – but we also see the empty terraces, and hear the bemused silences. Michel Platini blames the "malign" influence of money for creating a two tier system of haves and have nots. He's right, I suppose, but Matt has made me wonder who really are the "haves" in this equation. Those who still have their clubs, with a fan base rooted in the geographical area, who can afford to attend their matches, whose players earn scarcely more than they do and on occasion show a vestige of commitment – or the others, the ones who win everything.

Chapters

PREFACE

"We believe that an 'international round' of matches [Premier League games being played abroad] will enhance the strength [cash flow] of the Barclays Premier League as a competition [business]; create extra interest [profit] in all twenty Premier League clubs at home and abroad, and allow increased investment in talent development and acquisition facilities as well as our football development and community programs [more money to fund John Terry's wages]."

Premier League chairman Richard Scudamore – 2008

Shortly after the release of the original edition of *Theatre of Silence*, it was revealed that the Premier League were in talks about playing domestic games abroad. The plan was that each team would play one more game a season, taking the number of fixtures from 38 to 39. The prospect of a fixture such as Wigan v Bolton being played in Dubai for the benefit of a bit of extra cash was a public relations disaster, and fury was unleashed by both football supporters and the media. Personally I felt unmoved. My team play in an overpriced corporate bowl called the Emirates, to a different type of crowd who, in football terms, I simply can't relate to. Given those circumstances, the thought of a game in

New York or Rio seemed like a more interesting prospect compared to what is now the norm. But for the majority of fans, this proposal was a disgusting imposition on our national game; one liberty too far from the Premier League.

On the weekend that the 'games abroad' story broke, the BBC programme *Football Focus* ran a feature on the issue. The presenter Manish Bhasin kicked off the programme by asking the question: "Is our national game in danger of becoming just another brand?" The immediate response by many viewers surely being: it already is Manish, where have you been since 1992? Perhaps the following week he kicked off the show by asking the question: 'Is Richard Littlejohn in danger of becoming nasty, reactionary and condescending?'

So was football's soul in danger of being sold down the river by the prospect of Wolverhampton v Fulham exclusively live from Singapore? Let's have a look at the culture that was already in place within football at the break of this story:

* Unaffordable ticket pricing to those on a modest income.

* Players on more money a week than a person on an average wage will earn over the space of many years.

* Corporate clients of sponsors given ticketing priority over genuine supporters.

* Atmosphere in stadiums having become quiet and timid.

* Games played at times of the day that prioritise TV coverage ahead of the attending supporter.

* Stadiums named after commercial brands, along with overbearing flashing advertising hoardings that are installed on the touchlines.

* Sepp Blatter.

With all this evidence, who could blame the Premier League for believing that they could get away with anything? Sure there might be the odd grumble about these bold suggestions, but money talks and eventually the fans will come round.

What this highlighted was the way in which English fans had, and still are, taken for granted. Although extremely profitable in the eyes of the Premier League, the market in England had become saturated. Therefore, the time had come to expand even further into the foreign market. The Premier League were not worried about a backlash from English fans because they'd already gotten away with so much; that little bit more would be a doddle. But this time was different. This time the fans said no, and the Premier League backed down to avoid any form of protest.

So for the first time ever, the fans actually got one over the Premier League. It only took just under two decades for it to happen, but it did happen. It does beg the question: what if we had made more of a protest about the impositions that currently ruin our national game? Is it just me who hates the way that football has changed from one extreme to the other during the past twenty years? Clearly not – I can hardly find a genuine football supporter who disagrees with my grievances. I really want to find these guys and debate with them, but they're a rare breed. I'd love to find that person who believes that players are worth their wages and that Rupert Murdoch is a force for the common good. The typical response from fans that I get from *Theatre of Silence* is that, '*I agree with what you say, but there's nothing we can do to change it*'. Indeed, just like politics, we're consistently told that we have no influence in the way that things change. But surely the example of the 'games abroad' story hints that the power still lies with the masses.

Maybe by the time that you read this, Aston Villa will have played Newcastle United a Premier League fixture in Johannesburg. Don't doubt for a minute that the Premier League are finished with this one just yet. If this plan does ever surface, then the Premier League will have taken a gamble against the wishes of the people who made them so successful in the first place. Perhaps they believe that the commercial opportunities of the Premier League 'brand' abroad is worth more than the original fanbase. If that ever turns out to be the case then English fans will still have the opportunity to prove them wrong on a week to week basis. Without the loyal support of the English fans, the Premier League will have no worthy product to sell to the rest of the world. Not many people in China will want to watch a game on TV that has thousands of empty seats all over the stadium. The Premier League clubs should of course be grateful for the massive following they have in other countries; but to maintain that foreign support in the long term, it's more important for them to show more respect to the people, who have within them the power to make or break the world's most popular sporting league.

Sit down and shut up!

The following letter was sent to fans of Middlesbrough FC by the club in February 2009.

Dear block 53A supporter

Over the last few games this season the stewards have tried hard to persuade you all to sit down in this area of the ground.

The club are grateful of and encourage your noisy passionate support, but please remember that the Safety Certificate for the ground, issued by Middlesbrough Council, does not allow permanent standing within the seating areas.

I know when the action is exciting and when the team are shooting at the north end of the ground the instinct of every fan is to stand, I do not want to stop you doing this, but then please sit down. If you could adhere to this but still maintain your level of support then all parties will be happy.

We need you to work with the stewards towards a safe environment, this compromise is the way forward and respects the wishes of other fans, which want to sit in the same area as you but cannot stand.

I am receiving more and more complaints from our own fans also seated in this area about both the persistent standing and the constant banging and noise coming from the back of this stand.

Please stop, make us much noise as you like when we score, but this constant noise is driving some fans mad.

Yours sincerely

Sue Watson
Safety Officer

Letter of resignation

I sent this letter to Arsenal in 2007.

Managing Director
Arsenal Football Club
Emirates Stadium
75 Drayton Park
London N5 1BU

Dear Managing Director,

Please find enclosed my current silver membership card. Feel free to cross my name off the list for the following season and save the club the price of a second class stamp. I'd hate for you guys to waste twenty-three pence, because we all have to work hard to make the club as profitable as possible, and I'm just trying to do my bit. You see the other day, I realised that the last time I actually used this membership card to buy a ticket from the club was way back in winter 2004.

That was when I decided that I'd finally had enough of being treated like a gullible customer who has unconditional loyalty no matter how badly they are treated. The good news is that there are plenty of others on the waiting list for one of these silver membership cards and I'm sure that you will have no problem with replacing my custom. However, the bad news is that one day thousands of others will wake up and send you a similar kind of letter including their 'valuable' membership cards or season tickets. At this moment it doesn't seem like anything to be too concerned about, but give it time. All I will say is that if times get hard and the attendance comes down, please don't come back to the likes of me to give the club support, because we'll treat you with the same amount of respect that you currently give to us. You've marketed football to a new breed of consumer, therefore when things start to get tough, they are the ones you should demand loyalty from. Good luck, because you might need it.

A lot of fans will be surprised that I'm prepared to give up something so valuable as my silver membership – something that is in such demand and wanted by so many thousands of others. But in reality it's just a piece of plastic (costing £26 a year[1]) which gives me the right to apply for a match ticket. Next time I go to a restaurant maybe I should pay £26 to have a look at the menu? Of course as a silver member I appreciate the fact that I'm better off than a red member who pays £26 a year for the right to apply for a ticket only on the occasions when the tickets have not all been purchased by silver members. Yep, you guys are geniuses! I remember when the silver membership cards first came into effect, members got £1 off for every ticket purchased. That soon went and I can see why, as there's no way you can let us greedy bastards get away with so much as £1 a game.

Leaving Highbury was a difficult decision, but I could understand why any club would want to leave a 38,000 stadium for one that holds 60,000. In my naivety, I believed that a bigger capacity stadium would have allowed more of us to gain entry to the games at a more reasonable price. Not exactly a radical idea. Instead, the whole project was part of one big corporate money-making plan that has ripped to shreds the identity and heart of a

---

[1] By 2011 the cost of silver membership had risen to £39.

football club. Watch out Arsenal, because if I ever become a billionaire I'm buying the club outright and the first thing I'm going to do is sack the board. Okay this is unlikely to happen! But just in case it does, I'm giving you plenty of warning. I'm currently checking for oil in the Finsbury Park area. After lowering ticket prices the next thing I'd do is pay off your friends at Emirates Airlines and rename the ground 'The Arsenal Stadium'. I know it's a bit controversial to name a football stadium after a football club or area these days, but for some reason I thought the name seemed to fit.

It's sad for me to give up my membership, because I've been a club member at Arsenal in some capacity every year since 1986. But at this moment in time I've never felt so detached from the club and from football in general. I certainly don't see myself as the kind of consumer that you hold in your plans, and I can no longer continue giving you my money.

Kind regards
Matthew Bazell

P.S. Good luck in the Deloitte money league in the coming years. I hear we stand a good chance.

Chapter 1
"It's all gone quiet..."

"For as much as there is a great noise in the city caused by the hustling over large balls from which many evils might arise, which God forbid we commend, and forbid such a game to be used in the city in the future."

Edward II – 1314

On the 15th August 1987 my dad, my brother and I were having a kick-about in Finsbury Park, North London, just a quarter of a mile from the old Arsenal stadium, Highbury. I was ten years old at that time and had only been to Highbury a few times. This was the opening day of the 1987-88 season. Liverpool were in town and Arsenal under George Graham were a young team on the way up after a decade of mediocrity.

The crowd was massive that day: 54,703. Not far short of Arsenal's current ground capacity at the Emirates Airlines Stadium. The pictures from the TV and newspapers the next day would show Highbury so full that some fans had managed to climb on the roof of the old North Bank to gain the best view in the house. Images dramatic enough to give today's health and safety fanatics a fatal heart attack. I wasn't in the stadium that day, but I still felt an experience of live football that I've always remembered. The noise of the crowd that day was theatre on its own. The roars from the North Bank and Clock End could be felt in the fields of Finsbury Park and powered over the noise pollution of the Seven Sisters Road. Loud enough for the fields to have felt like the Highbury pitch itself. Although I wasn't inside the stadium I was in a good mood because one almighty roar told me that Arsenal had won the game 1-0. So you can imagine I was shocked to find out that we had actually lost the game 2-1. Liverpool would go on to win the title quite convincingly that season, losing only two games on the way. The noise that day was frightening. But it was great and it was seductive.

Nineteen years later, and midway into the 2005-06 season, I was at Highbury to watch Arsenal play Cardiff City in the FA Cup third round. Formerly a regular, my trips to Highbury had become a rarity and the Cardiff game would only be the second time I had been to the old stadium in its final season. My friend was late, and I was left waiting outside the stadium for him to arrive. A cheer went up, indicating that a goal had been scored. A cheer not seemingly loud enough to be that of the home crowd, so I assumed that the 6,000 Cardiff fans were celebrating an early 1-0 lead. So I was delighted to hear the PA announcer declare that Robert Pires had put Arsenal into the lead.

Whilst standing outside Highbury, I realised that if I was none the wiser I would have no idea that there was a football match going on inside being watched by 38,000 people. Then again, the horse shit all over Avenell Road and hot dog and burger stands would have been a slight giveaway. My friend arrived within about fifteen minutes of kick-off and we soon made our way inside the ground. When you arrive late at football matches nowadays, it can feel like you're a latecomer to the theatre or the cinema. The row of people that you ask to get up from their seats look unhappy to have been disturbed during the performance. Once in my seat, I noticed two fans a couple of rows in front of me having a conversation about the game. They were virtually whispering and it didn't sound anything more than a typical discussion on how the game was going. So why were they whispering? Perhaps because the modern football crowd is so quiet that they didn't want the surrounding fans overhearing their conversation. In the first half, one nearby fan stood up and shouted out, "For fuck's sake make some noise" before a steward told him to sit back down. Arsenal went 2-0 up early in the first half and the game was effectively over. I looked around me and started to analyse the faces of some of the 38,000 people who populated the football ground I used to consider a second home, and who now populate Arsenal's new stadium. I'm no psychiatrist, but I felt I had as much expertise to judge a football crowd as any Freudian or Jungian.

Despite the propaganda that football is now a more suitable environment for children, the average age of the modern day supporter is forty-three, and this was certainly reflected in the crowd that I analysed. In this crowd there were virtually no kids, no groups of teenagers, and not many old people either. This crowd was white, middle class and looked decidedly forty-three years old! The men and women around me had one dominant expression: a look of lethargy and detachment, to the point of boredom. It brought me to the conclusion that many people who do attend football today do so out of status and habit, rather than any genuine passion or sense of enjoyment. It's a pastime that they've chosen to be a part of their life, and to their credit they dedicate a lot of time and money to this pastime. However, the expressions on their faces forced me to question whether their time and money would be better spent elsewhere. It certainly reassured me that my decision not to be part of that world any more, on a full-time basis, was the correct one (I'd been absent as a regular since 2004). No one seems to smile at football any more, or even look like they're enjoying themselves. When did it all become so serious? The fans who do try and make some noise end up as lone voices and get given funny looks from others. Sitting in such a quiet atmosphere among nearly 40,000 people is a very disconcerting experience. It's a claustrophobic feeling of emptiness and non-belonging. This environment is the theatre of silence. A theatre where the audience applauds in the right places, stands up when they're supposed to, and whispers so as not to disturb anyone else. They're spectators watching a performance, rather than being part of it. They've not realised that crowd participation is also a vital part of the entertainment. It bothers me that this type of fan makes up a football crowd these days, but of course these people have every right to be there. They have every right to follow their team, which I don't doubt they really do care for, and I have no right telling other people how to behave at a football match. If they choose to watch a game in passive silence, then that's up to them and there's nothing wrong with that. Sometimes I like to sit back and watch a game of football quietly, especially if I attend a match as a neutral.

But the concern is for the people who are left on the outside looking in; the ones who have been replaced by the new affluent consumer. The thousands of fans who would create that passion from the stands, but who are now so isolated from the modern game that they will remain on the outside, unless there is a change.

As visitors to Highbury for the FA Cup third round, Cardiff fans brought with them one of the worst reputations for football violence in the country. The reputation is well deserved and it was clear that there was no shortage of Soul Crew (Cardiff's hooligan firm) in North London on the day of the game. After the match a three hundred strong mob of Arsenal's hooligan firm 'The Herd' made their way up the Blackstock Road en route to find the Soul Crew.

Now, of course, I don't condone hooliganism. Of all the things in this world to fight for, to fight for football seems like wasted energy. Hooliganism caused English clubs to be banned throughout Europe for five years from 1985, and is also the main reason that steel fences were put up in stadiums that ended with the deaths of ninety-six Liverpool fans at Hillsborough. Yet the sight of this Arsenal mob sat well with me for one reason, and that was the expressions on the faces of the new breed of fan in the area who were walking towards Highbury and Islington tube station. The new breed, despite their age, didn't attend football in the 1970s, 1980s and 1990s, so they'd probably never seen much of this at Arsenal before. Most of them would have been under the impression that Arsenal do not and never have had a hooligan firm. But they knew that this mob must have been Arsenal and not Cardiff, on account of the accents and the ethnic diversity. The confusion on people's faces interested me because the sight of this three hundred strong mean-looking firm didn't fit in with their modern commercial ideal of football. This sight was a throwback to another era, the so-called dark days of football. With the hooligans on one side and the new breed of consumer on the other, there was a contrast between two cultures who have each been responsible in their own way for 'dark days'. Dark days so different in application, but both in their own extreme way pushing out ordinary supporters.

The pendulum has swung from one extreme to the other. The game of the people has been crushed, in little more than a decade, and with barely a whimper of opposition, to the point where the sport has almost become meaningless. What once was a sport accessible for all is now a hobby for those who can afford it. This is scandalous and immoral, and does not deserve to be met with apathy.

What is the meaning of football now? Simple, to make vast profits. This is not a revelation. The people who run the game let us know this. Every fan who attends matches will also tell you that football's a business. That's why they pay a fortune for tickets. That's why they buy the team shirt with all the trimmings once or twice every season and subscribe to satellite television. The phrase "But football's a business now" is one that gets bandied about on a regular basis in defence (yes defence) of how the modern game is run. And that's it, argument over. Stop complaining and accept reality. Whatever the complaint might be about the integrity of the game, the phrase "But football's a business now" will soon finish all debate. It's an argument that tells fans to forget about the heart and soul of the club they support, and to accept the purpose and reality of the modern game. The purpose of the modern game being solely to exploit the gullible consumer, and the reality being that enough fans are docile enough to simply accept it. And consumers don't get more gullible than us football fans. You only have to look at the food that supporters eat at half-time to realise that they will put up with anything, and then go back for more.

So the question to my fellow supporters is simple: why do you keep going back for more? If football is just a ruthless business, and you know this, why go along with it? Why don't you turn the tables back on them? The business world is fickle and unmerciful, and as fans we're the financial backers who the industry depends on. They are totally at our mercy. So if your football club is making unrealistic financial demands on you, then ask yourself whether this business is becoming too expensive for you to carry on financially backing it. Maybe we should all be businessmen and think of ourselves. It's the way I feel about the game these days, so I'm going down the business route, along with everyone else within football. I'm going to think about my bank balance only. Therefore, being a shrewd businessman I believe it makes sense to abandon this over-expensive and morally redundant product by withdrawing my custom. I'm not anti-business because we all have the right to make a living and to prosper. But when I was a kid I didn't feel inspired to put up posters of Donald Trump on my wall, or pay good money to watch Ted Turner hold a board meeting in front of an adoring crowd.

Some argue, in defence of the modern game, that football has always been a business, which is true – but also irrelevant in regards to the argument that fans are being ripped off. Since the fall of the upper class amateur teams and the rise of the professionals, football clubs have been institutions with the aim to survive as well-run businesses. None of us had any objection to that concept. Football may have been a business twenty years ago. It may have been a business fifty years ago. It doesn't matter, for the simple reason that in those times the sport was affordable.

In this book, I make comparisons to global corporations and even slip in a Voltaire quote that most people associate with human rights struggles. Indeed those of you who feel indifferent to the corporate takeover of a sport that was once known as the 'people's game' might point out that there are more important issues in the world than the plight of those of us who can't afford to watch football anymore. Well, anyone who would think along those lines would be right. I would tend to agree that starving children in Africa is more scandalous and shameful than the price of a football ticket. But we'll leave that subject for people like Sir Bob Geldof to inform us on. For this book we'll stick to the injustice and exploitation within football. Secondly, what the bloody hell are you doing reading a book about football when you'd rather be reading one about saving the whale and the hole in the ozone layer! Go and get a refund now before you damage the book and they refuse to give you back your money. For those of you who lost the receipt, or spilt herbal tea on the front cover, I'm afraid that there is no chapter highlighting the threat of extinction to the orang-utan. But read on anyway: because the football world mirrors wider society. A lot of the time in a negative way, but sometimes in a positive way.

If British football is overrun with advertising and greed then maybe it's because Britain has become a more commercial, superficial place to live in. But if racism at football is no longer acceptable at our stadiums, then maybe it's because British society has become less tolerant of such bigotry. The main principle in football right now is no different to big businesses all over the world, and is also a principle that governments stand by.

That principle being: anything that brings in money is beneficial no matter what the consequences. The export of arms from the UK is seen as good for the economy while ignoring the damage this trade brings to the world and the number of lives it destroys. Then of course we send soldiers out to die, when the people we sold the weapons to in order to murder people suddenly turn out to be murderous tyrants. The short-term economy is also put ahead of the welfare of the planet's environment. I know that's an extreme comparison to make in relation to football. No football club is responsible for the slaughter of innocent civilians or for destroying a rain forest. But it's the same line of ruthless thinking: money comes ahead of every other principle.

To give one prime example of how the pursuit of money devalues the majesty of the game: FA Cup semi-finals being played at Wembley purely for the sake of a bit more revenue. It completely downgrades the final, costs fans of most clubs more money in travel, and takes away the uniqueness and excitement of two teams competing in a stadium that belongs to a neutral football club. I loved watching two teams compete in a semi-final at Villa Park, neither of whom were Aston Villa.

Advertising revenue is seen as good for football. Sometimes it is, and their money can go to fund good causes within a community. Lower division clubs rely on advertising for their very survival. But what if advertising goes so far as to reduce the capacity of a stadium in favour of advertising hoardings that keep out thousands of fans? This actually happens in the European Champions League. Can replacing fans with commercial hoardings really be good for a spectator sport? The genius behind it all is that now many fans view football with the same one-dimensional attitude: anything that brings money in is good for the club. Even if the thing that brings money into the club takes away the very soul and aesthetics of the game, and further alienates the supporter. Some fans now talk like bank managers or club directors in regards to what's best for their club, and that really is frightening.

This is not a book about falling out of love with football; it's about the game losing its heart to money, and some of us not willing to go down that route. I'm now a lost customer and lost customers are not good for business. I'm not unique in my feelings towards the modern game, therefore what you're about to read has to be considered a warning to the future of football.

I hope that by reading this book people will understand some of the reasons why many fans are turning their backs on the game. Sorry, let me rephrase that – trying to turn their back on the game. In a recent football-related conversation, I told a friend that "I've had it with football". My friend replied with "You've not had it with football. You're just a football cynic". The bad news is that my friend was 100 per cent right. Once football is in your blood it's virtually impossible to abandon it outright. No one who has ever been obsessed with the game can completely stop caring. I try to do my bit by not attending games and not purchasing club merchandise. As I've already said, common sense tells me that I should now abandon the industry – completely. That's the way it should be with a business if they treat their customers in the wrong way. However, this problem I'm faced with isn't quite the same thing as being dissatisfied with one supermarket and changing to another. I'm stuck with it, and will support Arsenal and England till the day I die. In 2006 I travelled to Madrid to be at the Bernabeu stadium to see Arsenal play the greatest club side of all time, Real Madrid; I travelled to Madrid at a time when I was more disillusioned with football than at any other time in my life. A month later I would then travel on a road trip through Europe to Turin to watch Arsenal play Italian giants Juventus. A month after that I would make the short trip to Paris to be present in the city where Arsenal played their first ever Champions League Final. A few years later, and as pissed off with football as ever, I travelled to the eternal city to watch Arsenal play Roma. These might be holidays but a major part of it is still the football. To be so disillusioned with something, but still prepared to travel to other countries and spend so much money to follow that same thing, is confusing to say the least. A funny kind of business we have here!

Chapter 2
The envy of the world?

"Right now the English Premier League is just about the definition of a great thing... Less than twenty years ago, English football was known more for rabid fans and decrepit stadiums than for the sort of classy crowd that now fills the suites at the stadiums of Chelsea and Manchester United."

Time magazine – 2007

In 1992 the top division of English football changed hands when the Premier League/Premiership was formed and replaced the old Football League, which had been established since 1888. The reason behind the Premier League was to re-brand football, make the game more commercially viable and to create more wealth for the top clubs. It has achieved its aim – the Premier League is indeed a money-making machine. By 2010, according to Deloitte, the combined annual revenue of the Premier League clubs was an incredible €2.3 billion a year. That figure is nearly triple the revenue generated in 1997, and nearly €1 billion a year more than the world's second most prosperous league – the Spanish La Liga. Who can argue with a success story like that?

There is no definitive right or wrong answer as to whether football is better or worse now than it was in years gone by. People do have a habit of romanticising the past and harping back to a golden era that never existed. I'm not going to do that. I'm not going to claim that football was perfect in the days gone by, because it wasn't, far from it. I'm not advocating a return to the days when stadiums were crumbling, when fans felt threatened by other fans, when black players had bananas thrown at them and when Vinnie Jones should have had bananas thrown at him but didn't. Football did need investment and a change of culture. That investment has to come from somewhere and, as a paying fan, I would have happily paid a bit more for a ticket if it meant better facilities and better players from overseas. However, the change that occurred and the financial burden placed upon supporters went beyond all justification. A mix between what we have now and what football was like in the days before the Premier League would have been the perfect compromise in modernising football, while maintaining what was already so great about the sport.

For example, an English game where the standard of football is as strong as anywhere in the world, but where people of all incomes can afford to watch their team play live. A game where the players are high earners, but not to the obscene level that distances them from the rest of society. A game where some fans can sing their hearts out on an open terrace, while other fans can sit and watch the game in a more family friendly environment. A game which has good relations with outside commercial interests, but not to the point where the corporate boys who work for the advertisers replace the true supporters in the stadiums. It's the good and bad things about modern football that will be featured in *Theatre of Silence*. A mix between the positive and negative things we have in the modern game, both at home and abroad. If the bad things about the modern game heavily outweigh the good things, then so be it. The argument therefore is that football has to make some reverse changes or risk losing more of its fan base.

In 2007 *Time* magazine ran a feature on English football in which it proclaimed the Premier League as being 'the envy of other sports leagues'. Being an American magazine, and with a corporate American way of thinking, *Time* hailed the Premier League as a roaring success for no other reason than being so financially prosperous. In reality though, the Premier League is the envy of other businessmen – but not football fans in other countries. I doubt very much that German football fans, who pay as little as €10 to watch their top teams play, feel much envy towards fans of English clubs who now have to pick and choose their games due to the extortionate cost of tickets. I also doubt that football fans in other countries, who are allowed the freedom to support their teams in an exuberant nature, feel that much envy towards 'classy' English crowds who now sit down quietly for the whole game. There are only a very small handful of teams in England who expect to finish in the top four Premier League places every single season: does that mean that fans of clubs such as Aston Villa, Bolton, Everton, Newcastle United and Sunderland should be envied for following annual mediocrity?

Those who believe the Premier League is such a fantastic product are looking at it only on a financial level and not a social one. More importantly the same attitude is shared by those who run football. It is this attitude alone in which they are potentially digging their own grave. If football can lose the support of a lifelong fan like myself, then what about this new 'classy' crowd that has latched on to the game because of fashion?

In the original edition of *Theatre of Silence* I wrote the following:

There is something that hasn't happened in Britain during the years of the Premier League, which football should fear happening again in the future. It's something that has happened many times before and is something that will no doubt happen again one day – especially in a country in which millions of people are living in debt. The thing I'm referring to is a recession. A wider economic recession within the country could seriously harm football in a way that it never has done before. In the past, football has survived these hard times for two very simple reasons:

1. The game was affordable entertainment. Therefore people could still attend matches even when undergoing hardship.

2. The players' wages were not high enough to burden the club.

Now the opposite is true for both player wages and admission prices. A wider economic recession is a reality that is unavoidable. We don't know when it will happen, or how bad it will be, but history proves that at some point in the future, our country will face some very hard times. The last time we fell on these times was in the early 1990s, around the same time that the Premier League was being formed. During a recession, people will not spend such crazy money to watch football when they are struggling to pay off the bills, the mortgage or the rent. So the consequence for football could very well be half-empty stadiums and players on wage bills higher than the club's weekly revenues. Who will envy the Premier League then? This is why the people who run the game have to abandon the policy of short-term greed; otherwise the bubble could soon explode right in their faces.

Well I suppose that prediction is a little bit right but also wrong. Yes, people are giving the game up because they can no longer afford it, and attendances at some clubs have fallen. But in general, enough loyal fans have stuck around to keep it going. In all fairness, football for the most part, so far, has survived the recession. However, it is far too early to judge what lies ahead. Clubs are in financial turmoil and it's the after effects of the recession that could be the most telling in the coming years. The culture of English football changed at a time when there was a lot of money going around in the UK economy. That money is disappearing fast. The cost of living is going up, and in real terms people's earnings are going down. Given those circumstances, can football, an expensive attraction, maintain its appeal to those who now have to be more conservative with their finances? No predictions in this edition though, let's just wait and see how it all pans out.

Chapter 3
To regulate, or not to regulate

"The situation [financial crisis in football] is like trying to impose sanity in a lunatics' asylum".

Gavin Brown – *Metro* 2010

Premier League debt list published in *The Guardian* in May 2010:

Arsenal £265 million
Aston Villa £114 million
Birmingham City £2.85 million
Blackburn Rovers £20 million
Bolton Wanderers £67 million
Burnley £13 million
Chelsea £726 million
Everton £41 million
Fulham £207 million
Hull City £15 million
Liverpool £394 million
Manchester City £37 million
Manchester United £717 million
Portsmouth £123 million
Spurs £80 million
Stoke City £17.4 million
Sunderland £46 million

West Ham United £48 million
Wigan Athletic £69 million
Wolverhampton Wanderers £0.3 million

Around the same time this list was published, UEFA announced plans to regulate football finances. The main regulation, to be gradually monitored from the 2011-12 season, and fully implemented from 2014-15, is that clubs have to balance their books and limit spending to within their turnover. Chelsea, who in recent years have made losses of hundreds of millions by spending far more than their annual turnover, complained. Not for their sake, no, but for the sake of small clubs who might one day benefit from a multi billionaire Russian oil tycoon. How unselfish of Chelsea to stick up for the little people. Chelsea chairman Bruce Buck insisted, "We don't think that maintaining the status quo is right". Slightly ironic, given that since 2003, Abramovich's millions have widened the gap, to the point where clubs without rich owners have about as much chance of breaking the status quo as Status Quo do of hanging up their guitars and calling it quits. In the eyes of many, this UEFA ruling is very welcome, as too many clubs are overspending themselves into administration.

Corrupt deregulation of the financial system was responsible for the global economic downfall that came to crisis point in 2008. Football has the same problem, apart from the fact that there was nothing to deregulate in the first place. Along with our beloved banks, professional football has been one of the worst adverts for the principles of free market/free enterprise. Regulation is a repressive word, and the term 'free enterprise' makes those who preach it sound like libertarians. In the banks' case, the corporate lowlifes who preached free enterprise had a dramatic change of philosophy when they went begging to the state for taxpayer bail outs. So much for the market sorting itself out – I guess the American filmmaker Michael Moore was right when he said, "They [global corporations] want socialism, but only for themselves". The problem with the banking crisis was that the financial terrorists running these institutions had no concern for the customers and indeed the bank itself. They lost billions, but it wasn't their money to lose, so they didn't care.

Football at the moment has self-regulation. So currently we get a mixed bag of well run clubs and poorly run clubs. Arsenal have been a good example of how to balance your books responsibly and they have an annual debt payment set up, that is well within the boundaries of the club's turnover. A little bit too good perhaps, Arsenal are one of the few clubs to have announced significant profit in recent years (£46 million in 2010) at the expense of their overcharged supporters. West Bromwich Albion have also been a good example of how to run a football club in a responsible way. They have been known as a 'yo-yo club', meaning that they get promoted and then relegated every season. Being a yo-yo club is not really a compliment, but unlike other clubs who drop out of the Premier League they account for the fact that relegation might happen. Therefore West Brom players have not been on contracts that become too high to pay in a lower division.

In contrast, so many other teams take huge risks and put players on wages that become un-payable in the Premier League itself, let alone the Football League. Take for example West Ham, who by 2010 were spending £67 million on player wages, when their annual turnover was £76 million. The classic case here has been Portsmouth, who by 2010 had a wage bill of £65 million when their annual turnover was only £60 million. The financial demise of Portsmouth was a reality check for many in football: yes, actions do have consequences. The words 'too big to fail' do not apply to football. Unfortunately British football clubs are not quite as lucky as banks in terms of state bailouts (I say British, because in 2001, Real Madrid got bailed out of over £177 million worth of debt when the local authority purchased their training ground for a figure of around £290 million which many believe was an over inflated price. Glad I'm not a taxpayer in Madrid who supports Atletico!).

Some modern football clubs are run like global corporations. By law, a corporation can be deemed as a person in terms of its human rights. The documentary feature film *The Corporation* did a personality study of a global corporation and deemed it to be a psychopath. Psychopaths need to be restrained, so here are a few suggestions on regulation in football:

1. <u>You cannot buy a football club on credit and then put the debt onto the club.</u>

In May 2010, the well respected *Guardian* sports journalist David Conn published an article on the finances of the Premier League, and the incredible levels of debt that the clubs have found themselves in. His assessment of Manchester United's financial situation is as follows: "*Scandalous. The grim details of the Glazer family's takeover finally dawned on the wider world after the prospectus in January (2010) for the family to borrow £500 million for the third time in four years. The Glazers have never put a cent into Manchester United, but have charged £12.9 million in management fees since 2006 and borrowed £10 million from the club in December 2008. Interest, fees and other charges on the debts the Glazers took onto the club, which they then made United responsible for paying, amounted to £460 million in four years.*"

The biggest scandal here is that everything the Glazers have done is totally legal and above board. Premier League chairman Richard Scudamore is quoted as saying, "I defend their right to buy the club in the way that they did". So assuming the Premier League are unlikely to act on this, UEFA need to step in and take action.

2. Clubs cannot spend more than €20 million on transfer fees during a season.

The one shortfall of the UEFA regulation regarding spending within a turnover, is that it won't make the leagues of Europe any more competitive. The clubs that top the Deloitte Money League will still have a massive advantage over everyone else. A UEFA transfer spending limit could be the answer to making football more unpredictable as a contest, and we'll look at this issue further in Chapter 12.

3. Clubs must allocate a certain percentage of domestic league match-day tickets for a price of no more than €20.

This regulation would be totally legal if applied in a certain way. The initial problem is that UEFA would have a very tough time getting a bill through court that tells private businesses (i.e. football clubs) how much they can charge their customers for the service they provide. However, the regulation would work by enforcing the same clauses that will apply to the regulation of spending within a club's turnover. The UEFA regulation laws will allow clubs to continue to overspend and not balance their books if they choose. But if they do overspend, then they will not be allowed to play in UEFA competition, such as the Europa Cup and Champions League – kerching! Apply the same laws to ticket pricing and clubs will have a very simple option: allocate a percentage of €20 tickets, if this isn't done, then you miss out on the financial fortunes of European football. Some might argue that this would lead to clubs breaking away from UEFA. It wouldn't, because high ticket pricing in domestic football is mainly a problem for English clubs. I suppose that they could break away and form their own league where they could charge outrageous prices...oh hold on, isn't that called the Premier League?

4. You cannot run a football club if you have a history of financially mismanaging a football club in the past.

Why has Peter Risdale still been running football clubs since his departure from Leeds in 2003? The former Leeds United chairman oversaw the financial mess that resulted in Leeds dropping two divisions, after gambling on regular Champions League football, and failing. In 2010 Risdale stepped down from Cardiff City having previously been in charge of Barnsley FC. At Cardiff, the fans turned against him fully when he allegedly misled them about club funds in the 2009-10 season. Cardiff set up a scheme where fans could pay for season tickets six months in advance, in order to raise funds for new signings. The benefit for fans being that if these signings were to help Cardiff get promoted, then they would have Premier League season tickets at Football League prices. Fantastic! Well apart from the fact that once the club got hold of the money it all went to pay off the debts. Risdale still qualifies as a 'fit and proper' person to run football clubs and I'm sure that even Gordon Gecko would fancy his chances of getting through that test. One strike and you're out, mate – new rule.

5. A club cannot move to a new stadium without providing a detailed account which proves that a ground-move will not plunge the club into serious financial trouble.

This has been a common problem for many clubs. Arsenal would have passed this test, as they had a good reason for moving – they didn't have enough seats at Highbury to meet the enormous demand for tickets. However, too many clubs move stadium without this demand and then fall into financial crisis. Simple cure: get an independent body to means-test the move.

6. An agreed percentage of turnover must be spent on maintaining and improving the infrastructure of the club.

Former player and current TV pundit Steve Claridge made an interesting point regarding Portsmouth's financial downfall: millions of pounds had gone through Pompey, and yet not a bean had gone towards the infrastructure and future of the club. The stadium was no better, the training facilities no better, and the youth academy no better. All those millions to go around and it all ended up in the hands of a just a few players and agents. In May 2010, Portsmouth's administrator had to lay off eighty-five backroom staff workers in order to make savings. Perhaps if the previous owners hadn't paid £450,000 in wages, over just eight months, to a third choice goalkeeper who never even played a game, then perhaps some of the unlucky eighty-five might still have a job in football.

The principle of free-enterprise ideologies is that government interference and regulation is bad; the market will sort itself out. This economic philosophy won a Nobel Prize for Milton Friedman, the 'godfather' of capitalism of this kind and self proclaimed 'libertarian'. Freidman was also the economic advisor to Ronald Reagan, a President whose financial deregulation led to a huge gulf in earnings between CEOs and regular workers. That Nobel Prize now looks to be one of the most misplaced awards since *Time* magazine voted Adolf Hitler Man of The Year in 1938. An unregulated free market is a proven failure. Anyone who still argues its case should be taken as seriously as a person who claims that the earth is flat, or that SportsDirect.com@St James' Park Stadium is a sensible name for a football ground. The English game has done nothing drastic to sort itself out, even in the face of record debts caused by reckless overspending. Football clubs are not regular businesses. These are institutions that serve communities. Portsmouth FC is simply too important to have been the business play thing of ruthless financial gamblers, as were Liverpool and Manchester United amongst others. If regulation is a dirty word, then football needs to get filthed-up, and quickly.

Chapter 4
Customer satisfaction

One difference between my bank and my football club, is that my bank has occasionally sent me mail asking for my opinion as a customer. Don't get me wrong, I did get plenty of mail from Arsenal when I was a club member. In fact I was forever being sent applications for Arsenal credit cards and Arsenal mobile phones (they still sent me junk-mail long after my letter of resignation).[2] They even asked me to go in to the Spanish housing market through a new property scheme: buy a villa in Spain and get a season ticket for free, etc.

They kept pursuing my custom, but never once asked if I was happy with the 'service provider'. Maybe it's time for the clubs to start sending out bank style customer satisfaction surveys to their club members and season ticket holders. Feel free to fill this in with regard to the club you support:

HOW SATISFIED ARE YOU WITH THE WAY YOUR FOOTBALL CLUB IS RUN?

---

[2] A friend of mine who supports Middlesbrough was sent an application for a Middlesbrough credit card, which had the marketing slogan *'Every true Boro fan should have one'*. My friend wrote a letter back to the club, informing them that being a 'true Boro fan' has nothing to do with making the club more profitable through credit card debts. Those who did take up the offer, signed up to an APR of 19.9% – bargain!

1. Are you satisfied that your football club understands your financial needs?

Very satisfied   Satisfied   Dissatisfied   Very pissed off

2. Are you satisfied with your club's dealings in the transfer market?

Very satisfied   Satisfied   Dissatisfied   Very pissed off

3. Are you satisfied that your club treats you as a loyal customer?

Very satisfied   Satisfied   Dissatisfied   Very pissed off

4. Are you satisfied with your club's appointments in management and coaching staff?

Very satisfied   Satisfied   Dissatisfied   Very pissed off

5. Are you satisfied with the players' performances on the pitch?

Very satisfied   Satisfied   Dissatisfied   Very pissed off

6. Are you satisfied with your board members, shareholders and directors?

Very satisfied   Satisfied   Dissatisfied   Very pissed off

7. Are you satisfied that the people who run your club have respect for the traditions and history of the club ahead of commercialism and corporate priorities?

Very satisfied   Satisfied   Dissatisfied   Very pissed off

HOW STRONGLY DO YOU AGREE OR DISAGREE WITH THE FOLLOWING STATEMENTS?

1. Most television football pundits could be replaced by a more straight talking and charismatic plank of wood.
Strongly agree   Agree   Disagree   Strongly disagree

2. Nicklas Bendtner gained an enormous amount of public sympathy when claiming that his £52,000 a week is justified, on the basis that his football career forces him to make sacrifices – such as not being able to go on skiing holidays.
Strongly agree   Agree   Disagree   Strongly disagree

3. In his TV commentary, Clive Tyldesley should do more to remind us of 'that balmy night in the Nou Camp' when Manchester United beat Bayern Munich in the 1999 Champions League Final.
Strongly agree   Agree   Disagree   Strongly disagree

4. Ashley Cole is respected more for his integrity as a person than he is for his talent as a footballer.
Strongly agree   Agree   Disagree   Strongly disagree

5. Chelsea have achieved success through shrewd transfer dealings on a tight budget.
Strongly agree   Agree   Disagree   Strongly disagree

6. Mario Balotelli should take life more seriously, smile less and try and develop more of an ego.
Strongly agree   Agree   Disagree   Strongly disagree

7. I would like more stadium DJs to pump out loud music every time a goal is scored.
Strongly agree   Agree   Disagree   Strongly disagree

8. Football needs to stop allocating so many match tickets to genuine supporters, and instead give a fairer share to its corporate sponsors.

Strongly agree   Agree   Disagree   Strongly disagree

9. Sepp Blatter sounds less like a man who should be in charge of the biggest sport on the planet and more like an internal organ of the body.

Strongly agree   Agree   Disagree   Strongly disagree

10. I would like Peter Risdale to be the new chairman of my football club.

Strongly agree   Agree   Disagree   Strongly disagree

An even better idea would be a little bit more democracy. Could we as fans have the opportunity to vote out club directors like building societies do? No doubt there are certain directors out there who wouldn't even get past the first ballot. Sounds like a crazy idea but it's a policy that two of the biggest clubs on the planet employ. At Barcelona and Real Madrid, the supporters are the ones that get to decide who heads the club by voting in a president via a fans' ballot. It could be pointed out that Catalonia is regarded as left-wing, and Barcelona FC simply incorporates the same social ideals as the region. England is a more capitalist society that doesn't quite share the same social principles. To change football in this way would mean changing the whole political ethos of the country, right?

Well, no. Germany is considered a capitalist society, and yet Bundesliga rules state that every club must be 51% owned by members and supporters. There's more than a strong argument to say that football clubs should be run by a community, not just a few flawed individuals who have the power to make decisions that affect thousands of people without being accountable, mentioning no Mike Ashleys…I mean names.

If those elected do a good job the fans will love them and vote them back in. If they don't do a good job or treat the club and the supporters with respect, then the fans will have a lot more power than to simply stage the odd protest or sing 'Sack the board' from the stands. Most governments rise and fall on this principle. The ones that don't are called dictatorships. Had the fans of the former Wimbledon FC had this power then the directors would not have been able to get away with relocating to Milton Keynes and creating a new football club. The same thing would have also applied to the fans of Brighton & Hove Albion, whose owner Bill Archer sold the ground off to developers for personal profit in 1996. Brighton received virtually no money from this sale and went fifteen years without a home of their own. A similar fate nearly happened to Wrexham FC in 2004, when owner Alex Hamilton tried to evict the club in order to sell the ground off to a property developer – a company owned by a certain Alex Hamilton! In 2005 the High Court ruled that Hamilton's company had improperly acquired the freehold to the ground and Wrexham ended up in the control of administrators. It's quite worrying to think that one person's greed can be so damaging to a community, and this is why fans need more genuine influence within their clubs. An organisation that promotes fan ownership of clubs is Supporters Direct, which can be found online at www.supporters-direct.org/

Chapter 5
The only league that counts

"If tomorrow, business becomes more important than the game itself, then football will no longer exist."

Aime Jacquet – 1998 French World Cup winning manager.

Today it is accepted that the most important thing in football is generating more money than your competition. Therefore I just don't understand what Chelsea were doing parading the streets of West London on an open top bus after the 2009-10 season. Okay, so they may have won some little football championship trophy for only the fourth time in their history, but these losers should have been crying into their wine glasses. They may have finished first place in the English Premiership in that year, but they only finished sixth place in the league that takes first priority. The only league that counts in modern football is the Deloitte Football Money League. The league that lists the twenty most prosperous football clubs in the world. Step forward the true champions for that year, Real Madrid.

THE DELOITTE FOOTBALL MONEY LEAGUE, FIGURES RELEASED 2010

This table is for annual revenue generated by the club only, not the wealth of whoever owns the clubs. The figure is taken before club expenditure and is in millions of euros.

1.	Real Madrid	€401.4
2.	Barcelona	€365.9
3.	Manchester United	€327.0
4.	Bayern Munich	€289.5
5.	Arsenal	€263.0
6.	Chelsea	€242.3
7.	Liverpool	€217.0
8.	Juventus	€203.2
9.	Inter Milan	€196.5
10.	AC Milan	€196.5
11.	Hamburg	€146.7
12.	AS Roma	€146.4
13.	Lyon	€139.6

14.	Marseille	€133.2
15.	Tottenham Hotspur	€132.7
16.	Schalke	€124.5
17.	Werder Bremen	€114.7
18.	Borussia Dortmund	€103.5
19.	Manchester City	€101.2
20.	Newcastle United	€101.0

Yet when this league was published in 2010, the Real Madrid fans were not out on the streets celebrating their success. In fact I was in the city of Madrid in May 2010, and the only open top bus I saw had Japanese tourists on the top deck instead of Cristiano Ronaldo and co. What happened was that Madrid dwelled on the fact that Barcelona kicked their backsides on the football field during this time, and they let it spoil the party. Barca could only finish in second place in the Deloitte Money League, and big deal that they won the European Champions League in the season when these financial results were relevant. The point is how many Kaka and Ronaldo shirts did they sell in that time? Exactly, they're amateurs. But despite all this glory, the ungrateful Real Madrid supporters were still not happy. In fact they're as bad as these whingeing Newcastle United fans who are always moaning about the state their team seems to be in. Newcastle made it into the 2010 Deloitte Money League, which was a fine effort for a club that got relegated in 2009. Yet their spoilt fans still complain about the fact that they haven't won a domestic trophy of any kind since Elvis was looking for his first major record deal.

Poor little Porto, doesn't your heart just bleed for these Rich List virgins. They may have won the Champions League in 2004, but I'm sure their fans would trade in that trophy any day, just to experience a glory similar to that of when West Ham broke into the Deloitte Money League in 2007. Not bad for a club who, in the same week as these results were published, were stranded in the relegation zone and looking to be on the way out of the Premiership. The reality is that a club like West Ham made it into the Deloitte Money League not because of success on the football field, but because of the high cost of following them.

The Deloitte Money League has almost taken the tone of being as important, if not more so, than the actual football leagues. It's certainly reported on by the media like a sporting league with news talk such as *Arsenal move up to fifth place... while Liverpool's season gets worse... they've slipped down to seventh.* In recent years it's been the benchmark as to who are considered the most successful clubs in the world. People have claimed Manchester United to be the world's biggest club because of finishing top of this Deloitte list on a number of occasions in recent years. Even the term 'most successful club' has been used to describe United because of this. It all depends on how you view football. If making the most money makes you the biggest club in the world, then so be it. A Real Madrid fan however, is probably more likely to point to the fact that they've won an incredible nine European Cups/Champions Leagues as a good enough reason to be able to call themselves the most successful or biggest football club; not because they generate more revenue than their rivals.

The club I support kicks ass this league. I've heard fellow fans gloat with pride: "We're one of the only clubs in the world to make profit". Well hurrah to that, what a wonderful triumph! Let's bring out the champagne, and hire the open top bus. My favourite line is when fans claim, "We're financially secure". No, a ruthless global business is financially secure, while you're struggling to pay for a match ticket. Sorry to be a spoiler, but financial success of this kind is nothing to be proud of, especially as it's built on corporate priorities and unaffordable regular match tickets. It fills me with no more emotion than knowing that the computer I own helps make Microsoft prosper.

Achievement in the Deloitte Money League might be considered by some as the highest honour in the game, but for true supporters, success in football will always be judged the old-fashioned way.

Chapter 6
The Game in the Balance – part 1

In football right now, too many things seem so misplaced and out of character with the aesthetics of the sport. From the music the club DJ blares out when a goal is scored, to the manic depressive fans who put everyone on a downer on radio phone-in shows. The positive things about football seem to be so heavily outweighed. So I put this theory to the test. In my left hand I placed what I, as just an ordinary fan who got disillusioned, consider to be the positives of the modern game mainly since the formation of the Premiership. In my right hand I placed the negatives. Let's have a look at the result:

<u>Positives</u>

Big screen football and 'illegal' foreign channels
International superstars and skill factor
Tackling racism
The back pass rule
Lower Division play-offs

<u>Negatives</u>

Player diving and gamesmanship
Television presentation
Americanisation of the game
Corporate priorities

24 /7 fixtures
Football's new owners
Ticket pricing
Cautions and petty laws
The new consumer
Stewarding and security
All-seater stadiums
Overbearing advertising and marketing
Annual kit changes and shirt numbering
Wage demands
Stadium design and identity
Lack of home-grown players
Radio phone-in shows
Lack of free speech
Player agents
Media sensationalism
FIFA rankings
Following England

After this little experiment I was taken to hospital with a suspected torn muscle in my right arm. Luckily I made a full recovery and got back into good enough shape to be able to type up a few details about these positives and negatives. Let's be positive first...

POSITIVES

Big screen football and 'illegal' foreign channels

"I think it's a greedy private company [Sky] trying to dictate to the small people what they can and cannot do, purely for profit. The law needs changing...If I wanted to buy a car I could go to any garage I like. Me, as a publican, if I want to show football, I can only go to the Sky garage, and I have to pay ten times the price of anybody else [in Europe]. I don't believe that's fair."

Pub Landlady Karen Murphy 2011

In the last few years I've gone from being a fan who regularly attended live matches to what they call an 'armchair supporter' (or perhaps now, a 'bar-stool supporter'). In other words – someone who follows their team via a television screen.

When you stop attending live games you become a lot more disconnected with the team you support. I'm not quite as joyous when they win, and not quite as downhearted when they lose. You also start to come out with these weird phrases, things you never used to say, stuff like "Who are we playing next weekend?"

With the cost of football now so high, many of football's forgotten fans fill up the pubs and bars instead of the rows of plastic seats. Sometimes the atmosphere in certain venues can be more electric than what you might experience in the actual stadiums. I've been in pubs that have erupted in celebration and seen a release of energy that was so familiar during the 'dark days' of football. I encounter a lot of people who actually prefer to follow their team in a pub or bar, because it's far more social and hassle free than going to the game. In a way, terrace culture has survived in these venues for the following reasons:

1. You can stand up if you want to.
2. You can watch the game in the company of your friends.
3. You can decide on the day of the game if you want to go and watch it.
4. It won't cost £40 to get into the pub.
5. There are no men in orange bibs, telling you what you can and can't say.

So what does it say about the modern game when so many supporters actually prefer watching the game in a pub for these reasons? I encountered a similar scenario when I was in Barcelona for an Arsenal away game. Me and my friends couldn't get match tickets so we watched the game with the locals in a bar just outside the Nou Camp. Spanish football is similar to ours in the sense that the crowd has been gentrified in recent years and ticket prices have been hiked up for big games. There wasn't much of an atmosphere coming from the ground but the fans in the bar were certainly passionate and very vocal.

In this day and age, fans of bigger clubs are lucky, in that we have the option to follow our teams from the television for virtually every game. On one level it is overload, but given the option we'd rather have it. Many bars and pubs now show Premiership matches on foreign channels, whereas there is a law in the UK stipulating that no British channel can broadcast a live match between 3.00pm and 5.00pm on a Saturday (a law in place to safeguard attendances in other games). At the time of writing, venues that broadcast the games on foreign channels are breaking the law. However, a court battle is taking place where Karen Murphy, a landlady in Portsmouth, is challenging this law. If she wins, this will be the broadcasting equivalent to the Bosman Ruling. If she loses I can't see that much changing; in this technological age, pubs and punters will still look for ways to get better value for money. In 2010 I actually had a uniformed police officer tell me that he watches the football on these (illegal) foreign channels because going to Spurs (his team) was too expensive and too corporate.

Watching football in pubs years ago was good, but it usually meant watching a small box not much better than what we had at home. Big screens are now the norm and we've probably got to the point now where we take for granted this enhancement. During a World Cup or European Championship, giant screens are put up all over the country (except in our capital city for no apparent reason) and even some cinemas have gone back to the tradition of showing big games on the silver screen. Sport just like the movies, looks so much better when bigger. But, I shall end this with a strong word of warning: I've been in pubs that have had *Celebrity Big Brother* and *X-Factor* showing on a big screen.

International superstars and skill factor

Those of us who have issues with the financial and social side of the English game have to also acknowledge that the standard of domestic football has improved since the formation of the Premier League. Can't argue with it, the play's more skilful and flamboyant and it's mainly down to the increase in top quality foreign players.

English club football suffered and fell behind as a result of the ban on our clubs in Europe between 1985 and 1990. Our teams with home grown players won plenty of major European honours before the ban; in fact we were second to none. But those five years did a lot of damage and the influence of imports since the ban was badly needed to get our teams back to a competitive standard. In theory, this should have also benefited the England team as our players regularly compete with these foreign talents. The national team has painfully underachieved throughout the Premier League years, but that is probably more down to the dominance of average foreign players who stifle home-grown talent (we'll get to that later).

It's somewhat surprising that it had taken so long for the English league to accept foreign players as a normal part of the game. The leagues in Spain and Italy had no issues with fielding the top foreign players from the very formations of their leagues in the 1930s. During the same period in time it would have been inconceivable that English teams would have regularly recruited players from overseas, and it highlights arrogance in their mentality over the years. In the early days of football we considered ourselves to be untouchable. So much so, that we didn't even bother to enter the World Cup until 1950, thus denying future generations of England fans a team jersey with more than just the one lonely star. A lot of the time, the opinion that England were the best could be justified by results and even the rest of the world still viewed England as the masters of the game. To give just one example, in 1948 Italy were rated by many as the best team in the world and were also officially the world champions. In that year, Italy played England who were seen by many as the unofficial world champions. This high profile game was played in Rome and England humiliated the world champions 4-0. This confirmed to the English the belief that they were still the masters of the game they invented. It wasn't until the famous England v Hungary game at Wembley in 1953 that this belief was finally blown to pieces in dramatic fashion. At the time, the Hungarian Olympic Champions had become the superpowers of European football and England were destroyed 6-3. It was the first time the inventors of the game had ever been beaten on home soil by overseas opposition (discounting Ireland). Eighty-one years of home superiority crushed in a game that cruelly proved to the English that Johnny Foreigner had developed better technique and that we were no longer the masters. Without this attitude of superiority and complacency, foreign players would have been a regular part of the English game decades before, but it wasn't until the late 1970s that it became normal to see players from overseas play for English teams.

By the mid 1990s English clubs were attracting the cream of the crop. At Highbury I saw Dennis Bergkamp make his debut for Arsenal back on the first day of the 1995-96 season against Middlesbrough. He failed to score and the press mauled him for supposedly making an unimpressive performance. My eye-witness impression was that of a player with more skill and finesse than I'd ever seen before on a football pitch. Watching him play live for the first time was a showcase in touch, passing ability and all-round technique. I was blown away; I knew this player was awesome despite what some elements of the media had to say.

The likes of Bergkamp also managed set a better example to home-grown players through their professionalism of the game and dedication to their own career. In order to keep up, the English players had to improve their habits and diets. Tony Adams and Lee Dixon both claimed that Arsene Wenger's ideas on nutrition and fitness added another two years to their professional careers. Dennis Wise once commented that when Gianfranco Zola first came to Chelsea in the late 1990s he put the other players to shame with his professionalism.

It might also be suggested that some foreign players not only play football better than us – but also speak better English. After playing in the Premier League for many seasons Liverpool's German midfielder Dietmar Hamann complained, "I still can't understand Jamie Carragher!" In fact this was a widespread opinion from most of Liverpool's foreign players who had mastered our language but hadn't quite mastered extreme scouse. If it makes them feel better, we don't understand Jamie Carragher either.

Tackling racism

"It [football] is colour blind. When for instance, in the 1970s, the Brazilian military government attempt to 'whiten' the national team, there was a huge popular and successful demand for the return of the black players who had been and were soon again selected on merit."

Melvyn Bragg

One of the worst things about 1970s and 1980s football was the sound of monkey noises from sections of the crowd directed towards black players. The abuse that players such as John Barnes, Cyril Regis and Luther Blissett had to put up with is now thankfully in the past in English football, a more positive example of how football had to change with society. Personally I've never heard monkey chanting at any football match in this country and I've been attending games regularly since the year 1986. The only time I've heard this type of racism was when I went to watch AC Milan play Lazio in Italy. Milan player Clarence Seedorf received the ball near the Lazio fans and a loud monkey chant went up by a sizable minority. I and the people I was with looked surprised by this, but to the rest of the crowd this seemed like just a normal part of the Italian game and was not an issue. In England now that would not be tolerated and action would have been taken.

Many of Europe's leagues have this problem, with the Spanish La Liga being the most high profile. In 2006 when playing for Barcelona, Cameroon striker Samuel Eto'o threatened to walk off the pitch after loud monkey chants were directed at him by large sections of Real Zaragoza supporters. Real Zaragoza's punishment for this was a €6,000 fine, far less than some of their top players would get paid in a week. This was not an isolated incident for Samuel Eto'o who had also received racist abuse at other Spanish football grounds from fans of Real Madrid, Atletico Madrid, and Racing Santander to name a few. Another high profile example was in February 2011, when French striker Djibril Cissé felt he had to leave the Greek league because of constant racial abuse from the crowd.

England still has plenty of racists at football grounds but the authorities have been coherent and clear about the consequences if this racism is displayed in any way. The *Let's Kick Racism Out of Football* campaign, which was founded in 1993, has been the most prominent voice and is an organisation funded by the main governing bodies of English football including the Premier League, FA and PFA.

Football is an industry that still gets labelled with a racism tag, usually from those outside of the game. Whether that tag is justified or not, those who point the finger should take a look at the industries they work in and see how integrated they are. Football is one of the few things we have where people of all races actually mix together. A game of park football in England will be far more racially integrated than for example a party held for workers of a typical media or advertising company. I've done work for the film and television industry as an extra since the year 2000. I've worked on hundreds of different TV and film productions and in that time I've not seen one black director or one black producer. Rather than being a 'who you know' industry, in football ability and character are all that matters.

Okay so there might be a lack of ethnic and social diversity in the very top jobs in football. Black footballers make up 25% of a team squad, yet even by 2011 there were only two black managers out of ninety league clubs. I've never seen or heard of any black board member, director or executive of a football club. It's a situation that didn't change during a time when racism on the pitch did. But this is the business side of the game, and it's no surprise that the people who run football clubs tend to look the same as the people who run other big corporations. To quote Les Ferdinand in 2011, "I watch our [Tottenham] games from the directors' box. 99% of the time I'm the only black person in there".

An accusation of racism directed at football is that no British Asian player has yet made the highest level or become a household name. For the amount of British Asians who play the game, that is surprising to say the least. I used to play for a predominantly Asian Sunday league team called Finsbury Park Monarchs. We played in a North East London league at Hackney

Marshes. The teams we played against in this league were all integrated with white and black players. The Asian players in our team, mostly Indian and Bangladeshi, were a bit smaller and less physical but they made up for it with skill and we would finish in mid-table and make the odd cup final. I never saw one example of racism directed towards our team (apart from the time when one of our Indian defenders called one of our white midfielders a 'paki'). However, the Finsbury Park Monarchs decided to switch leagues and go and play in the Asian League in North West London. All of a sudden the non-Asian players in the team like myself were then classed as 'foreigners' and we were only limited to four 'foreigners' to a game. Not for the first time in my life either, having already been classed as a 'foreigner' in the London Greek League. Maybe I should set up a London Aryan League and see how that goes down: *Sorry mate, only four players allowed who don't have blond hair and blue eyes!*

The reason this is a problem for the development of Asian players is that it's isolationist. Scouts searching for talent are less likely to watch games in these leagues. There's no use in running away from the realities of what you would be up against in the professional game. The best in football will include big ugly white and black guys, and Asians should face up to this reality rather than be left on the outside. Asians in Britain have not been playing football in great numbers for as long as other races, therefore they are adolescents in the sport. Their time will come, just as it has done with cricket. It took India and Pakistan decades to become major forces within the sport but they did get there. Hopefully it won't take decades for British Asians to make an impact in football and it is inevitable that some players will make that breakthrough in the near future. Football history proves that if you're good enough, your ethnic background is irrelevant.

One problem that I would cite would be the lack of black and Asian supporters attending professional football matches. It's ironic that in the 1970s and 1980s when racism was rife in football, it was far more common to see black supporters at clubs such as West Ham, Birmingham and Man City, to name just a few. For some football clubs to survive they need to find a way to bring more support in from ethnic minorities; because in many cities these are sizable minorities. A city like Birmingham is 30% non-white but this is not represented in the fan base of the local clubs like Aston Villa, Birmingham City, Wolves, Walsall and WBA. Other struggling clubs like Bradford, Blackburn, Burnley and Oldham also need to get in more fans from the ethnic minorities of their towns, as there is potential for a huge fan base which these clubs currently lack. In London more than most, football grounds are in communities with large ethnic backgrounds. Again this is not represented in the fans who attend football matches. Virtually every London Asian I know for some reason has chosen to support Liverpool! Ticket pricing could be a factor here, as black and Asian people are among the lower earners in British society; failing that, they have the money and just know a rip-off when they see one.

Arsenal and Spurs pride themselves in traditionally having lots of black people who attend games. With these two clubs there is very little recent history of a racism problem, although very small sections of the Arsenal support have been known for anti-Jewish songs that include references to gas chambers. This is no doubt influenced by Spurs fans calling themselves the 'Yids', but singing about Hitler and gas chambers clearly goes beyond football rivalry (this is not to be confused with a lot of Arsenal chants that include words like 'yids' and 'yido' when Arsenal fans sing these songs they are referring to Spurs, not Jews).

But even though Arsenal and Spurs have many black fans who attend games, the number is still hugely under-representative of the local fan base. At Arsenal and Spurs the integration comes in the pubs and bars of the surrounding areas. In these venues, a more equal mix of people watch the matches together on the big screens. That is real integration and comes about simply through football, so despite a few problems the positives surely outweigh the negatives. The game has done a great deal for unity and integration and deserves more credit for this than to simply be labelled as racist. In the football grounds themselves the authorities have made a real effort to combat racism and they have been very effective.

The back-pass law

Remember the days before the 1992 back-pass law? Before then, teams with a negative style could kill a game by going no further than their own 25 yard box and then playing the ball back to the keeper, who was allowed to pick it up, pass it back out again, only for the same scenario to be repeated. Can't pick it up any more mate, you'll just have to find more inventive reasons to waste time. This was a major change to the game at the time and it did face a lot of opposition. A couple of decades on and most people would concede that football's better off with this law. Okay, so there are countless other new rules, introduced by FIFA, that are not needed – but this one did improve the flow of a game. A positive for modern football, introduced for good reasons – thumps up for FIFA!

Lower division play-offs

Football at its best is about excitement and drama. Excitement and drama come about through a level of competition that is passionate, equally matched and competitive. That pretty much sums up the promotion deciders for the three lower divisions in England. The top two (top three in League 2) teams in the league automatically go up to the division above, leaving the next four teams to battle it out for the last promotion place. What we get with the play-offs is diversity in the teams that compete and unpredictability. It keeps the interest in lower division football intense throughout the whole season and plays a vital part in preventing clubs from going out of business altogether. Below the Premiership, a season is never over for any club and there is always something to fight for if a team can find a good spell of form. In 2004 Crystal Palace went from being near the relegation zone in Division 1 (now the Championship) to being in the Premiership in the space of about three months. What a contrast to the predictable nature of the top leagues in Europe. I've heard rumours that the Premier League is considering the same concept of the play-offs to decide the fourth Champions League spot. If such a plan ever does come into action then it's hard to see how it could go wrong. If we had a situation where a team who finishes in seventh spot is then in with a fighting chance of gaining a Champions League place, then that opens football up and gives a little bit of hope where there was no hope before.

NEGATIVES

Player diving and gamesmanship

"Players are conning each other, I'm glad I'm not playing any more, especially in the Premiership. I can't get my head round a player who rolls around then gets up thirty seconds later. I'd be embarrassed. Lads I've played with go down like they've been shot and it drives me crazy."

Roy Keane

After the 2007 League Cup Final, players from Arsenal and Chelsea were strongly criticised for a 'mass brawl' [a bit of effeminate pushing and shoving] that 'marred' [made a good talking point] the end of the game, which Chelsea won 2-1. During a radio debate on TalkSPORT many callers sounded just as angry as the hosts did about what a bad example these highly paid stars were setting to youngsters. One caller however made a brilliant point, that a good example was set to young people – because cards were issued and the offenders were seen to be punished. The caller pointed out that what really does set a bad example, on a regular basis, is when players cheat and are seen to get away with it.

I'm a qualified FA coach and work with kids between the ages of six and ten. Some of these young players are now copying their heroes in a culture that has damaged the integrity of football for the past two decades; severely harming the soul of the actual sport itself. I tell the kids I coach not to dive. One of them said to me, "I bet you dived when you were our age". I replied, "No I didn't, because the players we looked up to didn't".

The World Cup of 1990 was a notable point in time when the problem of diving and injury feigning was increasing. In the years since then, it's become an accepted part of football, with hardly a top-flight game going by without fit athletic sportsmen falling to the ground and re-enacting the Willem Dafoe death scene from *Platoon*. It has downgraded football from a 'man's game', to a sport for over-sized cry babies. Ironically, as football became less of a 'man's game', never before have advertisers and the media portrayed these guys as being brave gladiator style warriors. I must have missed that scene in *Gladiator* when Maximus feigned a flesh wound and rolled around the coliseum crying his eyes out. Excluding the odd isolated incident, I can't name any other sport in which the players fake an injury in order to gain an advantage or to punish an opponent. It is exclusive to football, and this culture is ruining what should be the greatest sport in the world.

The football authorities have been completely inept in dealing with the problem of player gamesmanship of this kind.

Since the late 1990s FIFA has run a *Fair Play* campaign which has been all gestures and no action. FIFA think that the best way to clamp down on bad sportsmanship is by having kids bring on banners reading FIFA FAIR PLAY before a game. Incredibly, this type of gesture hasn't done anything to solve the problem. It turns out that footballers only react to gestures such as fines and suspensions. There's an easy way to stop this cheating overnight, with a simple law involving video evidence by a panel after the game. If a player is found guilty of cheating by diving or feigning injury, then he receives something like a three match ban. If a player is found guilty of the same offence twice in a season then he receives something like a five match ban. Brian Clough once commented that if a manager was fined a week's wages for every time one of his players dived then it would solve the problem overnight. The football authorities are certainly quick to punish players for miss-timed tackles, shows of emotion and even voicing an opinion. Yet when a player tries to get another player punished by feigning injury the authorities do virtually nothing. The one time FIFA did act was during the 2009-10 season, when Arsenal striker Eduardo dived to gain a penalty against Celtic. FIFA handed out a fine and suspension to Eduardo. For some reason, that one dive caused media outrage, which was why FIFA chose to act. The whole scenario was completely inconsistent; did it set a precedent for FIFA to act against all future diving? No, diving continues on a regular basis and the governing bodies do nothing about it. When Eduardo dived against Celtic, we can be 100% sure that his dive wasn't the only one in top level football on that night.

Football supporters and the media must also all be consistent when it comes to diving. It's either wrong or it isn't. It can't just be wrong if it's a player of an opposition team who we dislike. I'm an Arsenal fan, and I'm prepared to admit that what Eduardo did against Celtic was wrong, and against the spirit of the game.

He deserved to be punished for it, but so have the countless others over the years of who are no less guilty.

Managers are certainly consistent in their views on diving – in that they're mostly a bunch of hypocrites. To give just one of many examples, here's Alex Mcleish's reaction to when one of his Birmingham City players dived to gain a penalty against Wigan in the 2009-10 season: "He [the defender] stuck his leg out, and when you do that you risk giving away a penalty". Of course he stuck his leg out, he's a defender! What was he supposed to do, strike a pose. The point Mcleish, is that your man dived, and had it been the other way round, you would be the first one to condemn both the dive and the standard of refereeing.

A great way to stop injury feigning and diving would be legalised thuggery. Yes legalised thuggery, now hear me out. If a player pretends that he's hurt his leg and been found guilty of cheating, then the leg should be made to pay the price. Let's say for example, that a player has gone down in a crumpled heap without any contact. He holds his shin in pain and slyly looks up to see the opposition player get a caution for an offence he never committed. The diver thinks that he's won the day, however the FA study the videotape and judge that he feigned injury to get a fellow professional penalised. As a punishment, the player who got the caution then gets to kick that player in the shin for real and as hard as he likes.

Not convinced with that one? Okay, a less violent method would be for TV evidence to be used during the game by a fourth official. People have mixed opinions on the introduction of instant video replays during the actual game. A very strong argument in its favour is that it would go some way towards solving this problem. Eduardo would not have dived against Celtic had he known that the incident would have been judged via a TV replay before a final decision was made.

Laws aside, it's a shame that the players themselves don't have more professional pride. Old pros such as Roy Keane, Ian Wright, Terry Butcher, Stuart Pearce, Julian Dicks and Tony Adams never once lowered themselves to that kind of cheating. Players who dive can also get themselves a reputation that works against them when they are genuinely fouled. England striker Andy Johnson became regarded as such an expert at diving and deceiving referees that whenever he did get fouled there were immediately cries of 'cheat'. Robert Pires and David Ginola also had many genuine free-kick and penalty appeals turned down due to the same reputation. When playing for Newcastle, Ginola once got sent off for receiving two yellow cards handed out to him for diving, when in fact TV replays showed that he had been genuinely fouled by the defender. I tell the kids I coach the story of the boy who cried wolf and how it relates to diving and injury feigning – Ginola does get a mention!

During the prime of Diego Maradona's career, one of the most impressive aspects of his game was his ability to stay on his feet and not go down when he was fouled. It was a part of his game that was to his advantage, as some of the best goals or set-ups he ever produced were times when he would keep his balance whilst being fouled. It was an honest schoolboy-like approach to playing football, but by the 1990 World Cup that part of his game had changed. In that tournament Maradona had reduced his style of play to diving whenever he thought he could con the referee. He would no longer try and stay on his feet when challenged, and the end result was that he never made the runs or passes that he was still capable of doing. It was sad to see such a great player, still in the prime of his career, lose such a noble and effective part of his game in favour of a pathetic style of cheating. Today's equivalent, Lionel Messi, appears to play the game with the right spirit; shame about his team-mates. In the 2010-11 season Barcelona played Real Madrid in the Champions League semi-final at the Bernabeu. In a highly anticipated game between the two strongest squads in the world, we witnessed 90 minutes of both teams trying to get each other sent off and constant harassment of the referee. Both legs of this semi-final were totally dishonest games of football – so dishonest, that even Cristiano Ronaldo complained of cheating! That's a bit like Jim Davidson accusing Bernard Manning of being crass. Fans and players of other sports, witness to such a football match, must scratch their heads in confusion at the fascination and glorification heaped upon what you could justifiably call a bunch of immoral, spoilt, cynical pricks!

What doesn't help matters is the justification of this problem. For example, football pundits who criticise a player for 'not going down when he could have done' to gain a penalty. Diving is now considered an art and players are referred to as 'clever' when they get away with it. If it is so clever why not just go the full way and have a Dive of The Month competition on *Match of the Day* (we could judge the winner by holding up scorecards). In the 2002 World Cup, Michael Owen was considered 'clever' for diving and gaining England a penalty kick which ultimately won us the game against Argentina. Yet had it been an Argentina player that dived he would have been described as devious, dishonest and a slimy con artist.

Another justification for this kind of cheating is that footballers are under enormous pressure to win games. Well if that is the case then maybe we should all conduct our lives by the same principle. Modern life is competitive and financially times are hard for many. Therefore due to these pressures is it perfectly acceptable for people to cheat on their tax returns? As long as they can get away with conning the Inland Revenue then fair enough, right? Somehow I don't think that any judge would accept that line of defence. Trying to get opponents penalised through diving and feigning injury should never be an accepted part of the game; it's a total contradiction of its origins. If getting someone punished for something they're innocent of is deemed acceptable, then what kind of example is football sending out to children and the rest of society?

And speaking of football pundits…

Television presentation

"I was doing the TV panels with the likes of Jimmy Hill, Jack Charlton, Malcolm Allison and Bill Shankly. It was like the football's *Who's Who* on the box at the time, and I was usually the one who said something that was seized upon by the press. I never did see the point of going on television, expected to voice an honest opinion, and then saying next to nothing or being cautious and particularly careful just to avoid upsetting somebody. There are too many supposed pundits who do exactly that now. What a life! Get yourself on TV, get paid a small fortune, smile a lot and say next to nowt. Now that's nice work if you can get it."

Brian Clough

What Brian Clough was referring to here, is that all too often, broadcasters choose presenters and analysts who can make an art form out of sitting on the fence. To put it in very simple terms, the pundits of years gone by were more entertaining and straight talking. Ian St. John and Jimmy Greaves were the main faces of football television coverage during the 1980s. The Saint and Greaves were both football legends turned presenters who fans felt an affinity for because they came across as down-to-earth and carried the image of two old boys discussing football in a pub or a bookmakers. Jimmy Greaves was not the most presentable man to ever appear on TV, and wouldn't get on the box today for that very reason – however he was funny, forthright and had charisma.

The two men combined brilliantly as the Saint would spend half the show laughing at Greavsie's comments.

On the BBC during the same period, Jimmy Hill and Terry Venables were the main football pundits, with Des Lynam presenting. It's easy to criticise someone like Jimmy Hill, but as a TV personality, he never lacked a different opinion and was never boring. Terry Venables would tear his hair out over Jimmy Hill's comments and the two of them would regularly enter into a heated debate. What we had back then was a contrast of personalities. What we have today is conformity of opinions and language. There are exceptions. Someone like Ian Wright went so far as to quit his job at the BBC as a football pundit because he felt that he wasn't allowed to express his views in the way that he wanted. Another exception to the usual conformity is BBC's Colin Murray, whose humorous and light-hearted presenting is in contrast with the regular style of football presentation.

That regular style would be for TV presenters and analysts to play it safe with everyone – with the exception of the poor old referee. The experts in the studio will look at about ten clips of an incident in slow motion, and then all agree that the referee made a bad decision and is incompetent. With everyone else they will tread very carefully by using clichés that don't quite say it all. Such as:

"He seemed to go down quite easily"
> **He's a diving cheat.**

"They're going through a transitional period right now"
> **They used to be a good team. Now they've fallen apart and are on the road to nowhere.**

"He'll be disappointed with that effort"
> **He gets paid ninety grand a week and he can't score from two yards out.**

Football TV presentation can, at times, be over the top and very hard on the eyes, ears and brain. This is supposed to be the golden age of television sports coverage. It is in the sense that there are many more live games on TV and the technology is far superior compared to years gone by. The high quality tracking cameras and HD slow motion replays can give us a better insight into a live game, which of course is a good thing. But sometimes the way the technology is applied can also make for uncomfortable viewing and this is mainly through the editing. I've got good eyesight and a low concentration span, but even my eyes and brain can't cope with the amount of edits per second and the jerky cameras. Unless a person has superhero eyesight that has the power to slow down motion, then the majority of after-match football clips are completely unwatchable (these clips are usually in the form of the good old musical montage). A montage of football clips will have as many edits per second as an MTV video. I've closed my eyes in cinemas during some films where the editing is so fast that it's impossible to have any idea of what is happening. Technically this style of cutting is very impressive, but as a viewer I find it very hard to watch. In older style sports presentation we simply got shown the best of the action – no other stylisation needed. The big thing now is 3D football which is getting a big push from Sky. The breakdown of it is this: we used to watch football in stadiums – got priced out of that, and now we're being told how uniquely lucky we are to pay more money for a 3D TV experience than what we used to pay for a live in the flesh experience. Thanks Murdoch!

Okay so we've dealt with 3D, boring pundits and fancy editors. Now it's time for a lot of English commentators to be shown the door. With Clive Tyldesley I would recommend that door read ROOM 101. And their replacements should be foreigners. Well why not? It's okay for players, managers, and even club owners to come from overseas, so why not the commentators? If they're better at it than our home-grown announcers then let's bring them in.

They've got more flair and exuberance, and what better way for a commentator to greet a goal than the South American style GOOOOOOOOOOOAAAAAALLLLLL...GGG...GOOOOAAAA LLLLL. Actually, Sky Sports do employ a similar tactic by giving viewers the option of watching fans as commentators, as opposed to the regular commentary. It's a promising idea but it doesn't really work, mainly because those involved in the commentary are, to put it politely, fucking horrendous! These biased fans scream when a goal is scored but it's hard on the ears and they sound like a cat being tortured or a Christina Aguilera record (or a cat being forced to listen to a Christina Aguilera record).

The South American style GOOOOAAAAAAALLLLL... has an operatic quality about it but, more than anything, these amigos sound like they're having a great time when calling the action; much more so than some of our English commentators who can sound so dour and uptight. Our home-grown announcers are also so quick to condemn everything from a pitch invasion to a player who shows emotion and exuberance. John Motson made his name in the 1970s when he commentated on a famous FA Cup giant killing, when non-league Hereford beat mighty Newcastle United 2-1 after being a goal down. The goals were greeted by the famous sight of hundreds of parka jacket clad kids running on to the pitch in celebration. It's footage the BBC repeats on a regular basis as iconic images associated with FA Cup giant killing. Today those Hereford pitch invaders would be deemed to be committing a criminal offence. This offence is punishable with a fine or custodial sentence, plus a place on the hooligan register and ban from every football ground in the country. This strict attitude in football is now reflected in the commentary. If the same attitude were around in 1966 then I would hate to think what Kenneth Wolstenholme's immortal lines in the World Cup Final would have sounded like... *'And some people are on the pitch.*

They think it's all over...What a disgrace...They should not be on the pitch...Where are the stewards...Dear oh dear...England have won the World Cup but I'm afraid it's been marred by these ugly scenes at the end.'

Kenneth Wolstenholme was a fine example of how British football commentary hasn't always been cheap and uninspiring. He, Brian Moore and David Coleman were all masters of their profession and their voices had a British movie star quality about them. The excitement in their tone when something dramatic happened was so spectacular and enjoyable. They also had a comic side and light-heartedness. In the 1966 FA Cup Final Everton beat Sheffield Wednesday 3-2 after coming back from being two goals behind. Everton's equalising goal sparked a one man pitch invasion from a fat, bald, suited-up scouser. He was chased from one half of the pitch to the other by police whom he avoided like a rugby player who brushes off the defence en route to scoring a try. Wolstenholme's commentary for this incident highlights a more relaxed attitude of the time and a sense of fun. He simply commented on the action in front of him. As one policeman rugby tackled the Everton fan on the edge of the 25 yard box, Wolstenholme shouted out, "*And a great tackle. Almost on the line.*" There is still one commentator around today who has the same style persona and that is Stuart Hall, the old *It's a knockout* presenter. He works on the radio for BBC Five Live and has that old-fashioned movie star voice along with a sense of fun. But they only let him commentate on low profile matches and it seems like he's just there as a gimmick rather than a serious commentator. Funny thing is though, despite the fact that he's not taken seriously, Hall is arguably the most entertaining and eloquent commentator they have. Football commentary used to be very simplistic; they only talked when the action required them to do so. The style today is very different. What we get now is non-stop blabbering and ninety minutes of analysis and speculation.

Speaking of which, Clive Tyldesley is rated by many as the top TV commentator. Indeed, he has won awards for his work, and he does have a very good knowledge of football tactics. Okay that's the plaudits over with – I and many others find his style of commentating exasperating, especially when along the lines of *Here we are in this football coliseum, where these two teams of gladiators are set to battle it out to the finish in front of a baying crowd.* Or even... *Welcome to Old Trafford the Theatre of Dreams, as tonight's stars get ready to act out in front of a packed auditorium. Which one of the performers is going to write the script blah blah blah...* Or how about *It's like Mourinho is the ultimate safe cracker looking to unpick a difficult lock, but he wants this vault door closed.* Eh?

This type of metaphoric commentary could possibly work if done by Orson Wells or Laurence Olivier. Those two actors carried a talent that should also be the basic requirement of a football commentator – a great voice. Clive Tyldesley is a self-confessed boyhood fan of Manchester United. Some might say that it shows when he commentates on Manchester United. Actually, it shows when he commentates on a game which has bugger-all to do with Manchester United: *The crowd here at Rochdale just 3,000. That's 87,000 less than you can cram in to the Nou Camp stadium...Which reminds me...who can ever forget that balmy night in Barcelona when Manchester United scored those two goals in injury time.* Clive Tyldesley has got himself such a reputation for blabbing on about that "balmy night" in the Nou Camp, that he now has to give money to charity for every time he mentions it in his commentary (someone hit the jackpot there). Here is my entry to the Clive Tyldesley Book of Easy-To-Make Up-Metaphors – Volume 3 *Well Ron, football commentary is an art form but right now we're lacking in Rembrandts and Michelangelos.* The art of sports commentary is simple: call the game, have a dramatic voice and project genuine emotion.

Today it seems too focused on pre-rehearsed fancy lines and 'clever' metaphors.

British football coverage has become far too paranoid about broadcasting anything slightly controversial. If there is a streaker on the pitch the camera will now focus on another part of the stadium and away from the incident. This rule is meant to keep off air anything that looks as if it condones what is banned in football. So by the same principle, Eva Mendes could run on to the pitch at Villa Park wearing just her earrings and yet we'd see nothing. And they class that as entertainment – for our viewing pleasure. So the question is – what's the more criminal? Okay I'll admit that Eva Mendes is unlikely to do this! Most streakers don't look like Hollywood actresses, but there have been some good ones over the years. There can even be value in a naked fat bloke running on to the pitch and being chased by stewards. During a Chelsea v Arsenal match in 2005, a bare-arsed Arsenal fan ran on to the pitch with the message *You can stick your Russian roubles up your...* along with an arrow running down his back and pointing to his posterior! This wasn't shown by Sky Sports who instead focused on the Chelsea team bench which showed Jose Mourinho laughing at the incident. Football is uncensored when the TV coverage comes from Europe or South America. When football is broadcast to us from other countries we get English commentary but the producing is done by a TV company in whatever country the game is played in. During the Euro 2004 final in Lisbon, a Spanish man ran on to the pitch and was chased by the stewards in Keystone Cop fashion. As the English commentator apologised for the uncensored Portuguese TV coverage, the viewer witnessed the pitch invader run towards one of the goals at high speed and jump into the top corner of the net. Where I watched the game the whole room cheered on this terrific long jump, while the English commentator came out with the usual disapproval.

It's also a good bet that when the Spaniard flew into the top corner of the net the South American commentators shouted out GOOOAAAAALLLL. As a TV viewer I'd rather be treated like an adult and do not need to be protected from these 'shocking images'.

So there you have it. Football presentation on television could be improved and the BBC, ITV and Sky should make me head of their sports coverage. I'd have operatic Brazilians shouting down your television screens within weeks. GOOOAAAAAALLL.

Americanisation of the game

For the most part I'm not anti-American. I've liked most Americans that I've met, and any country that gives the world blue jeans, rock and roll, and Hollywood has a lot of good things going for it. As for their sports, they carry a certain image and style which is different to the rest of the world – a style that doesn't really work when copied by the likes of Burton Albion. The best example of what I mean by this is the playing of music whenever a goal is scored, which we now have at many football grounds. The sound of the crowd cheering a goal is now drowned out by loud music that blares over the thousands of voices in the stadium. A football match for the most part is eighty-eight minutes of nothing exciting happening and two minutes of drama. Drama climaxing with perhaps a goal or two being scored, and yet this climax of a game is now being crowned by *Let Me Entertain You* from Robbie Williams, or more commonly *Tom Hark* from Piranhas (if I had a pound for every club that plays *Tom Hark* after a goal, I could afford to buy a large round of pies at Wembley Stadium).

So far the really big Premiership clubs haven't taken to playing music as yet, but many other Premiership clubs do, along with lots of lower division teams. I dislike this trend so much that in the 2004-05 Premiership season I was delighted to see Norwich City get relegated, for no other reason than their annoying habit of playing crap music every time they scored a goal at home. So Delia Smith, take note of Morrissey – hang the DJ.

Other such Americanisms include cheerleaders before the game or at half-time. Only the cheerleaders we football fans get are not the *Playboy* standard vixens who jump up and down for the likes of the Dallas Cowboys. No, we get twelve-year-old girls! This isn't just a Premiership thing and again is usually more common in the lower divisions.

This attempt at razzmatazz is a hopeless cause at the likes of Macclesfield, Grimsby and Rochdale. These poor girls come on to the pitch at grounds such as Hartlepool and look absolutely freezing. Cheerleaders in Hartlepool would be better off running out in pullovers, leg warmers, and carrying a mug of hot chocolate. It's certainly a long way from the days when brass bands used to perform on the pitch before the game. Okay, call me old fashioned, but at least there was some meaning to those bands as many of them had historic connections with the clubs. I suppose the basic problem with cheerleading is that it's just not very entertaining. Anyone ever come home after a football match and commented that, "The game was shit but at least the cheerleaders were on good form".

Nothing seems more American than insincere hugging. At a number of clubs, hugging between players goes on just before kick-off as a show of team unity. The beginning of a game can now sometimes look like a standard episode of *American Idol*. Cut the hugging out fellas! You don't have to prove to us that you all love one another. Hugging should only be reserved for when you actually do something worthwhile, like scoring a goal.

I had a taste of American sport when I was in Texas in 1998. I went to watch the Texas Rangers take on the Chicago Cubs in baseball. The stadium was fantastic and the game was a great one-off novelty experience. As for the fans, I got the feeling that many of them were there just for a good excuse to sit down and eat more hot dogs and pizzas; food did seem to be the main focus of attention. Waiters even come up to your seat to take your order. If that Americanism is ever imported to England, then at least it would stop fans leaving the game five minutes before half-time in order to be near the front of the burger queue (it's medically proven that football fans can't go a full ninety minutes without a feed). Then again, the thought of having waiters come to your seat to take your food order would make football feel like less of a sport than it already is, and more of a corporate/commercial day out.

I wouldn't get rid of every single Americanisation in the game, but most don't work in football and should be sent back to Uncle Sam, along with Starbucks, Lady Gaga, sound-bite politics, Paris Hilton and Simon Cowell (don't let the fact that Simon Cowell isn't an American get in the way of a worthy deportation). However, the fireworks and the ticker tape can stay, and I can't say enough about the *Rocky* theme tune that Manchester United play as a build up before each game!

Corporate priorities

Let me give you an example of an incident which opened my eyes to how corporate priorities were starting to step on the feet of genuine football supporters.

In the summer of 1998 I travelled to France to support England in the World Cup. In England's second group game we were to play Romania in the beautiful city of Toulouse in the south of France. The capacity of the stadium wasn't quite enough to accommodate the thousands of us who had made the journey to Toulouse. I was ticket-less along with quite a few thousand others. The average price for a black market ticket was around 2,000 francs (roughly £200) which was more than we were prepared to pay. An hour before the game and whilst on the look-out for tickets, we saw one England fan running away and waving a ticket in the air along with a huge Cheshire grin on his face. It made us laugh when we saw him being hopelessly chased by a fat ticket tout who was waving his hands in the air and shouting, "Mon billet... Mon billet". Well, I found it funny: at 2,000 francs for a black market ticket who was really the thief? I thought le tout got what he deserved.

Anyway, our search for tickets was hopeless. The prices were not coming down and lines of riot police stopped us from getting too near the ground. We sat down by a nearby wall in acceptance that we were going to miss out on a match we had travelled hundreds of miles to see. Our mood wasn't angry or bitter, we were just disappointed. That was until we looked to our left and saw a very large number of coaches that were parked up side by side. These coaches were not England or Romanian supporters' coaches. Each of these coaches had a sign on the front with names like McDonalds, Canon, Fuji Film, Coca Cola and so on. One large coach then pulled up right in front of us.

Out stepped a group of chino-wearing, shirts-tucked-in, office manager types with Carlsberg baseball caps. They showed their passes at the gate and walked through the line of riot police. None of us spoke a word to one another as there was no need to. It was a classic example of FIFA putting corporate priorities ahead of true football supporters. We felt resentful and had every right to be. We were all part of the official England Members Club (now known as *englandfans*) which is run by the FA. It's the only official way for England fans to purchase tickets for England games. The allocation the FA received was not enough for the amount of members who required tickets, because for the World Cup, and now all major sporting events, the governing bodies hand out huge allocations of tickets to corporate sponsors.[3]

The new football mentality is that anything that brings money into the game is good. The fact that thousands of loyal fans miss out on the chance of attending big games is insignificant in the greater scheme of things. What's important here is obscene prosperity for the few.

There was a time when getting into big games or a cup final was fairly achievable for loyal fans. That's changed dramatically; we might still make the trip, but we don't expect to get in.

In 2006, a group of us made the short journey to Paris to follow Arsenal to our first ever Champions League Final. As expected none of us got in the ground which was played in an 80,000 capacity stadium. For this game, the fans of the two competing clubs received 40,000 tickets between them in a match that would easily have sold out three or four times over. So the question is, where did the other 40,000 tickets go?

The same thing happened in the UEFA Cup Final of the same year when the genuine fans of Middlesbrough and Sevilla only got given a small portion of match tickets. For a fan of Middlesbrough this game would have been the biggest in the club's history. To see their team compete in the UEFA Cup Final meant everything to these supporters who have followed their team loyally through years of mediocrity. During the unsuccessful years these loyal fans are needed. Yet for the good times the same

---

[3] During this piece I originally spelt the word sponsors as 'sponcers'. A terrible example of spelling I admit. But when clicking on spell-check the first word that came up was 'spongers'. Yep that figures.

fans are shunned in place of corporate day trippers, so in a sense the real fans can never truly win either way.

Even fans outside the big leagues now have to put up with the corporate boys stealing all the tickets for the biggest game of the season. For the first ever Championship Play-off Final at the new Wembley Stadium in 2007, just under a third of tickets went to corporate hospitality, whilst thousands of loyal Derby County and West Bromwich Albion supporters were left with nothing.

Since France 98 football has become even more directed towards corporate hospitality. During this England v Romania match in Toulouse the amount of tickets that went to hospitality and sponsors was 24%. By the time of the World Cup in Germany 2006, the amount was 31%. That figure is actually more than the amount of tickets given to the fans of the two competing teams which was a mere 8% to each country. FIFA president Sepp Blatter insists that, "FIFA is proud of these long term partnerships. They are an essential component in staging the World Cup." Interesting, however, the World Cups of years gone by didn't need these essential components in order to stage a football tournament. The perception that there would be no World Cup without this corporate dominance is a lie. The job of the sponsor is to advertise, not take away a large percentage of the tickets from genuine supporters.

A year before the 2006 World Cup, the cost of membership to the England Members Club went from £25 a term to £60. This fee increase was marketed on the basis that the membership period included the World Cup, and that it was the only official way for fans to obtain tickets for England games. What they didn't yell too loudly, was the reality that for each England World Cup game only 8% of tickets would be sold to its members. Instead of paying the £60, I decided to withdraw my membership as it was a blatant attempt at cashing in on the World Cup before a ticket had even been put on sale. In hindsight I was right not to rejoin, because when it came down to the sale of World Cup tickets, thousands of loyal England members would be left with nothing. When England members attend games they are credited with loyalty points on their membership. Those with a high number of loyalty points get given a degree of priority when big game tickets get put on sale. Away games and low profile friendly matches will normally count for the most points. What morons! Real loyalty is getting that freebie by working for the right company, and these *going to away matches in Estonia and Belarus cave dwellers* need to get with the times and stop complaining.

The England Members Club/*englandfans* will claim that they are not the ones who make the rules over FIFA's ticketing priority. But they are run by the FA who are a representative of FIFA, and I don't hear too many protests from the English FA about the overbearing corporate side of football; they are all part of the same gravy train. It's because of these priorities that I haven't travelled to a World Cup since 1998. I figured that by buying a ticket off a tout to go to a FIFA World Cup match, I would be supporting a system that urinates from above on so many of us. Loyal fans get shunned when it comes to the big games, in favour of the corporate boys, so then the only logical conclusion is to shun the greedy buggers back.

Along with the disappointment of England not being given the right to host the 2018 World Cup, people should also consider the reality of what that tournament would have been like. The 1966 World Cup finals in England were attended by ordinary fans, who were there through their love of football, not because of who they worked for. England 2018 would have been so different; corporate hospitality would have been taken to a whole new level. After all, it was Euro 96 that made football fashionable in England, arguably more so than the formation of the Premier League. That tournament began the change of the social demographic in the English game and the Premier League were able to take advantage of this. A 2018 World Cup in England would have been hijacked by every Sir, lord, and celebrity under the sun. Ordinary Russians will find this out in the summer of 2018. They won't get a look in. As for Qatar 2022, well that's just despicable for so many reasons! Forget about corporate hospitality, who wants to watch the World Cup in a country with no football credibility, suspect human rights, alcohol bans, one major city, a lack of hotels to accommodate the masses, jail for kissing in public, and temperatures of around 50 degrees (God help the Irish if they qualify). In a country smaller than Wales, a description of Qatar's geography is as follows: *Much of the country consists of a low, barren, plain covered with sand.* Cheers Sepp, your corporate pals are more than welcome to that one. FIFA will be lucky if any of us bother to watch Qatar 2022 on the TV, let alone make the journey.

The 2010 World Cup highlighted the fact that FIFA has come to rely on the black market in order to fill stadiums. A lot of the corporate and hospitality boys didn't fancy the trip to South Africa, which meant that most games had large sections of empty seats. Genuine fans don't sell tickets and corporate packages being sold on the black market is something that I've seen with my own eyes during France 98. Tournaments held in prosperous countries allow FIFA to get away with this, but South Africa was different. I'm sure that regular football fans from the townships would have loved to have gone to these games but they were simply unaffordable. If FIFA cared at all about fans in Africa they would have charged virtually nothing for all tickets, and still gone on to make a hefty fortune from the most profitable sporting event in the world (a duty free fortune at that, as FIFA make host country governments sign a loophole freeing them from paying any tax). FIFA claim that they have to make as big a profit as possible from the World Cup, because it only comes around once every four years and is their only source of income. That's not true, in fact it's laughable. If you include the qualifiers, then World Cup matches are played three out of every four years. Of course then there's the Women's World Cup which isn't a bad earner. Along with EA Sports who do you think makes huge profit from FIFA's numerous console games for Nintendo and Xbox? FIFA products range from sportswear to clothing to DVDs which are sold all year round, every year. So this lack of profit is a real mystery; one can only assume that these enormous sums of money go to Oxfam and Water Aid, instead of Sepp and the boys. Of course these are just the legal profits I'm referring to. I didn't even mention bribery and corruption! For a book that exposes FIFA as the corrupt reptilians that they are, I would recommend *FOUL! – The Secret World of FIFA: Bribes, Vote Rigging and Ticket Scandals* by Andrew Jenkins.

So back to Toulouse, and one corporate fan showed a lot of class when he walked up to a friend of mine and put a ticket in his hand. My friend asked, "How much?" and the man replied, "Nothing" then walked off. The rest of us would have to settle for a bar with a television screen. When you can't get a ticket, it would be nice to think that your place in the stadium is being taken by somebody who cares just as much as you do. On that day in Toulouse and in the current climate in football, this is not a realistic consolation.

24/7 fixtures

"In the Mexico 1986 World Cup, TV companies made teams play in Mexico City at midday and with an altitude of 2,500 metres and high levels of smog and humidity. It was inhuman. They sold a bad football product to the world. You have to care for the game and defend it from the outside aggression of commercialisation."

Jorge Valdano – 1986 Argentine World Cup Winner

On October 6th 2007, a record was broken when only one Premiership fixture kicked off at 3.00pm on a Saturday. It was solely down to the influence of television. On that weekend, Sunderland fans were expected to be down in London for a televised game that kicked off at 12.00pm on a Sunday. It only took a month for that record to be equalled, when Derby County v West Ham United was the only 3.00pm fixture on Saturday November 10th. Anyone bother to watch *Match of the Day* that night?

But it's not just the television companies who have this influence on fixtures. The police now dictate the time of games due to our good friends health and safety. The police insist that high profile fixtures must now be played no later than 12.45pm so that fans do not have time to drink alcohol before kick-off. Fixtures such as Liverpool v Manchester United, Arsenal v Spurs, Everton v Liverpool, will now always be an early start. The major flaw in this law (apart from the fact that it's bloody annoying and ruins the build-ups to the biggest games of the season) is that supporters of both sides who want to drink will just stay in the pubs for longer after the game and will consume as much, if not more alcohol than they would do if the game were a 3.00pm kick off. The fans who watch the games on big screens in nearby pubs will also drink a lot more from an earlier time. In any case, since when did alcohol create tension or passion in a fixture like Aston Villa v Birmingham City?

Hooligans today are more concerned about criminal records than not being able to have a pint before clumping someone. Mobs from Liverpool and Manchester or Newcastle and Sunderland will happily fight one another whether they're drunk or sober, and alcohol plays a smaller role in organised football violence than is the common perception. A 12.45pm kick-off will finish at roughly 2.45pm. This leaves the rest of the afternoon for the firms of either side to try and find each other and socialise. In the 2006-07 season, one of the worst incidents of violence, in which ten people received stab wounds, was after a Chelsea v Spurs cup match that kicked off at 12.45pm. The following season, mobs from Arsenal and Spurs clashed in the back streets of Kings Cross after a league game that kicked off at 12.45pm. Don't those two incidents alone prove that having early kick-offs in order to prevent disorder is a failed concept?

The best example of this type of overzealous interfering from safety advisors and the police was the local derby between Wrexham and Chester City in December 2005. It was a fixture that hadn't been played for over one hundred years, so naturally there was a lot of excitement between the two sets of supporters. The kick-off time was originally scheduled for the evening of 28th December. It was likely to have been the first sell-out crowd Chester City had had since 2003. Enter the spoilers: the police and the safety advisors recommended that the game should be moved forward to a midday kick-off, even though the 28th of December was a normal working day so many fans would therefore miss the game. This interfering is so unnecessary because Chester City v Wrexham is not exactly West Ham v Millwall or Boca Juniors v River Plate. By this health and safety principle anything that is remotely high profile must be diluted.

Using alcohol as the excuse for early kick-off times is as ineffective as banning alcohol altogether before a game. During the 1998 World Cup in France I was caught up in an incident that was a direct result of this paranoia. England were playing Columbia in the small industrial town of Lens. The authorities insisted that every bar was to be closed as alcohol could cause fans to start trouble. There's nothing special about the town of Lens (let's think of it as the Swindon of France) and there's not much else to do there other than sit in a bar or a restaurant.

With virtually the whole town closed, thousands of England fans were left walking around getting bored. I ended up sitting near a large roundabout with a few hundred other England fans. A couple of supporters had walked into the road and draped St. George Cross flags over moving cars. As a result the police moved in with serious intent towards everyone who was in the area. Within seconds I and other England fans who had done nothing wrong were being chased down a tunnel by a massive mob of baton-wielding riot police. We spent the next five hours penned into an area so that we couldn't even leave the town. This alcohol ban was later described by British politicians, who were not in Lens, as a great success and an effective way of stopping football-related trouble. What that should tell us, is that the people who make laws for our benefit and apparent health and safety, actually have no idea about the reality of these situations. And that includes the police who should not have the right to dictate the time a football match is played. If the police had their way, then no event would ever be allowed to happen just in case somebody might want to attend it.

By 2006 an average of four out of ten Premiership fixtures did not kick off at the traditional 3:00pm on a Saturday afternoon. By the 2010-11 season, which started in August 2010, we reached a stage where a club like Arsenal had no 3pm kick offs for their away games until February 2011. Football is now played every day of the week and irregular kick-off times prioritise the TV viewer ahead of the supporter who attends the matches. Sky and ESPN, by law, cannot broadcast a live match at 3.00pm on a Saturday. But even if live football were allowed to be shown on TV at this time there would still be the same amount of live games on at midday. In the 2005-06 season, Manchester City and Everton kicked off on a Sunday at 11.30am for a Premiership fixture. This was to accommodate Sky television coverage as they tried to cram in as many live games as they could into that Sunday. A lot of people are still in a deep sleep at 11.30am on a Sunday, let alone in any mood to go to a football match. In recent years, Boxing Day had been a time when every team played on the same day. That's sacred no longer, as Murdoch and the boys at Sky now spread games over to December 27th.

Football was scheduled at 3pm to accommodate fans who worked early morning Saturday shifts. Average working hours may have changed, but 3pm still remains a convenient time to attend a game. It's after lunchtime and it gives fans the early afternoon to relax and get ready to go to the game. Most people work hard Monday to Friday and prefer a longer lie in bed on a Saturday morning. Yet for away fans who follow their teams up and down the country a 12.30pm kick-off will normally mean that they would have to wake up earlier than they would do for a work day. TV companies will schedule a game at this time between two teams located at different ends of the country. Later kick-offs can also be inconvenient. Fans of London clubs will be expected to travel to places like Newcastle for a game that kicks off at 5.15pm; by the time the game ends there are no more trains heading back to London until the following day. Of course the same thing applies when a team like Newcastle play in London at irregular times. In 2003 Newcastle United played at Arsenal on a Friday night for a Premiership fixture, meaning that overnight accommodation became an extra expense for the travelling fan.

In general, Friday is the one day of the week that doesn't feature heavily in the football calendar. It's actually a great time to go and watch a football match. It is at the start of the weekend and there is a good vibrant atmosphere. Maybe the Monday night live match should become the Friday night live match? Either way, the important thing to remember is that, in order to accommodate television coverage, a game from the weekend gets moved to a weekday. Therefore travelling fans should be more thoughtfully considered, and these games should feature teams in close proximity to one another.

With modern day fixture lists, the fans who attend every match must take a very large percentage of their annual holiday leave just to follow their football team each season. If away fans didn't attend these fixtures then the TV companies would have a product that is less saleable to the viewer, and the football clubs would lose out on gate receipts.

If that were to happen you can be sure that things would change very quickly. The TV companies and the football clubs have shown a terrible lack of respect for the attending fan and for this they should be met with a lack of respect in return.

Football's new owners

"We realise you [former Liverpool owners George Gillet and Tom Hicks] are only here for the profits, that you perceive Liverpool as an ATM shaped like a stadium... Tread carefully. Liverpool are not a mere business, English football clubs are not about bucks and mortar; when fans gather they don't talk about bottom lines but about shared heartaches and triumphs."

Henry Winter – Daily Telegraph 2007

Q: According to Wikipedia, which of the following five allegations did ex-President of Thailand Thaksin Shinawatra have levelled at him, when he took over at Manchester City in 2007?

(a) Human rights abuses
(b) Conflicts of interest
(c) Hostility towards a free press
(d) Treason
(e) Demagogy and dictatorship

A: All of them. Welcome to the English Premiership Mr Shinawatra!

Does it matter where owners are from? Should we be bothered by the fact that so many British companies are now controlled by foreigners? I consider myself fairly liberal minded, but this does bother me. Does that mean that I'm xenophobic? I don't think so. I certainly hope that it doesn't.

The sale of our football clubs to foreign owners once again mirrors a depressing trend in wider society. We sell off our institutions that made their names in this land: Rolls Royce, Aston Martin, British Steel, Manchester United, Liverpool etc. We tolerate the American firm Kraft buying a billion pound profit making British company like Cadburys on credit, and then sacking the local workforce in favour of cheaper labour outside the UK. In parallel we allow a man like Malcolm Glazer to buy a profit making British institution such as Manchester United, on credit, and then laying the debt from this sale on to the club.

2006-07 was the period of the foreign takeover in the Premiership. West Ham United, Portsmouth, Aston Villa, Liverpool and Manchester City were all bought out by foreign investors in a trend that hasn't gone out of fashion. In three out of five of those cases (Liverpool, Portsmouth and West Ham) the takeovers were disastrous. The reason that they've been such a shambles is that these are investors/gamblers with no connections to the business they have taken over. They weren't in it for the club and the supporters; they were in it for themselves.

British business is considered easy pickings, because this doesn't happen in other countries on anywhere near the same level. For example, it's very hard to imagine the likes of Fiat or Juventus being taken over by anyone but an Italian national. The root of this problem goes back to the 1980s and Mrs Thatcher; a Prime Minister so often mistaken for a patriot. She relaxed the regulation laws that made it difficult for non-nationals to take over our industries. It can be hard for British people to buy or even run businesses in other countries, but we'll sell off our family jewels to anyone for the sake of a bit of short term profit. The Americans would not tolerate a British business taking over one of their billion dollar profit making companies, and then sacking the local workforce in favour of cheaper labour abroad (okay, so they're very good at doing the sacking and outsourcing themselves, but that's not the point!).

When other countries don't accept outsiders running their businesses it's because they have pride in the traditions of their culture. If we the British carry the same feelings it's because we're horrible racist, xenophobic Little Englanders. I'm not arguing that a foreigner should not be allowed to buy a British business. I think that would be extreme and in some cases counterproductive. But our society has now already reached the other extreme with football being the prime example. When the Premiership is run by so many foreigners, is it any great surprise that the league couldn't care less about the England national team? Not that I would dare to label some of the current 'British' Premiership football club owners as patriots who care about the well being of the nation. You'll find that most of them are residents or registered outside of the mainland; coincidently, in places such as Jersey, Guernsey, Bermuda, Bahamas, and Switzerland. Many of the clubs you think of as *still British* are run by people who don't put anything back in to the country that allows them to prosper. A regular fan in the stands is likely to contribute more to the NHS than the bloke sitting in the directors' box.

One thing that every club in England has had in common over the last decade, is that they've had to find some way to compete on a level playing field with a club in West London, whose spending power since 2003 has dramatically upset the financial balance of English football. Chelsea set the ball rolling, and now we have an even bigger monster in the form of Manchester City, whose UAE owner's wealth dwarfs the fortune of Abramovich.

Chelsea alone cannot be blamed for ruining football, but they did provide the final nails in the coffin. What Abramovich's billions did was raise the bar even further at a time when football needed to be less money orientated. It needed to go back in the other direction, but instead the game became even more obsessed with making incredible sums of money. Other clubs justify high ticket prices and any other way to generate income on the grounds that they have to compete with the spending power of the Blues, and now City. In reality there is no possible way that the majority of clubs can ever compete with such market dominance, and what we've seen is a financial hierarchy that has taken away the dreams of those who have the ambition but not the spending power.

The big question is whether or not the foreign businessmen who are buying out our football clubs are prepared to invest more money into the club than what they get back. The fact that we refer to them as investors pretty much gives away that answer. The vast majority of them are highly unlikely to be modern equivalents of Jack Walker (with the exception of Abramovich and Sheikh Mansour). Jack Walker was a man who in the 1990s poured money into Blackburn Rovers because he wanted to see the team whom he supported as a boy win trophies. He didn't do it for financial gain, he did it because he cared deeply about Blackburn Rovers. He put far more money into the club than he was ever to get back. The same can be said of Sir Jack Hayward who pumped a huge part of his fortune into Wolverhampton Wanderers, not as an investment but because of love for his home town club. In the Premiership, a last bastion of that type of chairman has been Dave Whelan who owns Wigan Athletic. His track record is of someone who is not in the game to exploit it, or make money. Unlike some, when George Gillet referred to

Liverpool FC as a 'franchise', a lot of us knew straight away what his intentions were. He and his partner Tom Hicks put nothing back into Liverpool, not one penny. Their intention was solely to make a profit on their initial investment. As it happened their greed got the better of them and they failed miserably. In fact to quote an article by the comedian David Mitchell: "They're shit foreign tycoons. They're aims are reprehensible and they're not even up to achieving them."

By 2010, Liverpool were reported to be in takeover talks with a firm funded by the Chinese government. *The Guardian* columnist Marina Hyde summed it up rather well when she wrote: "What is the Premier League if not capitalism without democracy? China and Liverpool FC are made for each other." As it turned out, the Chinese deal never happened and instead Liverpool were bought out by another American firm NESV, who also own the Boston Red Socks (that's the last time I wear my Red Socks cap). This new group of Yanks may turn out to be good owners, they may turn out to be not so good owners, time will tell. One thing is for certain – they cannot possibly be any worse than Hicks and Gillet who came to represent the archetypal bad owners in football. It's important to remember that when Hicks and Gillet first bought Liverpool the widespread opinion was that they would be good for the club.

If a foreign billionaire, with a soul the size of the Grand Canyon, comes to Arsenal and actually moves the club away from corporate branding and lowers ticket prices, whilst at the same time investing in the team, then I will welcome that person with open arms. But if the new owners of other clubs are anything to go by, then that scenario is just a pipe dream.

Ticket pricing

I went to a West End cinema the other day to see the latest blockbuster movie. It is arguably the best cinema in the whole country. Great sound, giant screen, nice seats, impressive art deco surroundings. The ticket wasn't cheap – £13.50. I suppose that is quite a lot of money just to watch a film. Then again, I could have paid £20 for the cheapest seat at a League 1 ground. Cold weather, uncomfortable plastic seats, lower division football.

The issue of high ticket pricing is without doubt one of the key factors in the death of the People's Game, and the clearest manifestation of the big con. This whole issue will be featured in Chapter Seven. The question is simple: does the price we now pay for football represent value for money?

Cautions and petty laws

"In recent years the game has moved on rapidly, generally for the better. More games are televised, more money is spent, more games are played, even more laws are introduced. In fact so much change has occurred that sometimes I think we are getting away from what the thirteen original laws assume, that to play football all you need is honesty, courage and skill."

Sir Bobby Charlton

When I was in my early teens I used to play football at the New River astro turf in Haringey with friends from school. One day to all our surprise, we saw a true football legend heading a coaching session for youngsters on this same pitch. That legend was Sir Bobby Charlton. He saw us all gawping at him and he walked over to us for a chat. We were all star struck and hardly said a word to him, but he was very friendly. He told us that when he was a player he went his whole career without receiving one yellow card and that we should try and follow the same example.

Another high profile player never to have received a yellow card was Gary Lineker, who retired in the early 1990s. From the same era, England striker Alan Smith finished his career with just the one yellow card to his name. For an honest player to do the same today is almost impossible. It could only be achieved if a player went a whole career without making a tackle, without showing emotion and, more importantly, without playing a game.

A red card used to be a headline and even a yellow card was greeted with excitement from the TV commentator. Now most reds appear to come about through two yellows for two minor offences. The trend has spread so much that even the players themselves want to give out cautions. They're now waving their hands in the air and pretending to hold up cards; a gesture that actually should warrant a caution, yet usually goes unpunished.

The 2006 World Cup saw a record number of red cards and this record was broken as early as the second round of the competition. That tournament also saw a record number of yellow cards (345 in 64 matches). That record was a hard one to live up to and by the 2010 World Cup that yellow card figure did go down (240 in 64 matches), but the average was still 4.07 cautions per game. The result of all this means that players miss out on huge games because of cautions received in earlier rounds of the competition. The World Cup Final is the pinnacle for every professional footballer, and to be denied this pinnacle because of something so petty seems very unjust. This was highlighted in the 1990 World Cup semi-final when Paul Gascoigne received a yellow card (his second of the tournament) against Germany after a mistimed tackle and a bit of injury feigning from the German player. His reaction became iconic as he cried his eyes out in the knowledge that he would miss out on the chance to play in what would have been the biggest game of his life in the prime of his career. Less famously in 2006, Frenchman Louis Saha was suspended from the World Cup Final because of a yellow card received in the semi-final for what was arguably a fair tackle. There is no going back on these decisions, because for some reason FIFA refuse to overturn cautions even if the yellow or red card was undeserved. That stance seems completely absurd considering that revoking wrong decisions would allow players to play in games they don't deserve to be suspended for. In any case, a few strikes and you're out seems harsh to say the least. Yellow cards are now so common in tournaments that perhaps a player should have to receive at least one a game to warrant a suspension for a final. FIFA do not appear to understand the magnitude of how devastating it is for players to miss out on matches that define their careers and sporting history.

It's unfair to blame referees for the amount of yellow and red cards handed out in the modern game; they can only implement the laws that they are given. People in football demand both common sense and consistency from the referees, but to apply both is very difficult. Let's look at two scenarios that both warrant a red card, and see whether or not consistency and common sense can both be applied:

When the last defender brings down an attacking player, modern laws dictate that he has to be issued with a red card...

1. Goalkeeper A, who is the last defender, runs out of the 25 yard box and deliberately fouls the attacker. The goalkeeper is sent off, and a free kick is awarded outside the 25 yard box. From the resulting free kick the ball goes wide of the goal.

2. Goalkeeper B, who is the last defender, fouls the attacker, without intent, inside the 25 yard box. The goalkeeper is sent

off, and a penalty-kick is awarded. A goal is scored from the resulting penalty kick.

By being consistent, and by strictly applying the laws of the game, the referee must produce a red card on both these occasions. By using common sense, the referee can feel satisfied that Goalkeeper B made an honest attempt for the ball, and that the penalty kick alone is sufficient punishment for the foul.

The 2010 World Cup was a showcase of how football has become a non-contact game. The merest of contact resulted in free kicks and the referees were certainly not liberal in allowing play to flow.

We have to go back in football history to get to the root of where we are now. In fairness there was a need to give skilful players more protection from being fouled out of the game. The most notable example of this was in the 1982 World Cup when Diego Maradona was kicked and fouled constantly by players who would get away with this tactic unpunished. This limited Maradona's game and no matter how good a player he was, there was nothing he could do when every time he got the ball he was being physically assaulted. A similar fate happened to Pele when he was kicked out of the 1966 World Cup by aggressive opposition.

There was a need for stricter rules in favour of protection, but it's now swung too far in the other direction and players are being penalised for making non-dangerous genuine attempts at tackles. Players are punished for trivial matters such as removing their shirt, or celebrating a goal too close to the crowd. The football authorities appear to be paranoid about displays of emotion that might get a crowd up from their plastic seats and they want to punish players for anything that might encourage this. Games are being ruined because on too many occasions a player is sent off early in the match. These laws are cheating the paying spectators and are unfair on the managers and players who fall victim to these decisions.

Midway through the 2006 World Cup, FIFA president Sepp Blatter accused the England team of being boring en route to reaching the quarter finals. This was rich to say the least because if there's one man on earth who's been responsible for making football boring, then it's Sepp Blatter. He's the head of an organisation that has implemented laws which have taken away the physical edge from football and harmed the flow of a match. If the referee blowing the whistle and stopping the play so many times during a match is supposed to favour attacking play and make the game more exciting, then it has failed. Sepp Blatter should look back to the 1982 World Cup when Maradona was kicked out of the tournament because, despite some bad tackles, that tournament was arguably the greatest World Cup of all time, and was better and more real than the watered-down product that he now provides us with. As fans we want to see the best players protected from deliberate fouls, but we also want to see a side of the game that doesn't penalise physical but fair play. This is all a long way from the days of 1860 when Lord Kinnaird wrote a letter to Scottish team Queens Park before a match pleading, "Please let's have hacking. It's such fun!"

Much like the health and safety industry, the lawmakers in football can't leave well alone – something must always be done to justify positions. In 2007 the Football League proposed an idea in which regular league games that end in draws would be concluded by a penalty shoot-out. The motive behind this idea would be to make the game more exciting, even though it would most likely encourage more defensive play from weaker teams who would play for the draw. That's what happened when FIFA introduced the Golden Goal concept in the mid 1990s. After normal time the weaker teams would play for a penalty shoot out rather than get the Golden Goal that would end the match.

Football became the most popular sport in the world for what it is; it doesn't need to keep on being changed unless it's really necessary to do so.

Of all the pointless new rules in football the icing on the cake is the law that is enforced when a player gets up from being on the ground injured. In the years gone by there was a simple way to deal with this problem. Once the player got up from the ground after recovering from a knock, the player simply played on. That was far too logical to keep going so had to be dealt with by Sepp's men in suits who've probably never even kicked a ball before, but apparently understand the game better than anyone. Now once a player gets up and recovers from being injured he must walk off the pitch. Once he's off the pitch he must get waved back on by the referee. What next – text messages from the player to the referee asking for permission to re-join the game? The excuse being that the referee needs to be sure that the player still has all his senses after being fouled. In fact, each player could be sponsored by a phone company which would bring more revenue into the game, thus making football a better product. I'd better stop this piece now before I give ideas to anyone at FIFA and O2. Let's move on…

The new consumer

"The stadium is where Argentineans go to let off steam. Football belongs to simple players and poor people. These are people who for example can't afford to go to the opera. So they go to Boca [Juniors] or River [Plate] and that fuels the flames and their anger."

Diego Maradona

Before the World Cup in 2006, the BBC aired a programme in which Gary Lineker travelled to Argentina to meet Diego

Maradona. The programme featured Maradona attending a game at Boca Juniors, who are located in the docklands of Buenos Aires. It's the club in which he started his career and where he is now considered an honorary president and is worshipped by the fans as a god. Boca are one of the biggest clubs in the world and have a fanatical partisan support that is unrivalled in football. Maradona attends every game in his Boca shirt and watches the games with his family from his own outdoor executive box. The BBC documentary showed Maradona to be as passionate a supporter as he was a player. He couldn't sit still for one second and looked to have spent the whole game on his feet shouting, hanging over the edge of the executive box, singing, dancing and generally loving the experience of being at a football match. The greatest player the world has ever seen shows more passion as a football spectator than the majority of fans who now attend games in the English Premiership. Some people say that a football team would not function with eleven Peles or eleven Maradonas (I personally think that's bollocks!). Whether that be the case or not, I do know that if every stadium had 40,000 Maradonas in the crowd then no football match would ever be boring.

After the issue of ticket pricing, the reason I defected from football is because of the lack of passion from the Johnny Come Lately crowd, and the detachment which comes with that. The support shown by football fans in other countries is off the chart in comparison with the modern day Premier League supporter. But then English fans still hold on to this reputation as being the most passionate supporters in the world. In one sense we are, as English supporters are great in terms of attendance. We're a loyal bunch who stick with our teams even through bad times. Lower division games in England can produce crowds of 30,000 or more which is very rare in other countries. No one could possibly question the passion and dedication of a Torquay United fan who travels up to Carlisle for a mid-table match on a Tuesday night in winter. But what's harder to understand, is the apathy shown by supporters of teams who play the best football. It seems that the better football a team plays the more likely the fans are to leave the stadium before the end of the game. At certain grounds, one third of the stadium can be empty by the 89th minute. I once walked past the Emirates stadium during a game in which Arsenal were leading 4-0. The game still had about ten minutes to play and the thousands of home fans who were leaving in droves was an incredible sight; many of them running in a manner which suggested that they had just stolen something or were being chased by a pit bull.

One of the best European imports to these shores has to be the Poznan! Arms joined, backs turned away from the pitch and start bouncing in your thousands! Imported from the ultras of Polish club Lech Poznan, by Man City fans as an after goal celebration, it's a total contradiction to the usual experience in a modern English football stadium. Other than that, we have nothing to rival the kind of spectacle shown from say Boca Juniors, or other domestic teams from countries like Brazil, Holland, Italy, Germany, France, Greece and Croatia. The South American and European football fans can create a dramatic cauldron-like atmosphere with flags flying and flares smoking, and in this respect they put the new breed of English fans to shame. When I've been to some of these countries and attended a game, the noise and colour generated from the stands has been simply breathtaking.

This type of passion is not to be confused with hooliganism and violence. It is also true that in recent years there has been much more football-related crowd trouble in other countries than in England. After an Italian policeman was killed by fans in Sicily during a Palermo game in 2007, the publicity highlighted a problem that had become far worse in mainland Europe than in

England – the country which many Europeans have looked down upon as being the masters of hooliganism.

A month before the Sicily incident, Feyenoord from Holland had been thrown out of European competition due to crowd violence, in a punishment that had similarities to when English clubs were banned from Europe in 1985. The irony is that some countries in Europe (particularly Italy) are now likely to be looking towards England as an example of how to re-brand the game and sell it to a new 'consumer'. During the time of rising crowd trouble in Europe, and particularly after the death of the policeman in Sicily, there was a lot of backslapping by pundits in England along with clichés like: "It just shows you how far this country's come when you look at the trouble you now get abroad".

But the authorities in European football should not look at the English model as the perfect example of fan culture, because the exuberance from the crowd has reversed too far in the other direction. In this day and age in English football stadiums, fans get shouted at by other fans to 'sit down' if they dare to stand up in excitement when their team has a goal-scoring opportunity. The last game at which this happened to me was a North London derby between Arsenal and Spurs – a game which is marketed on the basis of being a 'highly charged affair'. So 'highly charged' that I can't even get up from my seat when I think that my team might score a goal! Despite the occasional bit of crowd trouble from a minority of fans in other countries, the atmosphere and sense of freedom in these stadiums makes you feel alive and part of something special. In contrast when I attend English football matches nowadays the whole environment makes me feel like I'm part of a glorified graveyard.

In the 2009-10 season a friend of mine who couldn't make the game, gave me a free ticket to watch Arsenal play Belgium side Standard Liege at the Emirates (the terms and conditions of my boycott do not include turning down free tickets). During the game I realised that, as a football fan, I had more in common with the noisy and intense fans from Belgium than the lifeless home crowd I was sitting with. A part of me almost wanted Liege to score against my team just because I felt their fans deserved it. Outside the ground a Liege fan complained to me about the lack of atmosphere. He had been disappointed in the home crowd because he was under the impression that English fans were the most passionate in the world; an opinion as out of date as his mullet.

The first chapter of this book featured Highbury in 2006 for a reason: this change of fan culture at a club like Arsenal hasn't just come about in the last few years. I've heard fellow supporters say things like: "The atmosphere was great until we left Highbury". That's bullshit. It's been a gradual process since the 1990s. However, we are now at the point where there is no longer a grey area. The crowd at a ground like the Emirates is a new breed. I first attended a game there in 2007. At halftime we were losing 1-0, and the man in front of me, who had been mute for the previous 45 minutes, commented to his friend, "No doubt there'll be some vigorous texting going on". Some vigorous texting! That should put the wind up the players. How about some vigorous chanting pal! A week or so before at the Emirates, a friend of mine told a chap in a business suit to put down his laptop, forget about his pie-charts and pay some attention to the game.

I've been honest and critical about my club's new breed of home supporters – now you can stick this in your pipe and smoke it: I've been to grounds all over the country in recent years and seen no better; despite reputations that some grounds still carry from a bygone age. The roar at St. James' Park was little more than a whimper. The newbie yuppie crowd at Stamford Bridge would cause no disturbance to a cinema audience. The 'Theatre of Dreams' at Old Trafford inspired the title of this book. White Hart Lane: it's so quiet at the Lane! Goodison Park: where's your famous atmosphere? Villa Park: shall we sing a song for you?

Anfield might occasionally produce a great atmosphere during a local derby or a big European night, but is like a morgue for the majority of games once the home crowd get *You'll never walk alone* over with just before kick-off. The demographic of people at a ground like Anfield has changed, yet people cling on to a false notion that is not there for most matches. At the time of writing the last game I attended was at Upton Park, which is a ground with a reputation for being full of noise and constant encouragement from the home crowd. Not so long ago that reputation was well deserved, but times have changed, even if people's perceptions haven't. The modern day West Ham crowd sing *I'm Forever Blowing Bubbles* just before kick-off and then sit down in silence for the rest of the match; expectation without encouragement. It's hard to find an example of a great English crowd in this era, with the possible exception of Portsmouth. Pompey fans have been noticeably vocal in recent years, none more so than in 2004 when Arsenal whipped their team 5-1 at Fratton Park on live TV. With every away goal that went in, the home crowd got louder and just wouldn't lie down. In Thierry Henry's post match interview the first thing he pointed out was how brilliant the Pompey fans were. Singing whilst their side are getting hammered was something I recall West Ham fans being good at in the early 1990s, no pun intended. *We only sing when we're losing!*

It could be argued that you still get a good atmosphere for the big games. For example, Old Trafford will still be loud and rowdy during a Liverpool or Man City game. But why would a fan only bother being supportive for a selected few games a season? In March 2011 Chelsea played FC Copenhagen at Stamford Bridge in the Champions League. The highlight of the game was the Danish fans who mocked the home crowd for their lack of support – in English. Foreign fans berating a British crowd with chants such as *Your support is fucking shit* and *Chelsea sing a song for us*. The argument for the quiet Chelsea fans is that they were already 2-0 up from the first leg; therefore the team didn't need much encouragement. *Who cares? It's only FC Copenhagen anyway.* Okay, but if that's the level of your apathy then why bother turning up to the stadium for such a high cost? For the home 'support' to sit there in silence whilst being cussed in English, by Danes, would highly embarrass me if I was part of that crowd. I suppose this is the significant dividing gap in culture between the new breed and the old school. People pay good money to sit down and be entertained, but my argument is that without the spectacle of a passionate crowd and without terrace humour, the drama is incomplete. The same principle applies to something like music. The best concerts I've attended have been the ones where the crowd complement the performers with equal energy and passion.

I have noticed that in recent years, crowds at music gigs have also become more timid and are now spectators/consumers rather than a vital part of the entertainment. If being amongst a boring football crowd is frustrating, then being amongst a similar crowd at, for example, a music gig is just downright depressing. It's as if a large section of society has had the energy sucked out of it, and has lost the ability to let off steam (other than the morons who let off steam by acting like aggressive drunken yobs, though maybe their behaviour is a result of that lost energy at football matches, music gigs etc?).

One explanation for this could be our TV culture. People are so used to watching entertainment on their TV screens that when they attend an event they simply stand still with their arms folded and wait to be entertained. Technology and gadgets have also had an effect, as so many people at events now seem to spend the whole time recording the match or concert on their mobile phone rather than experiencing with their own eyes what's in front of them. A bit like the kind of tourists who spend so much time behind a video camera that they only see the landmarks they visited on the home video of their holiday.

A lot of the people who make up football and music crowds today are the ones with the money and the contacts, and in modern day entertainment that's far more important than being a fan with passion. I'll give you an example of the kind of people who have these contacts and just why some events don't generate the kind of excitement from the crowd that the occasion warrants. One night in 2003 I had to cover for my sister on a house-sitting job for a couple who had tickets to see the Rolling Stones at Wembley Arena. I had actually tried to buy tickets for this gig but was quoted £180 a ticket by Wembley Arena. I would have liked to have seen the Stones play live, but for that price I would have expected to have had Jade Jagger sitting on my lap. I wasn't that surprised when the couple told me that their tickets came about through work and that they hadn't had to pay for them. I'd spoken to a few other people who had attended that Rolling Stones tour and none of them had paid money for their tickets. When tour organisers boast that a concert has sold out in just twenty minutes then it's probably because only twenty tickets got sold to the general public. I had only been house-sitting for around two and a half hours when the couple returned home. The timing seemed odd and I asked them if the concert had been cancelled. It turned out that they left the gig an hour early in order to beat the traffic – EXCUSE ME! These guys left a Rolling Stones concert an hour early because they wanted an easier ride home from one part of North London to the other. On that note, let me share with you something that I read off an internet fan forum from a disgruntled supporter: *Football is fucked end of, at Wembley a couple of weeks back a family of four were sat behind us, mummy, daddy and little Primrose and Edgar (I shit you not), they spent the whole game on their iPhones, then with ten minutes to go mummy pipes up "let's go darlings beat the rush". A fucking cup final it was still 1-1!*

Football is now considered family entertainment and it's great that the game is now supposedly a more suitable environment for women and children (although having said that I always felt comfortable and safe at football stadiums when I was a kid). But football being a family game is just one side of things. The other side includes young people who have energy to burn, and who will create the atmosphere in the stadiums. The truth is that without them the atmosphere is dead, and they shouldn't simply be dismissed and told that they have to sit down and be quiet. After all, football was originally founded on the very basis of young people letting off steam. There are many reasons why football crowds have become more timid over recent years. Stewarding and security, plus all-seater stadiums have certainly played a major part. Let's start with our friends in the orange bibs....

Stewarding and security

Gone are the days when we would see rival fans engage in full scale battles on the field of play as in the 1970s and 1980s. Other than nostalgic football thugs, most people would agree that this is a good thing, and that better and well managed crowd control has played a part in that change. But when fans are threatened with eviction if they even dare to wave around fake twenty pound notes with Ashley Cole's face on it – then some might just argue that football needs to be a lot less authoritarian in the way it treats its most important people. Before a Chelsea v Arsenal game in the 2006-07 season, it was reported that any fan caught with one of these fake notes that was mimicking Cole risked eviction from Stamford Bridge, for the crime of incitement. It would now appear that hurting the feelings of a £90,000 a week superstar is deemed worthy of being thrown out from a football ground.

The character Winston Smith from George Orwell's *Nineteen Eighty-Four* would not feel out of place in a football stadium these days. The camera surveillance is as overbearing as in the rest of our country, which is the CCTV capital of the world. Football stadiums are now very restricted environments where everyone must conform to the strict rules or face eviction. Very much like most nightclubs, which pretend to be places where people can lose themselves but tend to be the very opposite. Every year the football authorities find new things to ban and confiscate. At Upton Park for example, I witnessed a senior steward try to confiscate somebody's mobile phone just because that person took a photo of the game. If a fan has paid money for a ticket should they not have the right to take a photograph of themselves at the game from their mobile phone? Are the clubs worried that people are taking these photographs in order to sell them? If so, then why aren't professional sports photographers using Nokias and Sony Eriksons for that back page snap?

The list of banned items from football grounds ranges from the sensible to the ridiculous. Banning things like Stanley knives and beer bottles probably does make sense. But the traditional flag is now banned from some grounds as the bamboo flag pole is now perceived as a weapon. I can see where they're coming from as the flagpole does have a troubled history. In 1945 President Truman had to contemplate dropping flagpoles on Japanese cities in order to bring an end to the Second World War. A bamboo stick with a piece of cloth attached to it reading 'FA CUP WINNERS' wiped out the entire city of Hiroshima in seconds. Other weapons of mass destruction that have needed to be dealt with at football grounds include the dreaded bell. I've seen a Portsmouth fan get ejected at Highbury for standing up and ringing this deadly killing machine in support of his team. The other Portsmouth fans were unhappy at the stewards for this harsh treatment towards one of their fans. However, they have to realise that this bell could have suddenly flown out of the man's hand

and sliced off the head of a nearby spectator. Health and safety must take first priority, and without this type of enforcement we would never have heard the '*YOU'RE NOT RINGING ANY MORE*' chant directed at the Pompey fan as he was led out of the stadium.

The nearest I've come to being ejected from a football stadium by stewards was at Hull City in 1998. A group of us had committed the offence of singing '*YOU'RE SHIT AND YOU KNOW YOU ARE*' at the home team; a chant heard regularly at football grounds all over the country. At Hull City we were confronted by the head steward who told us that under the new Football Act, swearing is an offence at football grounds and that we would be ejected if we didn't stop it. My cousin informed him that the word 'shit' is in the English dictionary and that we were merely making an observation towards the style of football being played by the home team. The steward didn't buy that excuse and sounded like a policeman with his "I'm not prepared to argue" stance. For the record, after the final whistle we mentioned the word cunt (the English dictionary definition being "an unpleasant and stupid person"), informed him that he was one, and that if he wanted to eject us from the stadium he was now welcome to do so.

I haven't got a problem with the majority of people who do stewarding. Most are there to do a hassle free day's work and are not on a power trip. The money they get paid is peanuts and some companies that employ stewards take advantage of them. Many stewards will be expected to work six hours for an event, yet they will only get paid for five hours. This is because they are told that the first hour they work is 'preparation'. Is preparation not part of a day's work? In 2005 I very briefly worked for a stewarding and security firm that operated in this way, though I refused to work for them at football matches. I was with this firm so that I could occasionally work at events that I wanted to see but couldn't get tickets for, such as music gigs or a day at the races. Even so, I was still required to go through an induction that qualified me to work at football grounds. The induction was a showcase of paranoia and it showed me just how much ordinary football fans are viewed with contempt and suspicion. Every fan is under surveillance and every fan is considered a potential 'breach of the peace'. In my experience with this firm, the people I disliked were not the regular stewards but some of the supervisors and senior stewards. These are the people at football grounds who I feel are over-zealous and get off on power trips.

In the 2006-07 season, the Reading goalkeeper Marcus Hahnemann had a ritual of giving away his keeper's jersey to a lucky fan after the game. It was a simple way of thanking people for their support, and is the kind of gesture that the supporters always appreciate. But when approaching his own fans with his jersey after a match at Sheffield United, Hahnemann found himself surrounded by ten stewards who refused to allow him anywhere near the Reading supporters. Naturally Hahnemann was frustrated by the unnecessary interfering from the Sheffield United stewards and ended up in a verbal confrontation. The head of security at Sheffield United justified the behaviour from his staff by using the tiresome health and safety and risk assessment excuse. He claimed there was a risk of people getting crushed by a surge forward by eager fans wanting to get their hands on the souvenir. When listening to this sort of wisdom it's quite amazing to think that performers over the years have thrown souvenirs to their audience without creating scenes of death and carnage. Back to the real world, and what a sad state of affairs when security and stewarding has become so paranoid and aggressive, a player cannot even approach a fan to hand over a gift. Maybe stewards nationwide hold a particular grudge towards Reading FC players and supporters. In the 2009-10 season, Reading beat WBA 3-2 in a dramatic FA Cup tie at the Hawthorns. After the game the Reading players approached their own supporters to hand over shirts, but were met by a wall of monkeys in orange bibs, who then pushed the players back towards the halfway line. Confrontation then followed between the players and the stewards and as a result a good atmosphere turned nasty. What we have here is a fear from the authorities of any contact between players and supporters. When a player runs towards his own fans after scoring a goal, it's now met by a group of stewards flapping their arms about and getting in the way, as if they're breaking up a fight. Is there any need for this? Not really, if fans and players can't celebrate together then the game is harmed rather than enhanced.

The most over-zealous and aggressive display of stewarding I've ever witnessed was at Ipswich Town in 2000. Dennis Bergkamp had narrowly missed a goal-scoring chance that would have won Arsenal the game in the last minute of the match. A fan in the front row thought that Bergkamp had scored and he jumped out of his seat and over an advertising hoarding which was a couple of yards from where he was sitting. He soon realised that his excitement had taken him into an area of the stadium that was restricted, and he quickly got back into his seat. Within seconds about ten gorillas in orange bibs were on top of him before he was roughly dragged out of the stadium. The way the stewards jumped on him you would have thought that he was a sniper about to shoot the president – not a football fan who thought his team had just scored a winning goal in the last minute. The Ipswich stewards were like predators jumping on top of their prey, and from their expressions it was obvious that they relished imposing their authority. All a situation like that needed was a steward to have a quick word with the fan and to explain that jumping over the hoardings is not allowed. The fan involved in this incident is likely to have received a fine and a banning order from football.

In fact you don't even have to deliberately enter the field of play to get into trouble for doing so. In October 2010, Aston Villa played host to Birmingham City in a Midlands derby. At the start of the second half, the ball was booted out of play and towards the crowd in the Doug Ellis Stand. Nineteen-year-old Villa fan Kieran Comerford, who was on his way back to his seat after the halftime break, saw his chance, kept his eye on the ball, used his neck muscles to great effect, and directed a brilliant header back towards the pitch. The only problem for Kieran was that his balance wasn't so good. As he headed the ball he bumped into an advertising hoarding and accidentally flopped onto the pitch area. Charlie Chaplin would have been proud, Stan and Ollie would have tipped their hats, and Buster Keaton would have nodded his head in approval. The Villa crowd cheered and clapped, Fabio Capello took notice, and even *Match of The Day* showed the clip considering that Kieran's diving header was the major highlight of an uneventful 0-0 draw. So naturally the stewards grabbed him for entering the field of play and he was dragged out of the stadium and sent packing. This incident alone sums up the problem in English football today: it's a game where humour has been replaced with fear. Even more absurd than this is grabbing the attention of stewards and being removed from the ground for the crime of, wait for it, falling asleep in your seat! For fuck sake, how non-confrontational do you have to be in order to get chucked out of a football stadium? In 2003 this ended up a serious matter for Middlesbrough fan Adrian Car who was taken to court for this appalling act. His crime: being drunk in a sporting arena. A mate of mine was threatened with eviction from Elland Road for being a bit drunk. Not for being drunk and anything else – such as disorderly or abusive. Just for being a bit over limit on alcohol and it noticed in his walk to the toilet. My friend pointed out to the stewards that alcohol did happen to be on sale in this football stadium. As for Mr Car from Middlesbrough, he was convicted and ordered to pay £150, but justly it was overturned in an appeal. In the appeal, Judge Taylor said, "It is the right of every Englishman, at a football match to fall asleep if they want to. This is a prosecution that should never have been brought."

Stewards have lots of different uses. For example at the Emirates Stadium some now seem to have a good memory of knowing who should be sitting where. A common complaint that I am hearing from a lot of Arsenal fans is that they are having their season tickets confiscated, because they lent or sold their season ticket off for a game which they couldn't attend, and the person in that seat could not match their details with the name on the ticket. Arsenal will claim that this is in place to prevent ticket touting. On one level that sounds fair. On another level it sounds unfair in that fans can get punished just for loaning out season tickets to trusted people and are then mistaken for touts. Here is what could be behind it: Arsenal has a ticket exchange on their website where you can sell on your space in the stadium. The club take a cut from this sale and the fan does not receive the money until they re-new their season ticket the following season. When a person lends or sells their season ticket the club get no extra money, well, other than the extortionate amount that the season ticket got sold for in the first place. So when stewards monitor fans they're not always on the lookout for bad behaviour.

A problem with stewarding and security that hardly ever gets brought up is the financial burden that it places on the less affluent clubs. Lower league grounds have smaller crowds but a very large number of stewards on duty for each game. In my experience of attending lower league matches, more often than not, the number of stewards on duty seems totally disproportionate to the need. Most of the time the threat of crowd trouble is minimal and with so many empty seats you don't need anyone to direct you to your place in the stand, or to be there to help control the mass surge of people coming in and out. In the 2010-11 season I'd been to a League 1 game and felt that the number of stewards on duty was very high in relation to the size of the crowd and the threat of any disorder. I wondered if this was the club's doing, or whether or not the number was just the minimum requirement needed to maintain a safety certificate. I contacted the stadium manager and he told me that the number was over the minimum requirement, and that it usually is for most games. The clubs are safeguarding themselves which from a point of view is understandable. But it's a bit like putting ten locks on your door to prevent a burglary. One lock should be enough, two locks make it very safe, three locks and you're starting to go a bit over the top and paranoid. Ten locks and you should think about seeking help from someone. In relation to gate income, and the actual threat of safety being compromised, the amount of money spent on this orange bib presence should be looked at in a more pragmatic way. As fans we're not asking for this control. We don't require so many stewards and we don't want them. Rather than make us feel safe they're more likely to piss us off and actually create tension. Watch an old TV clip of a football match from the 1960s, 1970s and 1980s. Look out for the stewards in these clips. There aren't many. If it was a game where there was likely to be crowd trouble the police would be the ones to deal with it. If it was a low tension game then the police numbers would be far smaller. When I grew up watching football in the late 1980s the stewards were mostly fans of the home club and it was completely normal for them to cheer and punch the air in joy when a goal was scored.

Some stewards think they have the right to order people about in an environment totally out of their jurisdiction. For example in 2004 I ended up having an argument with a ticket seller at the box office at Arsenal. I had been queuing for tickets since 7:00am. It was a horrible cold rainy morning and after a couple of hours I had made it to the front of the queue. My membership details were unfairly questioned and I was refused tickets and treated with disdain by the man at the box office.[4] Feeling wet, tired and unappreciated I then felt it appropriate to tell the man at the box office to "Go fuck yourself" as I was walking off. As I was walking away I then had a steward rush up and raise his voice at me. What right did this traffic-cone look-alike think he had to do that? The box office at Highbury was on the street not in the stadium. What did he think he was going to do? Chuck me off the street into the stadium? Ban me from the street for life?

All this enforcement at football matches makes fans feel like children under the eye of a teacher. Here's a solution: any steward who is over-zealous and on a power trip should be singled out by the crowd and undermined throughout the rest of the game. At Upton Park the senior steward who tried to take away the camera phone from a fan spent the rest of the game having chants directed at him, and his snarling red face was a picture as the fans mocked him. In fact, I would have taken a picture of his face if it wasn't illegal.

All-seater stadiums

In November 2005 Tony Blair was asked on BBC's *Football Focus* about the possibilities of bringing back terracing. He made it clear that it was a terrible idea and that he wasn't prepared to even talk about the subject. A fine example of debate and democracy there from the man who was supposed to be the defender of our free speech. Now, just before going to print with the second edition of this book, there's been an interesting

---

[4] For the record, this incident was the straw that broke the camel's back. On that rainy day, I decided once and for all that my custom was not valued, and that's when I decided to stop attending football matches on a regular basis.

development. The Lib Dem Sports Spokesman Don Foster MP, backed by the Football Supporters Federation, has brought about a debate in which the return of terracing at top level football is being discussed. The Sports Minister Hugh Robertson will listen to the debate, even if so far he hasn't sounded enthusiastic about any change. He's a Tory – you would imagine that his natural instinct would be against terracing. The most significant bodies in the way of change are the FA, Football League and Premier League and in the first meeting to discuss this issue they voiced their opposition to it. According to a *Guardian* report, their opposition was not based on safety issues, but because *all-seat stadiums had been crucial in improving the game's fortunes and image since Hillsborough, and there is no major demand for standing.* No major demand, really? In 2007, the internet survey group the Football Fans Census asked 2,000 supporters if they would prefer to stand on the terraces and pay less. 74% said yes. More recently in 2011, the Football Supporters Federation did a survey in which 90% said that they favoured a choice to either sit or stand.

For the fans out there who don't want to see a return to terracing I have for them a proposition: you sit, we'll stand. It's a very simple arrangement, and one that was in place for well over one hundred years. Anyone who didn't want to stand on a terrace bought a seat. I certainly don't hear anyone advocating all-terraced stadiums. Such a concept would be extreme, un-inclusive, unfair, and more than anything else, selfish.

Nobody is insensitive to the reasons why we now have all-seater stadiums. In 1989, ninety-six people died on a terrace at Hillsborough due to people being crushed by overcrowding. In 1985, thirty-seven people died on a terrace in the Heysel stadium Brussels when a wall collapsed as a result of crowd trouble before the game. Were the terraces to blame for this? My argument is that they were not. At Hillsborough people died through under-investment, bad organisation, police errors and the steel fences which had more place in a zoo than a sporting arena. In Brussels in 1985, the crumbling Heysel stadium was not fit to hold any crowd, let alone one for a European Cup Final. In the same year, fifty-six people died in the Bradford City stadium fire in a seated end. There were no calls for a ban on seats at football matches, because the evidence tells us that there are lots of different elements that make up these tragic events. The same logic of thinking should have been applied after Hillsborough.

The nearest I've come to being seriously hurt in a football stadium was in a seated end at White Hart Lane during a North London derby. A large number of Arsenal fans were stood up in the gangway between the seats; I was one of them. Arsenal scored a goal and some people fell over leading to a domino effect pile up. I tumbled down, and people were falling down on top of me and others. As I tried to scramble out of the way and to the side, my upper chest/neck became wedged on a plastic seat – guillotine style! I couldn't move and could feel people still falling on me. At that particular moment in time I thought I was going to get seriously hurt in a football stadium. Not just any old stadium either – White Hart Lane. The thought of Heysel went through my mind at that time. Luckily the domino effect lost momentum before anyone was badly hurt. As we got up a man turned to me and said, "I thought we were goners there". A small bit of bruising on the chest and legs was luckily all that came of it.

I don't blame the seats alone because we chose to stand in the gangway. Does that incident prove to us terracing is bad news? No. A tumble like that would not have happened in a terrace because the steps are lower and there are barriers that prevent pile ups. On a gangway in a seated end the steps are higher and there is nothing to break the fall. It makes it easy to fall down. Some will say that if everyone just sat down then there could be no accidents. Okay that might be true. But only true in the same way that if all motor racing drivers drove slowly there would be no serious accidents in Formula 1. Such a scenario would kill the sport. Sitting down during some games goes against the natural emotions of so many fans. In the game where this pile up happened the atmosphere in the away end was red hot and the energy was intense; sitting down was not on the agenda and was never going to happen. The desire to stand up at games means that all seater stadiums can actually cause safety problems.

After the Hillsborough disaster Lord Justice Taylor outlined a law which meant that every top flight football ground in England had to be all-seater. The terraces were to be no more. Lord Justice Taylor probably came to this conclusion with the best of intentions, and he had the safety of football fans as his priority. But that does not mean that he was correct in his judgement. Many of us believe that his report was an overreaction to the Hillsborough disaster. Going back to the time, the people to blame for this were the football clubs who under-invested in the fans and let the stadiums rot. Back in the 1980s some stadiums were in a pitiful state. A week before the Hillsborough tragedy a friend of mine had been to Millwall's old Cold Blow Lane stadium. At the time he made a comment that, "One day someone's going to die at these stadiums". This comment was in reference to the facilities and nothing to do with Millwall fans. A week later a lot more than just one person died in the worst ever disaster in English football history. Back in the late 1980s these stadiums did need massive investment, but this could have incorporated terracing. Terraces can be clean, high-tech and, more importantly, they can be safe. No disaster similar to Hillsborough could happen in a terrace that has better security monitoring, better exits, all-ticket restrictions for big matches and, most importantly, no steel fences.

Terracing at top level European football is still alive in the Bundesliga. The Germans are proving to us that these sections are safe and that the Taylor Report was a reactionary measure.

Former European Champions Borussia Dortmund have safe-standing and have averaged attendances of over 73,000 in recent years, the fourth highest in Europe. Not bad for a club who up until the 2010-11 season, haven't had much on-field glory during the past decade. Such a high attendance figure for a team that has lacked success is down to two elements: the fun of standing at football and affordable tickets.

There can be no doubt that one of the main causes for high ticket pricing is the Taylor Report; its role in socially cleansing football has been huge. As a young teenager when the Taylor Report came into effect I knew instantly that entrance to the grounds would be harder and more expensive due to reduced capacity. In the first few years the change of ticket pricing wasn't that dramatic. However, all-seater stadiums were soon to be met with modern-day player wage demands and agent greed. The new arenas could not hold anywhere near the amount of spectators that the terraces were capable of. Highbury stadium at one time could hold 73,000 but after the Taylor Report its capacity was reduced to only 38,000. English football grounds in this modern era have never been bigger in structure, but the crowd capacities have never been smaller. Charlton Athletic's Valley was once the largest capacity league stadium in London, holding 75,000 due to one massive terrace that stretched from one end of the pitch to the other. Now the all-seater Valley only holds a mere 27,000. If stadiums such as St James Park, Eastlands and the Emirates had sections of terracing then the ground capacities would be near the 80,000 mark. If Old Trafford had sections of terracing then its capacity would be near 100,000. Think of the brand new 90,000 all-seater Wembley Stadium, and what the capacity could be with sections of open terracing. With such high ground capacities, football would no longer be exclusive to those with money and would soon return to being a game for all the people. The current situation is one where thousands of supporters are locked out of football grounds each week because there are not enough seats available to meet the demand.

Many kids are brought up on a culture of watching their team play on TV rather than attending the live match, because they don't have the means or money to get hold of a ticket. That alone is enough of an argument to be able to claim that all-seater stadiums have been a negative influence on football.

People talk about the comfort of all-seater stadiums, but what's so comfortable about sitting down on plastic in the cold outdoors in a cramped environment? Sitting down in comfort is being at home on a sofa watching the TV or reading a book, so when did this become the main principle of attending a football match?

Contrary to modern belief, the terraces were fun. They were practical and more than anything they had a sense of freedom. You could choose where you wanted to stand and watch the game. Now we pay more money to sit down where someone tells us. In the old Arsenal stadium before it became all-seated, I would watch the games in the West Stand Junior Gunners section. In this terrace I would walk from one end of the pitch to the other. So whatever goal Arsenal were shooting towards I could stand at that end and get an excellent view of the goal my team were shooting at. Back then, if you didn't like the person you were positioned next to in the ground, you simply moved to another spot. Nowadays if we're stuck next to a person who offends us we have to put up with that annoyance for the whole game. In fact I have to admit that, being someone who occasionally does shout and swear in football stadiums, I'm sure that I am that person who some people would rather move away from! But hey, don't blame me, blame Lord Justice Taylor and Mrs Thatcher. They decided that all football fans, regardless of manner and behaviour, should have to sit in the same sections.

Terraces provided drama. Every time the opposition at Highbury scored I used to be mesmerised by the sight of the away fans' goal celebrations. It was electric. In the old terraces the goal celebrations would resemble a pack of bees swarming around together. It was a moving sea of people and the energy was breathtaking and spectacular. Today, in this middle of the road all-seater environment, fans greet a goal by standing up, clapping for five seconds, and then sitting back down again. That release of energy is something that football has lost. I don't feel that old, not just yet, and I want to be on my feet at a time when I still have the energy and still have the knees.

When the terraces at top level football were knocked down in the early 1990s, it was devastating for a young football fan who liked to bounce up and down. I think I felt more of a loss when the old North Bank terrace was bulldozed than I did when Arsenal left Highbury altogether in 2006. By that point Highbury was still a magical and beautiful old stadium, but an important part of its soul had been lost for well over a decade. The season after the North Bank terrace was demolished in 1992-93, the atmosphere in the ground had become so quiet the club tried to improve things by blaring out pre-recorded Arsenal chants through loudspeakers. That was a real low point in my time as a football fan, and even today it's clear that supporters have not properly adjusted to the culture of all-seater stadiums. Although I miss the terraces, I do appreciate the fact that I was lucky enough to experience them and was part of the last generation of kids who did get that chance at top level football. I feel sorry for young fans who, unless laws get reversed, might never know of that culture and just how special it was. So when people refer to the "bad old days of terracing" I find it absurd, because there are thousands of us who remember those days as being some of the best times of our lives.

Don Foster MP is on the right side of this debate. Terracing needs to return. Football was far more enjoyable when you could wake up on the day of the match and make a decision to go to the game. Fans now have the hassle of trying to buy tickets online or over the phone for a game that is weeks or even months away. When a group of friends go to the cinema together they do not sit in separate seats in different sections of the cinema. When a party of people go to a restaurant they do not sit at separate tables and next to strangers. When football fans can't sit or stand together at a match, the game loses something right at the heart of its soul – community.

Overbearing advertising and marketing

The late, great American comedian, Bill Hicks, once described the advertising and marketing industry as the "ruiners of all things good" as well as "Satan's spawn filling the world with bile and garbage".

Now let me be the first to admit that I myself have made money out of football advertising, £250 to be exact. You see, back in 2004 I was Paul Scholes's body double for a Nike television commercial. Before you read on let me just clear something up – I'm not ginger. They dyed my hair and it took ten washes to get it out. To make matters worse Nike didn't even pay me for dyeing my hair as the production rules stated that I should only receive money for a haircut. Where's the justice in that? Shooting the commercial was great fun and it was an advert in which Thierry Henry was being chased around his house by other players contracted to Nike. No famous players were present unfortunately, just body doubles.[5] The back of me was seen in the advert as I chased Henry down a hallway along with several other

---

[5] Mikel Sylvestre's body double was a white guy! As was Claude Makelele's stunt double who had to be blacked up like a minstrel. Are there no black stunt men in Britain?

United players. I'd love to know how much the real Paul Scholes earned for that; more than £250 I suspect and he didn't even have to dye his hair.

This is not the sort of advertising that ruins football. If companies such as Nike and Adidas want to pay millions to players to promote their product then there's no harm in that. Sponsors will only pay players who perform well and who are worth the money. But what about a form of advertising that might affect a person's enjoyment of watching a game? What about the digital advertising touchline hoardings that are common throughout European football? Those who run the game were not content with motionless advertising hoardings, or ones that would occasionally flip from one advert to another.

They've imposed on us those which flash adverts at fans throughout the whole match and make the touchlines look like Times Square and the Las Vegas strip. The first club in England to have these installed was Manchester United, as always the pioneers of commercialism in football. These hoardings are horribly intrusive. My eyes sub-consciously get taken away from the actual game and towards these flashing messages from the likes of McDonalds, Pepsi, Nike and co. They are so imposing that I'm sure that they must be off-putting to the players – though the players will not complain, because the revenue from flashing hoardings goes to fund their high wages.

Other forms of entertainment are not violated in this way by overbearing advertising. When we go to the cinema to watch a movie, we get shown adverts before the trailers. Most of us accept this as being an important form of revenue for the cinemas. But imagine being in the cinema and having to put up with flashing advertising hoardings below the big screen – during the movie. It would no doubt affect a person's enjoyment of the film. It would symbolise the fact that the industry would rather the customer watch the advert than the film. It would not be tolerated and on this occasion, the moviegoer would not put up with an excuse such as 'it brings in more revenue for the Odeon'.

This style of advertising is aimed at the TV viewer as there are no flashing hoardings on the same side of the stadium as the main TV camera. The money-men of football were concerned that the game went a whole forty-five minutes without a commercial break, which is the same reason that football has never made it bigger in the USA. For football to break America it must have a credible TV deal, and US channels don't usually go more than five minutes without a commercial break, let alone forty-five minutes (when I was in America I saw a billboard advert for a TV station that boasted 'NO AD BREAK FOR TEN MINUTES – NO KIDDING!'). They've finally found a way to flash images into our heads throughout the whole ninety minutes and we're paying for the privilege. It's hard to believe that in the late 1970s and early 1980s, BBC sport had a conflict with the Football League about showing live football on TV because, for the first time, there were sponsors on the team shirt. The BBC were worried about breaching their own rules because they are not allowed to advertise any outside product. At the time they had no choice but to accept the change in football. Yet now they broadcast matches that feature flashing adverts for Nike and co and it goes completely unquestioned.

Barcelona and Real Madrid were both famous for rejecting the idea of having sponsors on their team shirts. The reason for this was that they felt no advertiser was worthy of having their name displayed on their proud kits. Real Madrid gave into shirt sponsorship at the start of the millennium with Siemens mobile being the advertiser with enough money to tempt them away from their pride. In 2006 Barcelona had their first ever shirt sponsor as they agreed to be sponsored by the UN's children's charity UNICEF, in a five-year deal worth €1.5 million a year. A truly unique deal in that the €1.5 million a year was to be paid by Barcelona, to UNICEF.

Barcelona President Joan Laporta said of the UNICEF deal: "It's an initiative with soul. It means winning the Champions League on a social level. It shows the world that our club is more than just a club." Traditionally, Barcelona fans were very hostile towards a shirt sponsor, but the UNICEF deal had strong social principles which were very hard to argue against. But how long can principles last in the current football climate? In 2011 Barcelona broke from all tradition and accepted a shirt sponsorship deal with the Qatar Foundation in a deal reported to be worth £125 million over five years. Modern day player wage demands and transfer fees have led them down a path which for so long they have managed to resist. *More than just a club* might soon be a cover for *Just another big business.* The 2006 UNICEF deal was a unique gesture until Aston Villa did the same thing for the children's hospice charity, Acorn, between the years 2008 and 2010. By 2011, financial problems forced Villa back to receiving money from regular shirt sponsorship, but they should be commended for sacrificing two years of income in favour of helping out a worthy cause.

The latest club to go down this route has been Italian side Fiorentina, who in 2010 decided to support Save the Children through funds and free kit sponsor promotion.

One of the last big clubs to break from the tradition of having no shirt sponsor at all, was La Liga club Atletico Bilbao from the Basque region of Spain. In 2008 they signed a three year deal with the oil company Petroner. Atletico Bilbao, just like Barcelona is viewed as a kind of national team by the fans. They are regarded as the unofficial national team of the Basqe region, in the way that Barcelona is seen as the unofficial national team of Catalonia. Of course national teams do not have shirt sponsors,[6] which is

---

[6] The Republic of Ireland shirts were once sponsored by car makers Opel.

surprising for the commercial age we live in. However, every year the game gets more obsessed with money and if football carries on the way it is right now, it wouldn't be that surprising to see sponsors on the national team shirts in the coming years.

Commercialism in football will go way beyond the mark if advertisers try to get involved in team affairs. For example, if the clients were to try and have an influence on which players actually play for a team then it would be unacceptable. There have been plenty of allegations in recent years that Nike has had too strong an influence in the Brazilian national team squad selection. These allegations hit a height just before and after the 1998 World Cup. Before the finals it was alleged that Nike were picking the Brazilian team in favour of the players who they had contracts with. After the World Cup Final between Brazil and France there were allegations and conspiracy theories that Nike had insisted that Ronaldo play, even though he was physically and mentally not right for the final. Ronaldo was Nike's highest profile player and it was perceived that for him not to play in the final would have been a big letdown for Nike. It does seem strange that Ronaldo played in this game. Even with his great reputation, no sane manager would have included him because he was quite clearly in such a bad way that night. But these remain allegations and conspiracy theories, because no one has officially spoken out, or come up with ultimate proof to back this up.

But if a sponsor was ever found guilty of interfering with team affairs, then they should be banned from any further involvement with the game. It wouldn't surprise a lot of people if this sort of interfering from sponsors does have a secret place in football, but never actually gets fully exposed. If it does go on, then I wonder how quick Sepp Blatter and FIFA would be to expose it; considering their own relationships with outside backers. The public's perception of their money-driven vision of football would no doubt be damaged by such a scandal. Instead of protecting the game from wrongdoing, FIFA has a history of being lukewarm to corruption and keeping matters firmly in-house.

Whereas some fans won't accept a club sponsor on the shirt, others seem complacent enough to let the very heart and soul of a club be bought out by outside interests. Europe has now fully embraced the American culture of naming the stadium after a brand instead of the team. The crowd at Arsenal are now even referred to by the media as the 'Emirates crowd' – not Arsenal supporters. Emirates Airlines are paying a lot of money for this honour, and what Arsenal gets from this deal will eventually be worth £100 million over a period of years. This £100 million means that Emirates have rights to the name of the stadium for fifteen years, and have the rights to sponsor the club shirt for eight years (this deal started in 2006). It is a lot of money and for these reasons I've had other Arsenal fans try and persuade me that it's a great deal for the club and that I should be pleased about it. So far they haven't got anywhere. I never cared how much money Emirates Airlines were prepared to pay because identity and pride do not have a price tag. The sum of £100 million also looks a lot less substantial when you consider that Arsenal make over £3 million for every home game and announced in 2010 an annual profit of nearly £50 million. As a fan, I feel that this stadium branding has been just another invasion on the traditions of the club I follow. The most important thing that a football club has is the stadium and the fans. The directors, players and advertisers will come and go, but the stadium and supporters will be around for longer. So to name a stadium after a chocolate bar or a packet of crisps takes away a huge part of the personality of a club (spare a quick thought for fans of York City whose stadium was briefly named the Kit-Kat Crescent). When we lose our identity and sell our soul to commercialism, what's left to follow? The corporate branding of a club like Arsenal is supposed to be the compromise for success on the field. If the team wins trophies the fans are kept happy. However, in the inevitable seasons when the club does not achieve success, the fans are left with a club that represents a corporate image and a belittled identity. Supporters of Coventry City are deprived of success; not much of a consolation that they now follow their team from the Tesco stand and the Jewson stand, and the Telent stand, at the recently built Ricoh Arena.

There are other options to make money in this way that do not sacrifice the soul of a club. For example the sponsor can have their name on the stadium, but not in a way that is more dominant than the symbols and name of the club itself. For example how about: THE ARSENAL STADIUM – IN PROUD ASSOCIATION WITH EMIRATES. That would be more acceptable because the stadium still carries the name of the club and the advertisers still get promotion. Real Madrid play in the Bernabeu stadium which is named after the Real Madrid legend Santiago Bernabeu. Above the stadium the word BERNABEU is lit up in big letters and you feel a great sense of history and tradition when you visit the ground. Certainly much more so than if their stadium were named after British Airways or Burger King. If the Nou Camp at Barcelona were named after American Airlines then Clive Tyldesley would have to use an extra three syllables in most sentences when commentating.

The greatest football venues in history have names that are part of football history: Old Trafford, San Siro, Anfield, Wembley, Nou Camp, Bernabeu, Maracana, Stade de France, Highbury, St James' Park, Olympic Stadium Munich, Villa Park, White Hart Lane, Parc des Princes, Velladrome, Hamden Park, Celtic Park, Ibrox, etc. Do we really want to sacrifice this for the likes of Emirates, Walkers Crisps, EDF Energy, T-Mobile, etc? It doesn't seem at all fair, or just, that the heritage we are passing down to future generations is a legacy of impersonal commercialism.

So much for football being a religion as some people pronounce it to be. Imagine walking down the road and passing the ADIDAS HOUSE OF WORSHIP or the TERRY'S CHOCOLATE ORANGE CATHEDRAL. Any mosque named after a commercial brand is simply unthinkable. Followers of these religions have a sense of devotion which is so strong that it can never be sold away to outside interests, and to have their place of worship named after a sponsor would belittle and cheapen their religion.

Alex Ferguson once questioned whether football fans should have to pay for admission any more, because of the amount of money the game generates from television and advertising. Of course the irony is that the more money football makes from things like advertising, the higher cost the supporters have had to pay at the turnstile. So as paying customers over the years we certainly haven't felt the benefits of advertising. Perhaps if commercialism had eased the admission burden for fans, then at least we'd have been left with a worthy consolation for their intrusion. However, to use just one of many examples: the Emirates sponsorship of the Arsenal stadium coincided with the highest ticket prices the club had ever seen.

And speaking of high ticket pricing...

Chapter 7
Value for money

"Our gate income will probably be the highest in the world. We will have 60,000 fans and higher priced tickets – and more premium [corporate] tickets than any other club in the UK."

Managing Director of Arsenal Keith Edelman – 2006.

When I read this quote in the *Evening Standard* I shook my head in disbelief, although it didn't tell me anything I didn't already know. Football's a rip-off, that's common knowledge. But what staggered me was that Keith Edelman happily admitted this fact, in what even sounded like a boastful fashion; as if Arsenal fans should be pleased about being charged such a high price for admission. Ten out of ten for honesty, but it sounded like a quote in which Edelman accidentally assumed that he was at an Arsenal board meeting and not in front of journalists who would then relate his intentions to the public.

How many businesses boast to their customers that they charge more than their rivals? Maybe this is a trend for the future of advertising which other industries should take a look at. I can picture a television advert from HMV. They have a new slogan for their marketing campaign: *HMV top dog for music. And with higher priced CDs we're making more money than our rivals.* Would that work? Maybe Edelman's words were in fact some sort of sly marketing ploy. When some season tickets are so expensive, owning one almost becomes a status symbol and an element of exclusiveness does work in attracting certain people to a product. In recent years, my team Arsenal has felt like a members' club in which there are people unable to get in because their names are not on the list. This exclusiveness might very well appeal to a lot of the fans who are on the inside, but it could be a dangerous game to play in the long term. A crowd that enjoys being exclusive and likes to follow a successful brand, will not be the ones who stick by that brand if that club becomes a mid-table team or worse. English football history does prove that no club can completely avoid a period of mediocrity or worse. Clubs such as Manchester United and Spurs spent a season of the 1970s outside of the top division. More recently, who would have thought that Leeds United would have gone from a Champions League semi-final with Real Madrid to a league match with Crewe Alexandra in just two seasons?

In 2007 the question: '*Do you think match tickets are good value for money?*' was asked to supporters via the internet survey group the Football Fans Census. The result was conclusive to say the least.

Do you think match tickets are good value for money?

YES – 12%
NO – 88%

Any other business in which 88% of customers thought that the company represented poor value for money would be in serious crisis. A year before this, the BBC programme *Football Focus* had asked the very same question and the result was exactly the same, with 88% of fans thinking that football represented poor value for money. Brian Barwick, the chairman of the FA at the time, responded to the BBC survey by saying, "I think we've got the balance just about right". Easy to say when you're the highly paid head of the FA who doesn't have to pay for access to football stadiums.

The study from the Football Fan Census surveyed 2,000 supporters, and emphatically makes it clear that supporters feel that the industry is not giving them value for money, from the gate admission to even the refreshments and merchandise that are sold at prices well over the odds. Other questions and results from the survey are as follows:

Should Premiership clubs use increased TV revenues to cut ticket prices?

Yes – 96%
No – 4%

Have you got into debt through following your team?

Yes – 20%
No – 80%

Do you go to matches less often, or more often than you used to?

Less often – 56%
More often – 8%
The same – 36%

Would you go to more games if tickets were cheaper and more available?

Yes – 86%
No – 14%

Would you be happy to pay more for tickets if it meant your club could afford to sign a top-class player?

Yes – 22%
No – 78%

Have you been to watch a team lower in the league than your own because it is cheaper?

Yes – 26%
No but I would in the future – 16%
No – 58%

What do you consider to be the biggest 'rip-off' at matches?

Ticket prices – 49%
Merchandise/ replica kit prices – 21%
Food and drink prices – 28%
Non-applicable – 2%

What doesn't fit with the results of these polls is the contradiction that football continues to draw big crowds, a fact that the Premier League, Football League and FA will happily point out. Football is a complacent industry, which is always a weakness in any field, especially one where most of the customers are not happy with the product they are buying into. When 86% of fans say that they would attend more games if the tickets were cheaper, then that is a clear indication that our stadiums could be fuller. Another more recent survey in 2010 (from the Virgin Index) concluded that an average of 25% of season ticket holders said they are considering not renewing for the following season. The two clubs with the highest percentage of fans considering this were at two different ends of the spectrum in terms of on-field aspirations: Manchester United and Wolverhampton.

Crowd numbers have fallen very slightly in recent years, making empty seats a commoner sight. If we go back to the start of the 2005-06 season, attendances were down at many Premiership clubs compared to the previous years. It was the first time top flight football had looked vulnerable for well over a decade. Most journalists and pundits put this attendance fall largely down to a lack of entertainment. At the start of the season there was a shortage of goals scored and lots of 0-0 draws. This was maybe one of the reasons for the drop in attendance, along with the uncompetitive and predictable nature of the Premiership. But football is not an industry where the majority of customers will buy into something on the basis of how much entertainment it provides. Most football matches provide average entertainment, and the truth is that for a lot of fans the whole experience of attending a game is more of a show of loyalty and passion than a pleasurable, stimulating experience. It's precisely because football isn't out and out entertainment that the clubs exploit the fans and get away with charging such outrageous prices.

Other than a surprising campaign by the *Sun* in 2007, aimed at lowering ticket prices in football (surprising in that a newspaper owned by Rupert Murdoch made a stand against free-market greed), the media over the years have very rarely made this subject a big issue, whether it be newspapers, TV or radio. Even though I have many disagreements with the *Sun*, as will become apparent in a later chapter about media sensationalism, you have to give credit where credit is due. Occasionally the *Sun* will take a stance against things like racism, animal cruelty and in the case of 2007, the rip-off culture in our national game. A cynical viewpoint will be that the owners of the *Sun* also part own Sky Sports, who have the rights to broadcast league football in England. Falling crowds throughout the leagues are not good for television entertainment, and no one wants to watch a match on TV with empty seats all over the stadium. If that was the case then Murdoch's media were smart in realising the problem, so that's not really a criticism.

The main argument from the *Sun's* campaign was that, with the amount of money that football generates from television and advertising, there is no justification other than greed for charging such outrageous prices. The problem with this campaign was that I'm referring to it as the *Sun's* 2007 campaign – because it ended nearly as quickly as it started. Hardly a word since, which is a great shame, because that campaign if sustained over a long period of time, was the best opportunity for clubs to realise that prices have to be reduced, not just by a tiny fraction – but dramatically. Certainly by more than the £8.35 that the *Sun* called for. When Bolton Wanderers responded to the *Sun's* campaign by announcing that they would be reducing season ticket prices by 10% for 2007-08, it was hailed by the newspaper as a great victory for the fans. Although any reduction in admission pricing should be welcomed, a 10% drop still maintains football as an overpriced attraction for its loyal followers. And this price reduction was only for season tickets, not matchday prices. Even if they did include matchday prices, 10% off a £36 ticket (the price Bolton charge away fans for grade A games) is not a great victory for football fans at all. In fact the £3.60 saved wouldn't even buy a pie at Wembley Stadium! In the same week, Chelsea boasted that they would be putting a freeze on ticket prices for the 2007-08 season. How commendable when the cheapest adult ticket for Chelsea home league games was already £45. Arsenal also boasted that they would lower ticket prices for Carling Cup matches. Equally as commendable given that the Carling Cup is a second-rate competition in which Arsenal field a second string team.

What's important to remember for most games, is that the so-called cheapest seats only make up a small percentage of tickets that go on sale, and would usually be the ones in the most demand. The availability of tickets therefore on offer to most fans will be the ones that are higher priced. To give just one example: Manchester United has nineteen different regular match-day ticket options ranging from £28 to £50. Only two of these options are for £28, eight are between £34 and £38, while the other nine are between £42 and £50.

On top of the price of admission, fans are also charged a booking fee for tickets bought over the phone and internet. At some clubs, tickets for certain games cannot be bought in person at the box office, meaning that a booking fee is unavoidable. The concept of a booking fee came about in the 1990s. Before then we bought tickets from living, breathing, paid human beings and never got charged booking fees. Now, we order tickets from non-paid computer systems and we get charged booking fees – work that one out! Tickets also come with a postage fee, not per transaction, but per ticket sold (same thing with the booking fee, one person buys five tickets and gets charged five booking fees). So if one person buys five tickets on behalf of themselves and four others, they end up paying five postage fees even though all the tickets are put in just one envelope.

Football presents itself as being a family game, but the financial burden on families to follow football is high. Let's take a Mother and Father with two children. They are on a reasonable household gross income of £40,000. If they are Chelsea fans then by using the most conservative and cheapest costs on season tickets, travel fares (all-zone London travelcards), food (£6 each) and a match day programme (one £3 programme per game) that family will spend roughly £2,200 on watching their team play home games each season. And that estimate doesn't include extra costs for cup games not covered by season tickets, club merchandise or anything else but the most affordable way for a family of four to follow their team for league games. The example I just gave also assumes that this family have been lucky enough to get four season tickets in the Family Enclosure, which is cheaper and of limited availability. £2,200 for this family to watch Chelsea home games each season is roughly 7.5% of their yearly net income. If this is the burden for a family on a reasonable income of £40,000, then what about a family whose chief wage earner is on minimum wage? Well after tax, a person who works a forty hour week on minimum wage (£5.93 per hour) will take home £200 per week. If that person wanted to take their partner and two children to a Chelsea grade A home game, then the cost involved would be:

Cheapest match tickets – (Family Enclosure, two adults, two juniors, booking fee not included): **£128**

Travel – Two adult all-zone London travelcards (children go free): **£16**

Food and drink – £6 each: **£24**

Match day programme – one programme amongst four people: **£3**

Total cost: **£171**

Again this is a very conservative estimate because it assumes they've been able to get tickets for the Family Enclosure. Even so, the total cost for this family for one football match will still be 85% of the main breadwinner's weekly net income.

I recently bumped into a friend who had brought his wife and two young sons along to a grade B Arsenal game, and had paid a face value price of £175 for tickets. This family travelled from Essex, so no doubt when including travel costs plus food and drink, the total price would easily top £200. As a former regular at Arsenal this man has had to limit the amount of times he takes his family to watch football each season because of the financial burden. This man earns a higher than average wage and runs his own business. So when they say that football's a 'family game', what they really mean is that football's a game for families who can afford to go.

Had tickets cost this much in the late 1980s and early 1990s when I was a junior, then I would not have been able to attend anywhere near as many matches as I managed to during that period. In the days when I had virtually no money the one thing I could always afford to do was go to watch football. In a cupboard in my room I have stashed away hundreds of tickets ranging from football matches, concerts, theatre and other sporting events like cricket and boxing. Recently I was rummaging around this cupboard full of memories and came across some nice little reminders, including the ticket of the first football match I ever attended. This was Arsenal v Everton in the West Stand lower tier in the year 1986. At the time Everton were the league champions and they won the game 1-0. The price on the ticket stub read £4.50 (adult price, not junior). Twenty years later in 2005-06, in the last ever season at Highbury, the same ticket was priced at £39. It doesn't take a mathematical genius to work out that this ticket price rise did not mirror the growth in annual wages in that twenty year period which was roughly £9,000 in 1986 and £23,000 in 2006. Even if the average person's wage had tripled in that time the equivalent price would be around the £13 mark not £39. In 1995 a seat in the Clock End at Highbury was £10. By 2005 it was up to £35, a 250% increase in cost. How many people's wages went up 250% in that ten year period? As I looked at other ticket stubs from the same era it brought back to me just how little it used to cost to follow your football team. Prices got hiked up to obscene levels in a very short period of time. Some German fans fear a similar imposition on their game and are determined not to be rolled over in the same way. In 2010, supporters of Borussia Dortmund boycotted an away game against

Schalke 04, in anger at increased ticket prices. The price they were protesting was €22. The season before they were charged €13.50 for the same fixture. Now to us in England either of those prices seems like a fair cop compared to what we are charged. Aside from a few exceptions, clubs in the Premier League will normally charge away fans somewhere between £30 and £50; a figure in the region of £50 sometimes being the only option for certain games. A spokesman for the Dortmund protest said, *"For the first time, the €20 mark has been crossed by a club and we are no longer willing to sit back and find out what happens next"*. In England, we know from experience what happens next, and we're paying a heavy price for it.

Without dissent, the accepted price just becomes higher with each passing year. Not to be outdone by the Premier League, UEFA imposed the most outrageous ticket pricing ever seen in football for the 2011 Champions League Final, held at Wembley. The cheapest ticket was £150, plus a cheeky £26 booking fee on top. Talk about a punch in the nose followed up by a kick in the teeth! They then had the gall to blame London for being an expensive city. Though quite what that has to do with the pricing structure for a one off football match never got explained; probably down to the fact that UEFA were talking bollocks. That minimum price will now be the benchmark for the Champions League Final. The next benchmark will be UEFA trying to emulate Superbowl prices, where the cheapest face value ticket for the final is reported to be around $800. About forty years earlier a Superbowl final ticket could be purchased for between $6 and $12.

When Arsenal moved to the Emirates Stadium, the *Daily Mirror* reported that the most expensive season ticket at Arsenal and indeed in the country is £100,000, which will buy you two seats over the space of three years as part of the exclusive Diamond Club membership. Executive boxes cost £65,000 per annum and can seat around ten people and are bought on three to five year leases. Other top tickets cost around £4,000 a season and have to be bought for a minimum of three seasons. I've been sent emails from Arsenal inviting me to pay £250 just to be on a waiting list for what they call the Club Level. In early 2011 it was reported that Arsenal were to become the first club to charge £100 for a regular match ticket (the actual figure was a price rise from £94 to £96). This price increase was attributed by Arsenal to the VAT rise from 17.5% to 20% in January 2011. What the club didn't mention was that their ticket prices never got reduced in line with the VAT drop from 17.5% to 15% in November 2008. By the end of the 2010-11 season the club announced a further increase of 6.5%, which of course did take the price of a regular match ticket to over £100.

Disabled fans now have to pay a high price to attend matches. Arsenal's disabled access to the games had always been for free at Highbury (after a very small membership fee was paid). Since the move to the Emirates in 2006, disabled season ticket prices have ranged between £442.50 and £1,250 a season. It had been claimed that disabled fans had insisted that they must pay. If this was the case then surely the fairest option would have been to let payment be optional. Those disabled fans who want to pay can, those who struggle won't have to pay full price, and there are plenty of disabled fans who do struggle to meet these prices. For instance, disabled Arsenal fan Jamie Brown didn't seem to be insisting too loudly that he should pay hundreds for his season ticket. He told the *Daily Mirror* that:

"Arsenal is my life. I don't know what I will do now. I can't work because I have spina bifida."

"All the fans in wheelchairs are in the same boat. The prices are beyond us."

"I've been going to Arsenal for seven years. The club says we should contribute and we're happy to do this. But the prices are way beyond our means. I've paid a deposit for the cheapest seat. But I can't afford it. And the view is rubbish."

What an ungrateful moaner this Mr Brown is. Doesn't he understand that it's his duty as much as anyone else's to sacrifice themselves financially so that some people within football can become even more prosperous than they already are? Okay, so Jamie Brown only gets £160 severe disability allowance a fortnight to live on. Big deal, where's my violin and box of tissues. What about the footballers who struggle to buy a Ferrari once every fortnight? I don't see anyone in wheelchairs crying for them. It will only take Mr Brown over five weeks' income to afford to watch his team play home games each season. And the state sponger has the audacity to complain about a little spina bifida as to why he can't work. Okay, spina bifida can leave a person paralysed from the waist down, but he should thank the money men in football for contributing towards his disability allowance through taxes. Of course that does discount the staggering number of football club owners/chairmen who have become residents/registered in tax havens and pay less tax than you and me. Let's also discount the footballers who avoid paying the Inland Revenue by having a large percentage of their wages paid into EFRBS tax loophole pension schemes. But I do hope that Jamie Brown can take some comfort in the knowledge that the more of his money that goes into football, the better back treatment the directors and shareholders can get through the top osteopaths.

This really is the mountain's peak of greed within the game. We've reached the stage where the poorest people in society like Jamie Brown are being cruelly shunned from top level football because of the financial strain of supporting a team. Suffering from spina bifida must be very difficult, but for someone like

Jamie Brown following Arsenal has clearly been one of the saving graces of his life. Now this saving grace is something that comes with a high price, to pay for the principle that people who are luckier in life can be super rich – instead of just very rich. Arsenal are not unique in this; it's now normal for Premiership clubs to charge disabled fans hundreds of pounds for season tickets. The carers are usually allowed free admission but then again this is in line with standard practice elsewhere. What's needed here is more of a price range based on incomes and whether a disabled person is working or on benefits. For example I think that someone like Professor Steven Hawking could afford to pay full price for a match ticket. However, someone like Jamie Brown should not be expected to pay hundreds of pounds for supporting his team when the price is beyond his range. Theatres and cinemas don't let disabled people in for free either, but they do have discount prices and more importantly they are usually one-off experiences, unlike a football season ticket which is an invoice for hundreds of pounds.[7]

Here's another quote from Keith Edelman as Arsenal moved stadium and were beginning a new corporate era. "We have 9,000 premium seats. 2,000 at club level and 7,000 at box level. The revenue from those seats alone is nearly that of the 38,000 at Highbury." Okay, so 9,000 corporate seats at Arsenal's 60,000 stadium generate as much revenue on matchday as the 38,000 capacity at Highbury used to. So why are the buggers charging such a high price for the other 51,000 fans? Why is Jamie Brown paying £442+ when at Highbury he got in for nothing? I suppose the easy answer to that question is – because they can. The likes of Arsenal can charge what they want because enough fans will cough up the money, and enough fans will also be on waiting lists and willing to pay the same prices.

---

[7] In general, season tickets cannot be paid in instalments. The full amount must be paid before the start of the season.

What's disheartening, is that it would appear that a large percentage of football fans seem apathetic about the predicament of people like Jamie Brown and indeed their own predicament. Their attitude is the classic "I'm all right Jack" mentality. But it does seem ironic that the same people who are happy to pay a high price for football are usually the same ones who moan about the cost of everything else on the planet. As I was writing the original edition of *Theatre of Silence* I had a debate with a Chelsea fan who claimed that football did represent very good value for money, and that if I didn't like paying top dollar to watch Arsenal then I should go and support Leyton Orient or Barnet. I think this chap was missing the point entirely. I'm an Arsenal fan and I follow my team whether we play good football or bad football. As luck would have it we play good football and have won many trophies since I've supported them. I'm allowed to be unhappy at the prices my club charge without being told that I don't appreciate good football. This man's argument assumes that successful clubs charge their fans more money than teams lower down the league. In the Premiership there's not a huge difference in ticket prices between the teams who finish top and the teams who finish bottom. In 2005-06, Birmingham City who were relegated that season, were more expensive to watch than Manchester United. In 2011-12, QPR hiked up prices to the point where the cheapest ticket for certain games was £47. The successful European teams who compete in the Champions League can be cheaper than lower division clubs in England. €200 or under for a domestic season ticket is normal for most top clubs outside of England.

Let's look at the two European Champions League finalists from 2010 and their admission pricing. Inter Milan's season tickets start from €200, while Bayern Munich's start from even less at a mere €120 for open terracing. If anyone ever tells you that clubs have to charge high prices in order to achieve success, please point this fact out to them. Also, if anyone claims that fans are happy to pay a high price in return for success, please bear in mind a recent conversation that I had with a 24-year-old West Ham fan: he told me that he actually hopes the Hammers get relegated from the Premiership, so that prices come down, meaning that he and his brother can afford to go to the games.

After pointing out cheaper European ticket pricing to the Chelsea fan, his comeback was that: "Everything in England is overpriced compared to Europe". Not true by any means, as anyone who's been to Europe since the euro came into effect will tell you. But let's give him the benefit of the doubt and say that he does have a point – surely then that's even more reason for English football to be affordable now. When trying to pay the mortgage, the council tax, the gas bills, the car insurance, the travel fares, the weekly food shop and everything else, do you really need to be hit with an £800 invoice from your club to pay for a one-year season ticket? The culture of professional football was not built on this principle. Football was an attraction that was accessible to people of all incomes.

If people like this particular Chelsea fan think that everything in England is a con then maybe it's because people like him say that: "Oh well it's what you've got to pay" (which he did indeed say) when faced with a blatant rip-off. Football fans in other countries would unleash fury if they were asked to pay the same prices we do for football tickets. Hypothetically, if ticket prices were too expensive in Italy the Italian fans would probably use two tactics.

1. Refuse to pay and protest by staying away.
2. Burn the club down!

Result: ticket prices in Italy come down. Problem solved. Not everything in England is a con if you make an effort to find value for money. And that value for money includes other forms of entertainment. I can go to my local cinema for £5.00, sit in a comfortable environment and watch a film of my choice. I know a good quality London West End cinema that offers admission to members from £1.50. I could walk into any major London museum such as the Natural History Museum or British Museum for free. Or I could go to the world famous Shakespeare Globe theatre and watch a live performance for just £5 on a warm summer evening. I'd do it regularly if I understood a word of what Shakespeare was on about (they have standing at the Globe – no Taylor Report in place yet). A top range ticket to watch the proms at the Royal Albert Hall can be purchased for as little as £12.50. Lower priced tickets start from £5. So-called middle class or upper class entertainment such as theatre and opera is now far cheaper than the so-called working class game of football. Tickets at the 'elite' Royal Opera House range from £6 to £140. Top drawer London West End theatres offer a cheaper night out than the London football clubs do on a cold wet weekday in January.

The lowest priced tickets for West End theatre averages at between £10 and £20. But if you don't think that this is very good value for a night out in London, then you could always try the nearest football club to Central London which is Millwall FC. The adult admission prices for Millwall, who in recent years have hovered between the Championship and League 1, are £22 to £27. A world class show at Covent Garden, or Millwall v Doncaster? It's entirely up to you. I very occasionally follow Millwall on the side and enjoy going down to the Den to watch a game. But here's the difference between something like theatre and football: people walk out of these kind of shows smiling and looking happier than many football fans do after spending over £30 to watch a 0-0 draw in the cold outdoors. Football can't claim to deliver the same customer satisfaction and this is where the problem lies when they charge such high prices in the name of entertainment. If you paid money to watch a West End show but felt the whole performance was poor, then the last thing you're going to do is pay money to watch the same show a week later.

So now we have legions of Mercedes, BMWs and 4x4s making their way to the ground which is something that never used to be seen before football became fashionable and expensive. The problem lies not in the fact that these people like football and want to go and watch it. The problem is that the new breed has completely taken over and pushed out so many others.

My argument is not that the middle classes or high earners shouldn't feel at home at football grounds. I'm not against any type of person going to football, but that's the whole point. Football can only be the people's game if it's accessible to all the people. Today, the game is accessible to high earners, or to people with little money but who dedicate all they have to supporting their club. The latter group of people therefore have to make sacrifices in other areas. So many of us don't fit into either of those two categories and so are unsure as to where we fit in with the modern game.

We're paying more for football now, but overall is the sport giving us more satisfaction and fulfilment? Is football more fun to attend now than it has been in the years gone by? If the answer is no then where's our value for money? If I had a Ford Fiesta but wanted a better car, I might buy a Jaguar. If I wanted a step up from that, then I would then buy a Ferrari. The more money I spend, the better product I should be getting. In football I'm paying far more money, but I'm not getting any more enjoyment out of the game than I was ten, fifteen, twenty years ago.

Of course football fans aren't the only ones who pay a high price in return for an environment where they are treated with contempt. For instance night clubbers, on a regular basis, before standing outside in a queue for an hour will:

1. Pay good money to get dirty looks from bouncers.
2. Get squashed like sardines in an overcrowded environment.
3. Queue at the bar for twenty minutes in order to buy an overpriced drink.
4. Listen to a bland choice of music they don't really like.
5. Give up on conversation because the music's too loud.
6. Claim they had a 'mad night' before taking out their frustrations in a drunken brawl later on in the evening.

But when a nightclub offers this kind of hospitality, anyone with a brain should easily come to the conclusion that they should never step foot into that particular establishment ever again. With football fans it's more complex than that. The brain doesn't always get to make the decisions as the heart gets in the way. It's tough to abandon something that has been part of your life from an early age. If you've followed a football club all your life then it becomes part of your identity. How easy can it be to temporarily or permanently abandon a part of your own identity? Scores of football fans would love to stage a form of protest by not buying match tickets. But many fans worry that if they do this, plenty of other fans will just take their place, and when this happens they've lost access to the club they support and will no longer have a way of even buying tickets. This is a tough decision for any fan to make and is the main reason why the clubs get away with treating fans so poorly. In the last few years I've let both my brain and my heart make the decision as to whether or not it's worth going to matches on a regular basis. If offered a season ticket by Arsenal (cheapest one £951) would I accept it? Fuck no! Absolutely not. The brain tells me that I'm sick and tired of paying well over the odds for something, just so that people who are already rich can be even richer. The heart is now telling me that I don't feel strongly enough towards the principles of the modern game to make that sacrifice anyway. I may be a football fanatic who still loves the game – but I'm not a mug. I will not pay a fortune to watch diving from overpaid players, to sit amongst boring fans, to have advertising shoved in my face and to be ordered about by people in orange bibs. In two words: screw 'em!

Chapter 8
Football in the future

I had this vision of the year 2050...

I'm in a pub called the Moon Under Water watching football on the big screen. This pub used to be known as The Freemasons Arms before it was taken over by a major chain. The government recently passed laws giving tax breaks to the big corporations for the more independent shops and pubs they take over. This was recommended by the Monopoly Commission which is headed by the wheelchair-bound old campaigner Rupert Murdoch. On the big screen, the commentary lets me know that the first five minutes of the first quarter "has been brought to you courtesy of the Carphone Warehouse".

In the stadium itself, the stewards and CCTV cameras are monitoring the crowd for instances of expressed subversive opinions. One spectator slyly hands a note to the person in the seat next to him. The note reads: *I'm not happy with the five in midfield. We need more support for the front man.* This message is picked up by CCTV cameras and the two fans are dragged out the stadium and banned from the ground for life. Of course the term 'football fan' has finally been replaced by the now popular and more suitable phrase 'football consumer.' Another consumer is being thrown out of the ground for wearing club colours that were not purchased from official outlets. Other consumers have been ejected for causing offences ranging from bringing their own food into the ground, to standing up and cheering when a goal is scored for more than the regulated five seconds.

At half-time, a big screen TV in the stadium displays all the other results from the Halliburton English Super League.

NIKE TOWN FC	**1-0**	REEBOK WANDERERS
STARBUCKS UNITED	**3-3**	AFC EMIRATES
MOSS SIDE MCDONALDS	**1-1**	CHELSEA BOOTS
ADIDAS ACADEMICALS	**2- 2**	ASTON MARTIN
NEWCASTLE BROWN ALE	**0-0**	THOMPSON HOTSPUR
LEICESTER & ALLIANCE	**3-2**	LEEDS BUILDING SOCIETY

The ref blows the whistle at the end of the final quarter and the consumers all leave the stadium and make their way home. Some are wearing baseball caps with the club's sponsor displayed on them. Wearing these baseball caps will soon be compulsory. They only cost €200 and the club receives money from the sponsor for every cap purchased. Some consumers are a little unsure about this marketing scheme, but they understand that anything which brings money into the club is the common goal that everyone should work towards.

Meanwhile at the other extreme of the culture spectrum, our nation's opera houses have been generating a lot of concern and are gaining publicity for all the wrong reasons. A news crew catches footage of a group of Puccini fans who are having a tear up with a mob of Wagner supporters outside the Royal Opera House in London's Covent Garden. The Puccini fans get the better of things early on, but the Wagner fans have stamina and end up having the rival mob on their toes. BBC news reporter Hayden Prutt is quickly on the scene and asks these opera fans why it is they choose to behave the way they do. "It's what you live for every weekend, going to opera, letting all that tension out," answers one gentleman with a broad Yorkshire accent. "Opera's about passion. Proper working man's entertainment."

Hayden Prutt then interviews a smartly dressed lady who is sitting outside a coffee shop in Covent Garden. Armed with a well spoken accent and plush mink coat she represents the traditional opera fan from yesteryear. She still attends, despite having grown disillusioned with the route that it has taken in recent years, and she hopes one day that opera will return to its true roots. Hayden Prutt asks her, "Can you remember a time when not all opera fans were poorly educated working class scum?"

"In the old days opera fans could sit together. There was no need for segregation. Why can't these people follow badger baiting instead?" she moans before ducking for cover to avoid a Wagner fan being thrown through the coffee shop window. Hayden Prutt looks down on the Wagner hooligan who is lying on the floor covered in glass. He points to the man. "However, morons like this can't claim to be real opera fans. They're just here for the fight. The real fans are still inside the auditorium watching the drama unfold."

Inside the Royal Opera house, the crowd are getting restless and irritable with what's been a lacklustre and poor performance of *Madam Butterfly*. One fan rises from his royal box and shouts out "SHIT, THIS IS FUCKING SHIT". Another upset fan in the lower circle calls out to the performers to "SHOW SOME PRIDE IN THE COSTUMES". The tension in the crowd rises even more with the poorly acted unconvincing suicide of Butterfly herself. This causes fights to break out in the stalls and even in the royal boxes, where some fans piss in wine glasses and throw the contents down on the people below. The Royal Opera House does not yet have steel fences between the crowd and the stage and it's not long before a stage invasion occurs and the performance is abandoned. Outside however, some fans have already left early in order to beat the traffic. Hayden Prutt is outside with them and gathers their thoughts on the night's entertainment.

"They're not fit to wear the costumes," grumbles a Geordie who is pushed out the way by a Scouser who whinges, "I've been watching *Madam Butterfly* for fifteen years and that's the worst performance I've ever seen. Should dock 'em all a week's wages. They're a disgrace."

"Will you be coming back next week to see the show?" asks Prutt. "I've been coming every week since the Puccini season started," replies the Geordie. "Hopefully things will improve, but so far I've watched the same crap show and the same crap actors for fucking weeks now and I'm sick of it."

In the same week, the BBC's controller Rupert Murdoch sends Hayden Prutt on a mission to Italy. He is there to report on opera fans who have travelled to Rome to watch the English National Opera perform a version of *Tosca* – in English. This is when modern day opera culture is at its most damaging to the reputation of England, as bare-chested groups of English opera fans parade the streets of Rome and sing classics such as *Nessun Dorma*. They drink beer and perform poorly acted death scenes in full view of the public. Even though England hasn't produced a world class opera tour for many years, these fans still believe that one day England will be top of the world. Throughout the piazzas of Rome, St. George Cross flags are tied to buildings and statues. One flag reads *Gilbert and Sullivan – Salford division*. As always with English opera tours, the shameful scenes overshadow the stage drama and there are calls for England to be banned from singing in Europe for at least five years.

Shortly after the Italy trip Hayden Prutt gets to appear as a guest on the long running political show *Question Time*. The question of opera violence comes up, along with other topics such as whether or not politics has been dumbed down in recent years. The host, Dame Kerry Katona MBE chairs to the best of her ability, in the bumbling but lovable way that makes her the nation's sweetheart. In this particular episode of *Question Time* she let slip with the word 'fuck' on just three occasions, and only smoked two cigarettes. After the show, the one subject that sticks with Hayden Prutt is the question of whether or not football has become too elitist. He doesn't feel as well informed on the subject as he'd like, so days later Prutt takes a camera crew to Soho Square to report on whether the sport needs to reach out to new fans in order to survive. He goes to visit the headquarters of the Football Consumers Association, which is now run by the Premier League. He gets an interview with the chairman, Lord Cornelius Dunseith. Hayden kicks off the interview with the most fundamental question in football:

Prutt – Cornelius. Is it fair to say that football is too elitist?

Dunseith – You see Hayden old boy, what we need to understand is that football has a certain etiquette that needs to be respected. You cannot have people coming to the football who behave in a way unfitting to the culture of the brand we offer.

Prutt – Behaviour such as?

Dunseith – Talking too loudly. Standing up during a performance. Have you heard the tale about the person who one day shouted out to the players? It was one of those moments when you just wanted to curl up and die. He did, horribly. But all credit to the players that day as they dealt with it very professionally and just continued with the game.

Prutt – But ordinary people feel that they don't belong at the football. That somehow this is a pastime for the elite only and for people with money.

Dunseith – There are no signs up banning the working classes from coming to football matches. They can come to the football if they want to.

Prutt – How much would a ticket cost them?

Dunseith – Tickets for the upper circle at most grounds start at around a grand a game. But the good news is that the clubs have agreed a freeze on ticket pricing for the next year.

Prutt – That's very commendable.

Dunseith – Yes. And if a person is on a low income but has savings, then there's no reason why at one time in their life, they couldn't just splash out on a day at the football.

Prutt – Their savings?

Dunseith – They might not live to see those savings anyway because the life expectancy of the lower classes is... er... well, lower.

Prutt – But their savings?

Dunseith – Well you can't take it with you when you pop off, and we're always willing to issue a ticket against the value of your property.

Prutt – So you'd welcome these people at football stadiums?

Dunseith – Bums on seats dear boy, bums on seats. And if your bum's not on a seat during the game then your bum will be on the back seat of a police car. Ha ha, get it?

Prutt – That's very good. One from *Clive Tyldesley Easy-To-Make-Up Puns, Volume 6* I believe.

Dunseith – The very one. A genius of the day, a bloody genius. Some say Lord Byron. Some say William Shakespeare. Some might even say William Blake. I say Clive Tyldesley.

Prutt – Sir Clive Tyldesley.

Dunseith – Of course. Dear Clive. You know that he requested to have his ashes spread on the turf at the American Airlines Nou Camp Arena in Barcelona? Said that when he was gone he'll want people to come and visit him there just so they'll never forget that balmy night in that same stadium, when Manchester United came back against all odds, and when David Beckham and Ryan Giggs...

Prutt – We're going off the point a bit.

Dunseith – Yes. Anyway this is complete nonsense. At football grounds there are plenty of people from very poor backgrounds who attend every game of the season.

Prutt – Really? Do you have a special deal then for low earners?

Dunseith – Yes that's the one. The special deal – or the new deal, or something like that. The government were even kind enough to scrap the minimum wage law just so we'd be willing to offer these people employment and give them hope.

Prutt – So these people you refer to are actually hot dog sellers in the stands?

Dunseith – Don't be a fool Prutt. Hot dogs are banned from stadiums, health and safety. Could be used as a missile, take no chances. No, these people sell match-day programmes, ice cream tubs and binoculars.

Prutt – You just mentioned health and safety. You seem very concerned about unruly behaviour from the consumers you represent. What are your methods in clamping down on the troublemakers?

Dunseith – We never have any trouble at our football grounds. In fact we've hardly had one major incident for anything more than the usual bit of over-exuberant talking, or not wearing official club merchandise.

Prutt – Why is this?

Dunseith – Zero tolerance. We're not prepared to put up with crime at our football stadiums. We have a highly advanced way of predicting crime and stopping the criminals before they have time to fight, swear, vandalise or pillage.

Prutt – Explain.

Dunseith – One of the best indicators of disorder is social class. The newspaper we read is a good indication of our social class. For example, scum read the *Mirror*. Therefore, we run spot checks on the consumers, and if they are found to be reading the wrong sort of newspaper, there is a fair chance they are hooligans. So we chuck the buggers out.

Prutt – And does this system work?

Dunseith – Well, you just have to look at the statistics. Although, due to our zero tolerance policy, the crowd trouble ratio is very high, most of the consumers haven't actually done anything, so in fact actual trouble inside football grounds is very low.

Prutt – So football stadiums are a safe place to be?

Dunseith – Yes dear boy. If you're a law abiding football consumer, your chances of getting caught up in disorder are very low. Because it's far more likely you'll be ejected from the ground first.

Prutt – I'm sure that all consumers will drink to that…

Dunseith – As long as those drinks are purchased from the club bar though Hayden. Look, clubs are not afraid to use tough methods in dealing with scum at our stadiums. Take for example Nike Town FC, run by the American chap Randy Bastard Junior. Last year they never had to make one arrest, nor did they have one unruly incident.

Prutt – Impressive. How did they achieve this?

Dunseith – They, along with the police, made it a criminal offence to watch Nike Town FC play. So they played out the whole season to an empty stadium. The owners of the club were not prepared to let a minority of idiots ruin the enjoyment for the decent fans of Nike Town.

Prutt – But with an empty stadium didn't that cost them financially?

Dunseith – No Prutt, because you do these things after the season tickets have been renewed and paid for. And not only that, it leaves so much more space to fill the rest of the ground with flashing advertising banners and billboards. Genius, bloody genius. They deserved that Deloitte Money League Championship last season.

Prutt – And the consumers were happy with this?

Dunseith – It brought more revenue to the club didn't it?

Prutt – I assume so.

Dunseith – Well then, don't ask stupid questions.

Sepp Blatter reveals the amount of tickets that will be sold to fans for the 2014 World Cup Finals.

Don't try this today kids. Well not unless you want a banning order.

Nineteen year old Ricky Regan got a three year ban, plus a £500 fine for lighting up this flare at Stamford Bridge.

Fans enjoying the game on a terrace, without worrying about how much the admission cost them. By the way, notice any stewards?

Man United fans going crazy. Terrace culture survives in venues like this one.

The ultras at Boca Juniors.

The ultras in the English Premiership.

The Riverside Stadium in Middlesbrough. At one time original, now the design model for the majority of newly built football stadiums.
Courtesy of Stephen Pickup.

Anyone seen a pub around here? This is Darlington's new stadium, which highlights the trend of clubs moving away from the community.
Courtesy of Jamie Mash.

Spreading the word on overpriced pies!

And spreading it directly outside the Emirates Stadium.

Well said that banner.
Courtesy of Gerry Fagbemi.

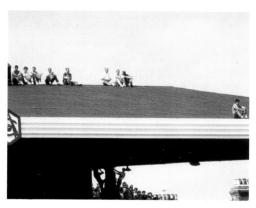

*Health and Safety advisers please look away now. Gooners on the
old North Bank for the opening day of the 1987-88 season.*
Courtesy of Doug Poole.

That's what you get for sitting on the roof without permission!
The End, 80 Years of life on the Terraces, Tom Watt; First
published, Evening Standard.

Born in hope. FC United of Manchester fans, young and old, have a club they truly believe in.
Courtesy of Mick Dean.

Love United Hate Glazer. FC United of Manchester fans cheer on an historic FA Cup win against Rochdale in 2010.
Courtesy of Mick Dean.

Chapter 9
The people's game

"I would love to have an investigation to find out who invented football. We will never have to build him a statue or monument. He will always be part of history along with the greatest geniuses that ever existed. Those who invented penicillin, the telephone, television and gravity are the greatest geniuses of all time. But whoever invented football should be worshipped as a God."

Hugo Sanchez – Real Madrid and Mexico legend

As Brits it's right that we should know about the dark side of our history and the number of wrongs we've caused in certain parts of the world. But we should also pay homage and appreciate our country's gifts to the world in culture through things like sport, music, literature, engineering and science. In these fields you could argue that our track record is unrivalled and undervalued. If there is a discussion about 'Britishness' or 'what it means to be British', clichés such as tolerance, fairness, and politeness are brought up, yet rarely does anyone mention creativity or ingenuity. Very rarely do people cite culture. Quite the opposite, I've heard many people insist that the English have no recognisable culture other than royal pageantry, cream teas and Morris dancing, They say that familiarity breeds contempt; we perceive culture as being something foreign, colourful and exotic, which it no doubt is. But it is also something that we exported to the rest of the world.

When Brazilians play beach football it's something that has come about through the influence of English culture. When India played host to Pakistan in the 2011 Cricket World Cup semi-final it brought both nations to a standstill. The focus of their attention was an English invention. When the Rolling Stones performed in front of a million fans on the Copacabana beach in Brazil, the people of that country were watching a combination of British and American pop culture.

In the last chapter we had a look into the future. Now let's go back in time. We're in a pub in London's Covent Garden called the Freemasons Arms. The date is 26th October 1863. Representatives of eleven football clubs have popped in for a quick pint and a chat about a spiffing idea they've all had about creating a new world phenomenon. The directors and executives of these eleven clubs start to get excited about an idea they've had of creating a unique brand – a business. Something with which they could exploit members of the general public for profit. A new social scene where they could sell lots of replica shirts of up-and-coming football giants like the Old Etonians and Royal Engineers. They had plans to play this new game in front of thousands of spectators who would spend lots of money on merchandise, pies and season tickets in well-decorated Victorian corporate boxes. They could even foresee a time when they could film the games and then sell the cinematic rights on for billions of pounds to the local picture palaces, where men with slick moustaches would watch games projected onto the big screens (look at the old film footage for proof that the game was ten times faster in the late 1800s). These chaps in the Freemasons Arms were out to make a fortune. Hold on a second, that's not true, I'm lying. These men were sports enthusiasts who played a crucial role in one of England and Scotland's greatest gifts to world culture. They drew a clear line in the rules between football and rugby and the Football Association was founded. The rules later drawn up from the FA would form the modern game as we know it today. A small book containing just thirteen laws would by this day and age be responsible for 1.5 million football teams and 300,000 recognised clubs around the world. The Freemasons Arms is still going strong, but doesn't do that much to advertise its heritage. I get the feeling it's more of a rugby pub, but come on fellas, make an effort. It's an important part of history and something to be proud of.

Prior to the late 1800s, there had been lots of rowdy ball games played in England dating back to at least 1314, usually with the ball being an inflated pig's bladder – sometimes, according to legend, with the ball being a severed head! Even before that time, legend has it that in the city of Chester, the Anglo-Saxons played football with the heads of defeated Danish invaders. According to historians, the ball games played around town centres in the fourteenth century were a rough and physical kick and rush free-for-all; a tactic that the Wimbledon team of the 1980s and 1990s used with some degree of success. In 1314 Edward II banned these games with the threat of imprisonment for anyone who disobeyed the law. Edward III also banned football as it was stopping young men from practising their archery, which at the time was vital for England in times of war. In later centuries in England and Scotland, whole towns would compete against each other in which the field of play would stretch from one town to the other. Some of these towns still carry on the tradition to this day.

There are some Italians who claim that football first started in Florence from a game by the name of Calcio, but that claim is a load of coglioni! Calcio bears more resemblance to football hooliganism than Association Football. It's legal thuggery in which bare-chested Italians in colourful baggy trousers spend more time punching opponents and team-mates than worrying about where the ball might be. And more importantly, Calcio is not a game played with the feet, unless you count the occasions when the players kick each other in the head. In fairness there are similarities to football, and Calcio was for the time revolutionary. It is arguably the platform of a style of team sport that resembles games like rugby, NFL, hockey and football. The ball is round, the pitch is rectangular and two teams (twenty-seven players/hooligans on each side) compete against each other to get the ball to the opponents' end of the pitch. But claiming Calcio to be the original football is like the inventors of medieval music claiming the credit for inventing rock and roll. Football has a style of its own, different from Calcio in rules, tactics, method, skill and finesse. Calcio is still played in Florence to this day and is possibly the most violent barbaric team game in the world. It makes Aussie Rules, ice hockey, IKEA openings and WWE all look like a non-contact game of tag.

Some people, including Sepp Blatter, claim that football originated in China centuries ago, but once again that claim is a load of fang pi! The Chinese version was far less similar to football than even Calcio; it was no more than a docile game of non competitive kick-ups. Going by re-enactments that I've seen, a few guys hover in a small square grid and occasionally kick a ball in the air and try and control it when it comes down – not really much of a spectator sport.

The men in the Freemasons Arms in 1863 were from the upper classes. The pioneers and players of football were from the elitist public schools such as Eton, Charterhouse and Harrow. In these early years the working classes would have had little or nothing to do with football. Sport owes a great deal to the people of these hierarchic public schools, but football could only expand and draw huge crowds by being a game devoid of any class barriers. It's interesting, that the elite of Britain created a sport that would arguably become the main representative of working class culture and lifestyle.

Through the efforts of missionaries, football became popular in working class towns in the Midlands and Northern England. The teams in these towns and cities were formed in local pubs, factories, social clubs and churches who saw sport as healthy and good for local communities. To use two examples: Manchester United was formed by railway workers and Celtic FC was founded by the Catholic community in Glasgow.

In 1883 the balance of football changed forever when Blackburn Olympic FC won the FA Cup by beating Old Etonians in the final. The oldest cup competition in the world had started in 1872 and prior to Olympic's win, the first twelve years of the competition had been dominated by the upper class amateur teams like Wanderers and Old Etonians. Blackburn Olympic, who folded ten years later, were the first working class team to win a major football trophy. It was a landmark game as after that final in 1883, the public school amateur teams fell away while the teams from working class towns became the dominant forces of football. It's worth noting, that as soon as football became popular amongst the working classes, the upper classes dropped it like a bad habit and played rugby instead. The sport had become the People's Game and would continue to be for decades to follow. All of the working class teams that created the first ever football league in 1888 are still famous names in English football and have league status.[8] It wasn't until one hundred years after the formation of the first ever football league, that the owners of football clubs in England deserted the very people who built these institutions and made them the great names that now are marketed as brands and products.

So let's quickly go forward again to the modern day in search of something that resembles the People's Game. In the

---

[8] Everton, Bolton, Aston Villa, Blackburn, WBA, Wolves, Stoke, Notts County, Burnley, Preston North End, Derby and Accrington were the teams who formed the world's first ever football league.

summer of 2005, football was put in the shade by what was described as the greatest Ashes series of all time between England and Australia. At the beginning of the last day of the final test series, England were in a great position to retain the Ashes for the first time in seventeen years. All they had to do was stay in bat for the day or build up a lead so big that the Aussies wouldn't have enough time in the day to win the game. The day started off fairly well, but wickets soon started to fall. With four wickets already down, Freddy Flintoff was then caught by Shane Warne, and all of a sudden England had only five wickets in hand and a lead of only 126. After being in such a great position, it looked like England were going to fall short on the final day and fail to recapture the Ashes. At this point I felt devastated and turned off the television for the third time in about fifteen minutes. A couple of minutes later I turned the television back on and endured the tension which was almost too much to take. I soon realised that for the first time, another sport had as much of an emotional hold over me as football. I'd always been a big cricket fan but the Ashes of 2005 were special and reinforced what a great game it is.

England won the series and a lot of people who had never watched cricket before jumped on to the Ashes bandwagon in similar fashion to the way people jumped on the football bandwagon in the late 1990s. During the summer of 2005, people reacted positively to cricket because England played well, but also because as a sport it still felt traditional and authentic. It didn't feel corrupted or belittled by corporate branding, agents or overpaid players (though some Pakistan players in recent years have done a great job in combating that perception of non-corruption).

The English and Australian players all competed with great sportsmanship and integrity; there were certainly no accusations directed towards them of being overpaid, spoilt, distant, pampered, wide boy cheats. The live terrestrial coverage on Channel 4 was very good, and most importantly accessible to anyone with a television set. At the time of this Ashes series, the perceived upper class game of cricket did almost feel like the People's Game for these traditional reasons. It was claimed that cricket had burst the football bubble. It hadn't, but what cricket had shown the nation in 2005 was an example of integrity and professional pride that football had lost both on and off the field. During the summer of 2005 it was a sport that encapsulated a sense of old-fashioned romance. Those who lived near the Oval stadium got a view of the game from their windows; I'll always remember the TV pictures of people sitting on rooftops enjoying the cricket and the sunshine with a can of beer. It brought back memories of the way football used to be when fans would sit on the stadium rooftops during a sell-out game.

Since that time it could be argued that cricket has never quite felt the same way. In 2005 the exclusive television rights of all England games were sold to Sky Sports, taking the game off terrestrial for the first time. Is this a problem for the future of cricket in terms of attracting as bigger fan base as possible? It most probably is. The 2005 Ashes series would not have achieved the same popularity had it not been aired on terrestrial television. The Sky deal has been a short-term solution where the cricket authorities have put the popularity of the sport second to a better cash deal. The simple fact is that many of us just don't watch live cricket on TV anymore. As a non-subscriber to Rupert Murdoch's media I've lost an interest in the game since the Sky deal and have drifted away; occasionally watching the highlights, which is not much of a substitute.

For the live experience in the stadium, cricket can offer better value for money than football does. Ticket prices for international test matches are very similar to Premiership matches. However, with test cricket you get the whole afternoon as opposed to ninety minutes. A fairer comparison would be to compare the ticket prices of 20-20 cricket which is a shorter game. An adult ticket to watch a Middlesex 20-20 championship match at Lords is £20, which is a price that won't be enough to get you into many English football grounds.

Domestic rugby, both Union and League, can certainly claim to offer much more affordable admission than football. For the Rugby Union European Cup Final (biggest game in the Union calendar) at Wembley Stadium in 2010, adult tickets started from just £5 (just 50p more than the pies on sale in the same stadium!). The counter argument will be that rugby is not as popular as football; therefore they have to charge less to attract a bigger following. Perhaps, but then there are plenty of empty seats in football stadiums in all four divisions in England. Being unfashionable isn't preventing them from charging high admission. A £5 football ticket is about as common as a non-confrontational episode of *EastEnders*. By being less popular it also means that rugby doesn't generate anywhere near as much revenue from TV and advertising, but it maintains cheap admission pricing. A similar comparison to ticket pricing in football would be international rugby. Prices to watch England at Twickenham mirror what you'd pay in the Premier League. Those prices are clearly reflected in the crowds that you get in these games: richer people with money who sit down and expect to be entertained.

The nearest thing to experiencing what football used to be like before the Premiership is Rugby League's Super League. The sport is now the epitome of working class sporting culture. The stadiums, the fans, the players, the atmosphere - it does feel like being in a time warp. I know of people who have stopped going to football in northern towns and cities in favour of Rugby League. I recently encountered a group of Manchester United fans who instead of going to Old Trafford on a regular basis now prefer to follow Warrington Wolves in the Super League. At Warrington, adult match day tickets start from £17 while season tickets start from £191. One of the reasons for affordable ticket pricing in

Rugby League is down to a player wage cap. The players are well paid, just not to the point which totally distances them from the supporters. There is also standing at many rugby stadiums which gives the sport that time warp feel, well from the point of view of a football fan of course. Like cricket, at rugby stadiums there is a more relaxed attitude towards the fans from the stewards. You can get away with far more than you can at football and there is good humour and banter between the crowd and the players (more so at cricket, where players and fans tend to interact in light hearted exchanges). Modern football is so deprived of humour; the culture of money resulting in everyone being so serious and fearful. What's community without humour, and what's football without a sense of community?

All sports have their issues with disgruntled fans, and none can claim to be perfect. For example in the case of cricket, we don't have the antithesis of football. Instead what we have is a grey area of good and bad examples.

So whether or not other sports can lay claim to being the People's Game is most certainly debatable. For professional football to lay that claim is now non-debatable – it simply isn't, and hasn't been for around two decades. A spectator sport cannot claim to be the People's Game when its admission prices have totally excluded a large portion of society; the very same demographic of society that the game once belonged to.

I suppose the difference here is that no other sport has ever claimed to be the People's Game, other than football. It means we judge it differently and place certain standards upon it. Many of us have grown up with a belief that the game has a duty to be accessible to everyone, and this is because of its long history of being so.

Football as a pastime does still belong to the masses. It's the game that millions of us play in the street or in the park with our friends and families. Whatever happens in the professional game, football as a sport is still the People's Game and always will be.

We don't have to buy into the money driven culture of the big leagues to love football or to draw inspiration from it. The sport as a whole became the People's Game because all you ever needed was a ball, or failing that a tin can. No one has ever been excluded from this culture and they never will be.

So what of the men who created the Football Association in the Freemasons Arms back in 1863? Could they have had any idea that what they were pioneering would spread across the globe to become the world game? Could they have imagined how much joy, drama, pain and ecstasy they would be responsible for? Would they have dreamed that an estimated billion people would tune in to the World Cup Final; the ultimate pinnacle of the thirteen laws that they drew up? Could they have imagined that this ultimate pinnacle would be in the hands of a man like Sepp Blatter? These were people who were fiercely opposed to the professional game and believed in sport being amateur – much like the attitude in rugby until it turned professional in recent years. In the early days of football many of the players came from comfortable backgrounds so to not get paid for playing was not a big issue. When football was taken over by businessmen, and played predominantly by the working classes, the game had no choice but to become professional, and rightly so. But if these men were so opposed to the professional game then one can only imagine what they'd think of players earning over £200,000 in a week. I'm sure they would feel great pride at creating a game that took the world by storm. But they might also look down at the money-driven game as it stands today, and feel that what they created all those years ago has become somewhat lost.

Chapter 10
The game in the balance – part 2

Negatives continued

Annual kit changes and shirt numbering

It's quite impressive that there's enough polyester in this world just to deal with the city of Newcastle, let alone all the other kit changes that go on every summer. The Newcastle kit 'changes' regularly, but for those of us not paying attention to minute detail, it appears to be black and white stripes with black shorts every season.

An annual kit change was something that Manchester United would be heavily criticised for, but is now common for all clubs. Classic club colours on the away strips are no longer respected because of the influence of manufacturers in their quest to maximise profits. Tradition is nothing, kit sales in other parts of the world is the bigger priority.

Annual kit changes, we are regularly told, are more of a problem for parents than for those of us without children. I don't wear colours to games and don't feel compelled to buy football replica shirts. Neither do I have anyone putting pressure on me to buy the latest team kit. It's claimed that children get teased by their friends if they wear an old football team kit instead of the most up-to-date one, and this is the common complaint as to why annual kit changes are a problem for many families. But is there a myth in all this? I coach children and I never see examples of this sort of teasing that we're told goes on regularly. Many of these kids wear old football tops and in truth it goes totally unnoticed. They might get some stick for the team badge on their kit, but certainly not for the year in which the kit was made by low paid workers in the third world. Even I have to dish out the odd comment when one of my group comes in wearing a shirt with a badge displaying a pigeon balancing on a beach ball. So called teasing for wearing an out of date football kit never happened in my old secondary school either, and that place could be a ruthless and harsh environment on a good day. Kids would get horribly ridiculed for wearing the 'wrong' trainers etc, but not for wearing an old football shirt. Children today face the same harshness and are expected to own mobile phones and other such gadgets. Let's say that some kids do get teased for not having the latest team kit; it does seem rather trivial compared to the other peer pressures they now face.

The problem with annual kit changes is in the retail price, which in England is usually around £45 just for a team shirt. Compared to the euro zone that's a bargain – a replica shirt over there can be in the region of €75 to €90. That's a lot of money for something that should be for free – yes, free! Football fans are now walking billboards. All over the country landlords get paid decent sums of money for allowing advertisers to put up commercial billboards on their properties. But football fans do it the other way round. We like to pay someone else so that we can advertise for them. The Manchester United kit is an advertisement for AON and the fans are paying a lot of money for the privilege to promote this product. On modern football kits the most prominent and domineering feature is the sponsor. But who can blame the advertisers or the football clubs for this when the fans continue to lap it up? Unlike attendance at matches, is having the very latest replica kit an essential part of supporting your team – when you've already got a whole frigging wardrobe full of the previous ones? If some supporters enjoy buying a new team kit every year and are happy to do so, fair enough. If others don't like this concept but still buy into it, then it's hard to see how they can have a major complaint. Those who believe that replica shirts are a con, but still buy them, should withdraw their custom and it won't be long before we see the prices come down. Case in point: directly after the 2010 World Cup, hardly anyone bought the England top and so prices were reduced dramatically, even going down to as low as £15. £15 for a team shirt – well, that's probably about right for something that is cheap to make and sold in bundles.

Last time I counted there were eleven players to a team. Traditionally, goalkeeper is number 1, your right back is 2, your left back 3, centre backs are 5 and 6, midfield starts at 4 and so on. Today, shirt numbering at football goes even higher than the amount of years it's been since Spurs last won the title (sorry Spurs fans, that's two cheap digs in two pages. Okay no more, this book is supposed to be non-partisan). After looking at each Premiership team's website, the highest squad number I could find was at Arsenal, who had a player with the number 53: at the time of writing, three years more than Spurs' last title win (that's a statistic not a dig!). The method behind it is sneaky but smart, because there's no actual need for squad numbering. The whole purpose of it is to encourage fans to spend more money by getting the player name and number printed on a newly bought team shirt.

Having the name of a club legend along with the team number printed on a shirt isn't a bad idea. But it makes less sense to have the name of a current player on your back, who could leave the club the next day for a slightly better wage deal elsewhere; then we see fans burn their replica shirts like we did when Fernando Torres moved from Liverpool to Chelsea. Fans upset because the mercenary they bought left them for someone else. New solution: don't buy into it and then you won't have to burn any shirts.

And speaking of those big wage deals...

Wage demands

"And what would have happened without any of this investment? Would top flight football have stopped? Would tickets to matches be even more expensive? Or would Wayne Rooney just have had to settle for cheaper whores?"
Comedian David Mitchell

During a match I attended in the early to mid 1990s (I can't remember the exact year), a disgruntled fan behind me shouted out something along the lines of 'Two thousand pounds a week and that's the best you can do, you're shit'. I remember that well, because it was the first indication I had to what top footballers earn. I was so relieved to find out that players made good money because I felt they really deserved it. I recalled this to a fellow fan recently and his response was: "Oh yeah, I remember that feeling too. Fuck me, when did that feeling go?"

When Roy Keane famously criticised the lack of atmosphere (and provision of prawn sandwiches) at Old Trafford after a Champions League game against Dynamo Kiev, he should have taken his pay cheque into consideration. When some players demand somewhere between £50,000 and £250,000 a week, a large percentage of that money comes from the paying spectators through a massive rise in ticket pricing. This no doubt changes the type of fan that populates football grounds, and it would be fair to assume that most of the fans at a ground like Old Trafford are probably not hard-up kids from Salford who might actually bring the passion that some players also demand. Thierry Henry also complained about the thousands of Arsenal fans who leave the Emirates Stadium early in order to beat the rush and get an easier ride home. There are plenty of priced out fans who would stay till the end, but what's more important to the players – £100,000 a week, or better support? The fans that Roy Keane and Thierry Henry criticised are the ones that footballers themselves are responsible for, due to obscene wage demands that have gone beyond any logic and justification. I agree with what Roy Keane said about the lack of passion from the fans, but would he have compromised 1% (£500) of his weekly wages for more encouragement from the stands at Old Trafford?

I don't think that anyone's against high wages in football for those who deserve it. After all, they are the masters of the most popular game on the planet. They provide drama and they carry the responsibilities and pressures of being in the public eye. Johan Cruyff once said, "If a whole stadium is filled each week, and millions of fans are watching you on television, then we want to see some of the profit also". What Cruyff argues for here is basic economic fairness which you can't really put a credible counter argument against. What these athletes do is far more than *just kicking a ball about* and nobody can seriously say that footballers do not deserve to be well paid for what they do. Especially when they generate such wealth and enjoyment for others. But when a victim of the 2005 London bombings who lost both legs and an internal organ receives less compensation to live on for the rest of his life than some players' weekly salary, then just maybe the wages footballers now earn have gone beyond both common sense and value.[9] It's certainly a contrast with 1960 when Jimmy

---

[9] Danny Biddle lost both legs and an internal organ in the 2005 London terrorist attack. The Criminal Injuries Compensation Board awarded him just £118,000.

Hill successfully led a campaign to put an end to the maximum wage for footballers, which at the time was £20 a week.

"The maximum wage went because we had the public on our side. We got them to understand the unfairness of the situation where there was a limit, however talented that player might be, compared to say a bank manager or a cricketer, that his salary was tied forever. It was public opinion that got rid of the maximum wage." – **Jimmy Hill**

The supportive public opinion that Jimmy Hill spoke of would today no doubt swing in the other direction. The general public look at the salaries some footballers now earn in both disbelief and disgust. Especially in comparison to the wages of those who quite literally save lives in the jobs that they do.

Public opinion today would favour a cap on footballers' wages. To give just one example: in 2010 readers of the mainstream football magazine *FOUR-FOUR-TWO* were asked if they favoured a salary cap, 66% said that they did, and 49% also favoured performance related pay. The main stumbling block to a wage cap is that the European Union could step in and deem it illegal, because it is a restriction of earnings (the European Union is a fine example of how hard it is to apply both consistency and common sense). A restriction of earnings! Even when any self imposed wage cap in football would probably be no less than £100,000 a week?

How about a wage cap of £12,000 a week? At least then we'd be spared from hearing the phase "That's more than I earn in a whole year" when talking about the money these guys earn. A person on minimum wage, who works full-time, will earn around £12,000 a year (before tax). A footballer who thinks that £12,000 a week is an insult would still be free to move on to another profession where they think they could earn a better wage. Or they could get a second job in a supermarket which they could fit in after training. With any luck that second job could earn them another £12,000 a year to live on. Let's be frank, most top flight players are not worth as much as £12,000 a week (£624,000 a year). It is a fine wage and one that would still maintain footballers among the highest earners in society. Truly great players who believe they are worth more than £624,000 a year would be able to sleep easy, because they will earn far bigger sums of money through things like sponsorship, advertising and computer game royalties. It is by these other means that top footballers earn most of their fortune. Lionel Messi's annual earnings are reported to be in the region of £30 million a year, but only a third of that comes through his weekly contract at Barcelona. The mega bucks that Messi earns through other means do not burden the paying spectator in admission prices. Players who think they're worth more than £12,000 a week, but who don't earn money through these other means are perhaps not worth as much as they think they are, because sponsors unlike football clubs don't pay high figures for those with no value. I don't like to play on a stereotype such as accusing footballers of being stupid, because they're not. Tactical awareness on a football field shows intelligence, and I bet that an IQ test taken by footballers wouldn't be that much different from the national average. On the other hand though, football is part of a culture in which someone like Graham Le Saux was deemed an 'intellectual' simply because of reading *The Guardian*. What do they nickname a man who does crosswords – Einstein? Put it this way: I don't think there are too many footballers out there who would make £12,000 a week as anthropologists.

The Premiership has the highest wage bill in world football at around £1.4 billion per annum. By the start of the 2010-11 season the highest paid Premiership player was Yaya Toure who signed a deal for Manchester City worth a reported £220,000 per week. Not bad wages for a guy who very rarely got into the

Barcelona first eleven in the previous season. A few months later in October 2010, Wayne Rooney became the highest paid weekly wage earner in European football on a sum reported to be somewhere between £220,000 and £250,000 per week. Again, not bad wages for a guy whose performances aspired to look average in the World Cup of that year. Rooney was in the worst form of his career, Manchester United were completely ridden with debt, the world was in financial meltdown, and yet United agreed to double his wages – unbelievable. Tactfully though, this wage increase for Rooney did come in the very same week as our government announced huge spending cuts and the loss of tens of thousands of jobs.

To say that this gulf in wages between 'normal' people and footballers makes fans feel distant from the players is of course an understatement. Players can be multi-million pound superstars before they've even achieved success in their careers. Young players strut around with Rolex watches before we've even heard of them; set up for life before they've even scored a first team goal. It certainly makes it hard for fans to feel sympathy towards a player who is going through a difficult moment in his career. Why should fans feel sorry for a person who earns tens of thousands a week for not doing his job properly? Empathy is also lacking in regard to footballers earning time off from work. Again this is down to the salaries that have created a distance between players and supporters. Just one week after the 2010 World Cup Final, Premiership teams were playing friendly matches in preparation for the new season. No matter how much money a person is paid, the human body still has its limitations. All professional athletes need time to refresh their bodies after a long tough season, and players should come back to pre-season training gagging for football, not feeling like they haven't had a holiday. But now the attitude from many fans and journalists will be that if players are so highly paid then they should simply get on with the job instead of complaining. When fans believe that they can no longer feel affinity and sympathy towards players, then it takes away the humanity from the game and makes football devoid of good spirit. Even the gulf in wages between players at the same club must surely cause tension and problems. A player who performs well on £20,000 a week has every right to feel aggrieved when his team-mate who earns £100,000 a week is out of form and on the substitute bench. In the MSL, David Beckham earns more money in one day at LA Galaxy than most of his team-mates will earn in a whole year. That is potentially very unhealthy for team unity, and his reported £500,000 a week could be viewed with resentment from many of his team-mates if he doesn't perform to a decent standard for every game. But then how do you perform to a £500,000 a week standard? Sell more replica shirts is the answer, though that would be no consolation to the rest of the Galaxy team who have bills to pay.

Let's look at some arguments that are commonly used for footballers earning such incredible sums of money:

- If you look at the annual revenue of the clubs, the players' wages are in line with those figures. After all, they're the talent who bring in the money; therefore they should see most of the financial benefits.

Correct, in relation to club revenue (except in the case of Chelsea and Manchester City) it's true that player wages are justified and they're getting their fair share. However, it doesn't take a genius to work out that player salary demands have forced the clubs to increase their revenues. This is why our tickets are so expensive and why football prostitutes itself to every advertiser and TV network that can provide the funds to pay for these huge wage demands. But even the best slice of these revenues hasn't been enough, so what we've seen is clubs spending more on player wages than their annual turnover.

- Football is a short-lived career. Retirement for most players will come in their mid-thirties. They have to set themselves up for when they retire.

True, football is a short lived career, but so are all sports. So let's compare a footballer's predicament to athletes of another high-profile sport (or in this case, sports entertainment). Wrestlers contracted to the WWE (formally known as WWF) have a massive global superstar profile and are watched by millions of people around the world each week. Professional wrestling is different to other sports because the final outcome of a match is pre-arranged. In fact the regular WWE weekly TV show *RAW* is more like a soap opera with writers and rehearsals. But the competitors themselves are still athletes with pressures to be successful and entertaining in their profession. On average they're asked to compete a minimum of four nights a week in non-televised house shows (footballers moan at two games a week). Their dedication to their sport inevitably leaves them with lifelong injuries. There's nothing fake about being slammed though a table or being smashed round the skull with a chair. Former Minnesota state governor, Hollywood actor and former WWE wrestler Jessie 'The Body' Ventura said of wrestling: "My advice to anyone thinking of becoming a wrestler is 'be prepared to live in pain for the rest of your life'." It's believed that the highest paid WWE performers are on wage figures between $1-2 million a year. The average yearly wage for most wrestlers contracted to WWE will be far lower. Their sacrifice for a successful career is more than athletes in most other sports. A footballer might one day need a hip or knee replacement. For a wrestler, there is a real risk of ending up in a wheelchair at an early age. Or worse, between the years 1997 and 2006, sixty-five professional wrestlers died before their fortieth birthday. Since that statistic, which was revealed in 2006, there has been no slowdown in wrestlers dying young. The point I'm getting at here is that a wrestler will find it hard to have another career due to these sacrifices. They spend a lot of time on the road travelling from state to state as they work at least four to five times a week in a vast country and travel to each corner of the globe on world tours. A boxer will also sacrifice any form of social life in favour of training to be ready for a big fight.

In contrast a footballer will train for two or three hours a day and play one or two games a week. These guys have plenty of time to study other areas of working life to prepare them for when they retire from football; much more so than athletes in other sports who make do with grants below the average yearly wage. Look at our Olympic athletes, some of whom train for eight hours a day, in return for just £12,000 a year. When Chris Hoy won three gold medals at the 2008 Beijing Olympics he was on £24,000 a year – a figure which for some footballers represents a good night out in Mayfair. In that year, the England captain John Terry earned far more from his basic wage than every British Olympic 2008 medallist combined. Our Olympic team finished the highest we have done in years with forty-seven medals, while two months earlier England sat out of Euro 2008 having failed to even qualify.

In any case, what makes some professional footballers think they're important enough to retire from working life altogether in their mid-thirties? The majority of people will have to work well into their sixties before they can retire. There's no reason why a career in football should hold anyone back from doing other things and learning other trades. In the 1970s my uncle was a professional footballer while he studied in his spare time, eventually taking an economics degree on retirement leading to a new career as a teacher. So the argument that footballers need to earn tens of thousands a week because they will have a short career, isn't a strong one. Especially when some of them talk of too much spare time and boredom (not stupidity and lack of imagination) as being the main reason for blowing hundreds of thousands away on gambling.

- Statistics show that the best jobs in society still go to a small minority of people who are privately educated. Many players still come from poorer backgrounds and football gives them a better chance of gaining wealth than in other areas of life.

It is good to see poor kids do well for themselves from sport, because there's very little chance of them becoming CEOs or bank managers. However, the result of such player wealth is that people from the very same communities get ostracised from the game. Kids from poor backgrounds don't go to football any more because ticket prices go up with player wages. So in general, modern day player salaries have also done a lot of harm for less affluent communities.

- If there were to be a UEFA wage cap then some of the best players in the world might move away from Europe to the United States or Saudi Arabia, where they could potentially earn more money.

Well if that were the case for some players then we should simply say – you're free to go buddy. Surely the leagues of Europe would be better off without such one-dimensional mercenaries. If they were to choose to play in a second rate league for the sake of a little bit more cash, then that would only prove their hearts were more concerned with 'The Benjamins' than a great legacy within the sport. Let them waste their career in the MSL, or the desert, because the truth is that a great legacy for a player can only be achieved in the big leagues of Europe and South America.

- Clubs are ruthless with players. If a player is no use to them, or has gone past his sell by date, the club mercilessly gets rid of them. Therefore why should players show any loyalty and not be just as ruthless?

This is an incredibly strong argument. It's undeniable – sport is ruthless towards talent that is no longer any use. It's all very well demanding loyalty from players, but where is the loyalty towards them when we don't need them any longer. This is why as fans we don't object to players doing well for themselves because fickleness is only around the corner from both ourselves and the management of the clubs. We don't begrudge these people earning good money. However, what we find so disheartening is when this isn't enough and when an obsession with earning more and more takes over – which leads us onto the next and final argument for such high salaries.

- Players moving from one club to another for better money are no different than regular people moving from one job to another for the same reason.

Total crap! How can anyone possibly compare a regular person's move from a £20,000 a year job – to a £40,000 a year job, with a footballer who changes allegiance because he'll get £100,000 a week at one club instead of his current £80,000 a week? When a regular person's annual wage rises, it might mean that they could possibly obtain a mortgage, or buy a car, or stay out of debt etc. In other words, that pay rise goes a long way in changing the lifestyle of that person. When John Terry got a wage rise in 2009 from £130,000 per week – to £150,000 per week – how did his life change other than the digits on his monthly pay slip? How was the future of his grandchildren any more rosy? This increase in wages came about after it appeared to many people that Terry was using the option of a move to Man City as a bargaining point for this new deal. This all-out pursuit of more and more wealth is when a lot of us feel that a player is nothing more than a ruthless mercenary.

The question is whether or not footballers can offer good value for what they earn. Just like bankers and CEOs, many in the game have this incredible talent of making a king's ransom from failure. The amount of footballers who have earned tens of thousands of pounds per week for very little in return is a list that is too long.

Robbie Fowler was a great striker and a down-to-earth honest character within football, and because of that I don't like to highlight his example. However, Fowler was on such a high contract at Leeds United, that when he was transferred to Manchester City in 2003, Leeds United were subsidising a percentage of his weekly wage. Even by 2006 when Robbie Fowler had re-joined Liverpool from Manchester City, Leeds were still paying him a reported weekly wage of £20,000. Hypothetically, had Liverpool played Leeds in the 2005-06 season and had Fowler scored for Liverpool, then Leeds would have been paying a player a weekly salary for scoring against them. During this whole period, Fowler was a shadow of the player he once was, and certainly not worth the riches that he was being rewarded with.

It's not just the players who can earn big money for little in return. The men at the FA who negotiated Sven Goran Eriksson's wages should be sedated and restrained to prevent them from ever printing out another contract (damn it, too late, they had their hands free to print out some more). Long after the 2006 World Cup, Sven Goran Eriksson was receiving £90,000 a week for NOT managing England. With the exception of the current England manager, the rest of the country is not managing England either, so where's our £90,000 a week? Eriksson earned a reported £25 million in wages from his time managing England, and a further £3.2 million for not managing England in a deal that ended in summer 2007, one year after leaving the job as England manager. The FA didn't learn from this experience. Steve McLaren was also paid off as England manager, and had they sacked Capello after the 2010 World Cup, he would have had a compensation package of around £20 million. To hand out £5 million a year contracts for any longer than two years, to someone who you might have to sack, is just incredibly bad business and football quite literally pays for it on a regular basis.

What causes a lot of resentment amongst fans is that too many players don't seem to appreciate just how lucky they are. Instead they give us the impression that they are worth even more. When Michael Ballack signed for Chelsea in 2006 he became the highest paid player in England on a contract worth £130,000 a week. Despite this, Ballack still moaned about the cost of house prices in London, and to say that he was better off renting because buying was too expensive! Not even his hefty advertising deals on top of his basic salary could get him out of this unfortunate predicament, and as a nation we all felt united with Ballack during his time of financial hardship. In 2009 I played a sports photographer in a commercial for the German firm Commerzbank which stared Ballack. The rumour on set was that he was on around £500,000 for this World Cup related advert. As I looked at the German star on the pitch that day I remember thinking *that poor man, he can't even afford to buy a roof over his head. Maybe if us extras weren't on a whopping £90 minus commission for a ten hour day, then they could have paid him a little bit more than half a million for his five hour day.*

The ultimate indignity was that despite public pressure, the government ignored Ballack's problem and did nothing to create more affordable housing for first time buyers who earn £130,000 a week.

In September 2006 Ashley Cole began a successful new career as a stand up comedian, and had the nation in stitches with the "I didn't join Chelsea for the money" gag. Cole left Arsenal after describing the £55,000 he was offered as "taking the piss". He wanted £60,000 a week and when offered only £55,000 Cole claimed that, "I nearly swerved the car off the road. I was so incensed. I was trembling with anger." Cole moaned that an extra £5,000 a week was "nothing", even though that figure over the space of a year amounts to £250,000. Ashley Cole's agent was also upset over his client's offer and was reported to have described Cole as "a slave". No doubt that people in the third world who are working in sweatshops for fifty pence an hour can also empathise with Cole's rough treatment. It's been over two hundred years since the abolition of the Atlantic slave trade, but it's shameful to learn that even in this day and age, human beings are being made offers to earn millions of pounds for playing football at their own free will. Why are Amnesty International making such a fuss about things like torture and world poverty, and yet at the same time saying absolutely nothing on the issue of Premiership footballer slavery? When Arsenal offered Cole £55,000 a week, it was as if they put him in chains, dragged him on to an overcrowded boat, took him across the ocean in torturous conditions, brutally whipped him, sowed his arse cheeks together to hide dysentery and then sold him off to a wealthy landowner who would then work him to death.

In this case, the word 'slave' would be in reference to the legality of a contract that ties the player to a club, for however many years the player signs on. Once contracted, a player cannot play for anyone else without the club's permission, or until the contract runs out. Even though in reality, when a player decides he wants to leave a club he is always allowed to go, as managers do not want players who are uncommitted. These contracts are the most valuable asset a footballer has, even though some might complain about restriction of movement; they allow players to earn incredible sums of money whilst not performing well, or even performing at all. It's what separates them from athletes in other sports whose earnings come about on the basis of how well they perform. Sportsmen such as Tiger Woods and Roger Federer have earned their millions through tournament winnings, appearance money and advertising deals, not weekly contracts where they get paid a fixed fee regardless of the standard of their performance. If they're injured they simply don't get paid.

Ashley Cole did in fact receive £60,000 a week in his last season at Arsenal before moving to Chelsea for £90,000 a week. In his last season for Arsenal, Cole spent most of the time laid off with injury and played only a handful of games. Any 'slave' who earns £60,000 a week for not even working isn't doing too badly. And one last thing – since when did slaves have agents?

Stadium designs and identity

"I'm not against change in football or clubs moving. But I enjoyed going to see Derby County at the Baseball Ground more than I enjoy going to see Derby County at Pride Park."
Alan Green – BBC FIVE LIVE

A common complaint about Britain today is that every high street now looks the same. The perception is that no matter what city or town you go to you'll be met with the same shops, the same food chains, the same pub chains, the same buildings and a general lack of individual character. So many sectors of society seem to be overwhelmed by a dominant one-dimensional vision. Capitalism of this extreme kind shares similarities with state communism, in that it holds back real choice and individuality. Football grounds are now losing that individual character. There is no reason that clubs should feel obliged to stay in the same stadium and never move to a different location. But what's disappointing is that the plans for these new stadiums are all so similar in character; or more to the point, lack of character.

It's as if the same design plan gets passed around to every club that moves home. The template for these plans is the Riverside stadium in Middlesbrough which opened in 1993. It was the first stadium of its kind in England, but it now has many replicas. The only difference will be either a larger or smaller version of the same stadium and with different coloured seats depending on the team colours of that club. All four sides of the ground are of simple design and virtually identical, with no stand-out features. Not long after the opening of the Riverside, Derby County moved into Pride Park and a new trend had begun; Pride Park was the Riverside's twin, only with black seats instead of red.

The goal-posts and goal-nets themselves now all look the same in every football ground. To some people that might sound trivial but years ago everything about each football ground had a unique and individual touch to it. The locations for these new stadiums also follow a similar pattern. Traditionally football clubs were located in the heart of communities. Football grounds that were surrounded by houses and pubs represented a certain romance about the game which is disappearing very fast. Most new stadiums are built in areas where you'd usually expect to find a retail park; now we find Coventry City, Stoke City, Reading FC, Sunderland, Hull City, Manchester City etc. In 2008 Colchester United moved to the countryside, to a place named Cuckoo Farm and named the stadium, without irony, the Community Stadium.

In fairness to Colchester they had a justified reason to move because their previous home, Layer Road, only held 6,000 which wasn't big enough for their fan-base after they got promoted from League 1 to the Championship in 2007. I contacted the supporters club of Colchester United to get a general idea on how they felt about the move. The overall impression I got was that the fans believed they had no option but to relocate; but that they've also lost an important element which made them love being Colchester fans. One supporter by the name of Jamie, who overall did feel the move was for the best, told me: *"The old ground had seventy+ years of history, memories and tradition. Being squeezed onto a terrace, being within touching distance of the pitch, all the memories, all the history and the noise you could generate by being in such an enclosed stand made for a very special experience. Win, lose or draw. That is what no new stadium can recreate, not without a lot of time anyway. At Layer Road, it was a small, tight-knit family club and you felt like you were part of something, rather than just a number who put a few hundred quid in the bank every season. I know that the business side of football has changed so much, but it does feel a lot less like a family club now, because we too have tried to go after corporate money. I'm just pleased we didn't name the ground Cuckoo Farm, can you imagine the chants from the away end!"*

On that note, spare a quick thought for fans of Shrewsbury Town who for many years played at Gay Meadow. Actually spare a thought for them since they left Gay Meadow in 2007. Despite a name that was easy to take the piss out of, it was a traditional and homely football stadium located in a central part of the town. Now Shrewsbury fans have to travel out of town to the New Meadow, which like Cuckoo Farm is surrounded by fields and has no rail links. I hope for the sake of clubs like Colchester and Shrewsbury that moving so far out won't harm future attendances. My major concern is that only the hardcore supporters will go to most games, leaving the more casual followers uninspired to go through the hassle of bus connections or trying to find a parking space. So far, both clubs have managed to maintain the same comparable attendance figures with those of the previous stadiums. Time will tell if making home away from a community will be detrimental to attracting a future fan base.

The powers that be seem to embrace this vision where everything looks and sounds the same – just so long as it's a cost saver. For example one of the most iconic and recognisable things about Britain is the regal looking black taxi. Transport for London have now introduced a Mercedes people-carrier as the new 'British' black cab, with the one consolation being *at least it's still black*. Things such as this belittle the symbolism and personality of this country and make life that little bit more charmless. When people talk about Britain losing its identity it's usually in a debate over immigration. Okay, but it wasn't asylum seekers who sold off two of my favourite Central London pubs to property developers, and turned numerous others into All Bar One style gastro pubs, with white walls and laminate flooring. Nor was it them who put ugly glass panels over a fourteenth century market square in Norwich city centre, or gave planning permission for a glass shopping mall to be built in the middle of the unique and world famous Camden Stables Market.

As a consumer I don't want to be presented with the same options every single time I make a journey to the high street. Neither do I, as a football fan, want to see the same style stadium every time I go to watch a game. These new sporting arenas are a perfect representation of how we've lost a sense of decor over the years in favour of saving a bit of cash. This country used to care deeply about decoration and style in the smallest of things, from a street sign, to a lamppost, to a shop front, to a post box, to a railing. This has been replaced with the attitude that bland street furniture is a better option, because it's less complicated to construct and slightly cheaper. There's no principle to architecture any more, other than keeping costs as low as possible and selling high. There used to be rules, standards and a sense of wider responsibility. Designs in philosophies such art deco, classical, gothic, Georgian, and modernist, were mathematically intended to be pleasing on the eye. The art deco East Stand at Highbury stadium was made with the intention of looking beautiful. Today there is no principle to the construction of most football stadiums other than *get me the design plans for the Riverside.*

There is the odd exception to this, as some stadiums that have been built in recent years have been practical in meeting attendance demands, whilst also being a little bit different in structure. Bolton Wanderers and Huddersfield Town have stadiums from the 1990s that fit into that category. Brighton's new stadium also differs from the typical Riverside Stadium trend.

Arsenal's 60,000 capacity Emirates Stadium in Ashburton Grove is one that the jury is still out on. The club made a massive error in the first years of its opening by doing nothing to make it feel like an Arsenal stadium; it felt neutral with its horrible concrete and glass exterior. The four sides of the ground had names like the Orange Quadrant and Blue Quadrant, instead of more meaningful titles. The new Wembley still has this and needs to follow Arsenal's example by realising that fans feel no affection towards this style of blandness. Arsenal have made strides to redeem the original problem by adding murals, plaques and giving the stands names like North Bank, Clock End etc. But it's just a start; Emirates still lacks the special features of Highbury and is also the most unashamedly corporate stadium on the planet, aimed more towards the wealthy than the average fan. It's not unique or original either, because the Emirates is a replica of the Benfica stadium in Lisbon which opened in 2003. That matters. As fans we do like to feel that our club is unique to other clubs in all ways. I was so proud of Highbury because I knew there was no other stadium in the world like it.

In recent years Spurs, West Ham, Liverpool and Everton have been trying to follow Arsenal's path and move to a new home. As a business model, a new corporate style stadium could turn out to be financially lucrative for these clubs. But speaking from experience as a football fan, what the club loses is so much more meaningful. A lot of Arsenal fans think back to Highbury and wish that a redevelopment could have been achieved in order to increase the capacity. I won't claim this to be the opinion of the majority of Arsenal fans because I can't speak for them, but I certainly know of a great many who do feel this way. Highbury's so sad to look at now, even though the East Stand survives because of the Listed Buildings Act. The flats on this site are basic and aesthetically dull, along with being unaffordable to most of us – sounds a bit like the Emirates.

How necessary are these relocations? On so many occasions clubs move home when there is no demand for extra capacity. In most cases a stadium move is not met with higher attendances so really what's the point; where are the benefits? The directors that make these decisions usually bugger off to another job within a couple of years, leaving the fans with the consequences of a vision that belonged to somebody else and not them. West Ham's successful bid to take over the Olympic Stadium went by with hardly anyone asking the question: does the club require a stadium bigger than Upton Park for the majority of games? Answer: probably not, as most West Ham games are not complete sell outs. Hammers fans who I spoke to had no desire to move from Upton Park and were hoping that the OPLC would favour Tottenham's bid. Then again, every Tottenham fan I spoke to hoped that that the OPLC would favour West Ham's bid! Meanwhile every Leyton Orient fan hoped that both bids would be unsuccessful and neither Tottenham nor West Ham would be able to make home on what Barry Hearn described as "our patch of London". A lot of Leyton Orient fans live in the borough of

Newham. I hope they won't be too upset by the cruel irony that a council loan is going to help West Ham move into the Olympic Stadium after 2012. In 2011 an over publicised bearded troll who goes by the name of Alan Sugar said that Haringey council should "put their hands in their pockets and give Tottenham Hotspur an incentive to stay in the borough". Excuse me Mr Sugar, my part of Haringey is two miles from Arsenal and four miles from Spurs. Most of us don't support that lot up the road. I would suggest that in a time of deep cuts, Haringey council put their hands in their pockets for the vulnerable people of the borough – not a multi-million pound generating football club.

There is nothing wrong in principle with football clubs moving to new locations, but the move should always be done in a way that maintains a sense of originality, identity, history and most important of all community. Sometimes the better option is to put more money into the current stadium and redevelop. In the 1960s, beautiful Georgian and Victorian homes were seen as outdated and not worth re-developing. As a result they were knocked down and up went concrete tower blocks all over the country. At the time these tower blocks were seen as new and dynamic. Today it is clear that this decision was disastrous as tower blocks made many areas of our cities ugly, and more importantly were not good enough for people to live in. You only have to look at the current price of a redeveloped Georgian or Victorian terrace for proof that they had plenty of life left in them.

Lack of home-grown players

"The English are being punished for the fact that there are very few English players in the Premier League, as clubs use better foreign players from around the world. The Thierry Henrys, the Dennis Bergkamps, the Gianfranco

Zolas of the past I don't have a problem with. But the ones that are probably clogging up the system, for me, are the next level down – the ones that are cheap at the time and might end up being great players."

Franz Beckenbauer 2010

When Celtic beat Inter Milan in the 1967 European Cup Final, virtually the whole team were from Glasgow. The successful Arsenal teams that I grew up with in the 1980s and 1990s were built on a foundation of London and Essex born talent. When we signed foreign players it was exciting, as fans we were all for it. Forward the clock a bit and a similar feeling is there when we field an English player; it's become something new and exotic.

At the start of the 2006-07 season, 60% of Premiership squad players were not eligible to play for the English national side. During the same period in the Italian Serie A, only 27% of players were not eligible to play for Italy. That statistic alone raised a big debate, not least because England failed miserably in the 2006 World Cup, while Italy won the competition. By the start of the 2010-11 season, in excess of 60% of squad players in the Premiership were not eligible to play for England. 2010 World Cup winners Spain do not have the same problem with their domestic league. Around 70% of La Liga players are eligible to play for the Spanish national team. The current lack of home grown players in English football is a dramatic change from the opening day of the first Premiership season in 1992-93, when only eleven players in the whole league were foreigners. Once again, we have seen a change that was needed, but one that has gone from one extreme to another.

To complain about the lack of home grown players in the Premiership does not contradict the fact that we also like to see international superstars play for our teams. The best players in the world will always be welcome to play in England. Most of us don't mind the majority of our teams being foreign, as long as they play with skill and commitment. We don't object to foreigners at all, we just don't want to see English players completely shunned. In recent years Arsenal have had a reputation more than any other for the lack of home-grown players. When Arsenal played Real Madrid in 2006, only two English players were in the starting line-up. That's the starting line-up of Real Madrid by the way. Arsenal didn't field one Englishman. When a top team like Arsenal does not field any English players, then it has to be damaging to the national side. But this is not Arsene Wenger's fault because it's not his obligation to field an Arsenal team on the basis of helping the English national team. If he feels that his best eleven are foreigners, then that is the team he should start with.

It is hard to argue with Wenger when he says, "Sport is competition. Competition is based on merit." If having too many overseas players in the Premiership is damaging to the national team, then the governing bodies of English football are the ones who should be calling for changes.

In 2007 Sepp Blatter, of all people, decided to do the talking on behalf of the England manager. He proposed bringing in laws that would limit the number of foreigners in the European leagues. The Premier League response was very hostile to this proposal. Every single quote from the Premier League spokesmen made it clear that they would be against any form of limitations on overseas players. Of course, why should the Premier League (who have three out of twelve representatives on the FA board) give a damn about the English national side? The Premier League is run by the Premiership clubs themselves. Their prime concern is making money, and luckily for them, people are very quick to forget history. In Chapter two, I said that the reason for the formation of the Premier League was to re-brand football, make the game more commercially viable and to generate more money for the top clubs. Well there was also another reason given for its formation, one which most people appear to have forgotten about. The FA claimed that the introduction of the Premier League would benefit the England team. A statement in 1991 from the FA told us that: *"The prospect of success for the England team would, at once, be enhanced"*. Enhanced how? The last time England progressed so far as a World Cup semi-final was in 1990, two years before the formation of the Premier League.

Since then following England has been one disappointment after another. In fairness, I suppose that just the one failure in the Premier League master plan isn't too bad going. Why be upset by the continued underachievement of the England team, when the Premiership clubs are selling so many more replica shirts and corporate packages? Cheer up England fans, because even though our much-hyped, much-pampered, overpaid, gutless team of prima donnas can't even trap a ball, our Premier League stands alone as the money-making champion of world football. Eat your hearts out Brazil!

Limitations on foreign players are likely to face problems from bureaucratic EU working laws. For a proposal to stand a chance of being made law, it would need strong support from bodies like the Premier League and the FA. A proposal perhaps along these lines: *A team must have in the starting line up, at least three players who are eligible to play for the country in which the domestic league is based.* I made that one up myself, but I don't think it's too earth shattering. If anything, I think that a lot of fans would prefer a law that goes way further than just three players. One ruling that did get passed in 2006 was a law that required every team in Europe to have at least two squad players that have come up from the clubs' youth academies. But due to the nature of this law, foreign players can be included in this, just as long as they've spent two years at the club before they reach the age of twenty-one. For example, Cesc Fabregas when at Arsenal would have, under this law, be classed as a home-grown player, because he signed from Barcelona when he was sixteen. The biggest worry for the future of the England team is that many professional youth academies are now dominated by young foreign players.

The crazy nature of the transfer market is the main reason why a club like Arsenal has rejected English players in favour of foreigners. English players are so heavily overpriced, and with little justification considering that our so-called best players seem to have trouble at fancy tricks – such as passing the ball accurately to the feet of a team-mate. Foreign players simply offer better value for money and have brought success to a club like Arsenal. The question of why English players are so expensive has never been answered. Let's face it, when Thierry Henry got bought by Wenger for around the same price as Frances Jeffers, it's obvious why the percentage of foreign players in the Premiership has grown every season.

Football phone-ins

So what's my problem with these audio fan forums? In principle I like the idea; actually some of them are pretty good. Fans get the opportunity to voice their opinions on live radio. The problem is that too many of the presenters and fans that take part tend to be the kind of people who need to get out more and try new things. In football phone-ins there appears to be only one thing wrong with football – referees. When listening to phone-in shows it makes it even harder to understand why on earth any sane person would aspire to be a referee or linesman. The fans and presenters get so angry at a human error by someone who's trying to be neutral in a very difficult and pressured environment. How bored must you be on a Saturday evening to feel the urge to phone up TalkSPORT and complain about a 'wrong' offside decision?

I'm not saying I've never been angry at a referee or shouted at the man with the whistle if I think he's wrong. Yet when I've done that it's spur of the moment, irrational, biased, and it's not personal. A couple of hours after the game I won't feel the need to phone up national radio and bore the whole country about a handball that wasn't given.

The presenters encourage this berating of referees on a weekly basis. I'd like to see them try and referee a Sunday league match at Hackney Marshes between two unfit pub sides in a slow-paced game, let alone a fast-paced professional game. They'd last about ten minutes before being chased off the field by former felons and escaping to the car park. I once refereed a match between two under-sixteen school teams. I thought I did a pretty good job and got most decisions right, but it taught me that to get every decision right as a referee is impossible because you just can't see everything that's going on. A player isn't expected to have a 100% pass rate throughout a match, so why is a referee expected to spot every handball or every foul?

A lot of these radio presenters can hardly be described as sporting experts. Let me give you some names of people who have presented football phone-ins in recent years: David Mellor, Richard Littlejohn, Gary Newbon, Terry Christian, Adrian Durham and Mike Parry. Former Conservative MP David Mellor was one of the first hosts of a football radio phone-in and presented the *606* show on BBC Five Live. The problem with Mellor was that he couldn't really relate with the fans who didn't want to sit down in their plastic seats for the entire game. After a few years he was replaced by Richard Littlejohn who's just a bad idea in general. Littlejohn is an unpleasant bigot who is also the only person in the country to see no irony in his catchphrase '*You couldn't make it up*'. Richard Littlejohn can feel free to sue me for calling him an 'unpleasant bigot' but I have more than enough evidence to back that up. His newspaper articles and TV appearances portray a nasty individual, devoid of any wit, charm, common sense or objectivity.

Gary Newbon presents phone-in shows for Sky Sports. If you were to shoot him for being a football expert you'd be gunning down an innocent man. He also comes across as being completely out of touch with many fans. I recall one show Gary Newbon hosted on TalkSPORT, when a Chelsea fan phoned in to talk about the rising cost of following his team. The fan complained that he had forked out well over £100 to take his young son to a Chelsea game. Newbon's response was along the lines of: "Don't come on here and tell me about how much you had to pay to watch your team. This is a football show. I'm not here to talk about how expensive your ticket is." Charming! My question to Gary Newbon therefore would be: how often do you pay money to go to football matches? Pundits and journalists who work in football do not have to pay to gain access to football stadiums. Maybe if he did have to pay for tickets, and were on an average wage, then it might dawn on him that ticket pricing in football is an issue for some people. BBC phone-in presenter Alan Green seems to be on the right side of things, despite his regular referee bashing. Here's how his manner differs from the regular phone-in presenter: he's always on the side of the fans, very respectful, and never gives the impression that his opinions are of any more value than those of his callers. Most importantly of all, his opinions appear genuine and not there to manipulate and deliberately wind people up in order to boost ratings.

One of the most popular phone-ins in recent years has been TalkSPORT's weekday morning show that was presented by Alan Brazil and Mike Parry. It was second only to Classic FM in ratings for commercial radio. Big boned host Mike 'Porky' Parry talks a lot of rubbish and is well known for it. For example, he once suggested removing September 11th from the calendar because it holds bad memories. He also advocated that British footballers wear Union Jack armbands in support of the Iraq war.

Despite his obvious flaws, he is thick-skinned enough to accept it when callers phone in and recommend that he goes back to the mug-farm. In late 2005 I was in a bar in London's Haymarket during a night of Champions League football. It turned out that Mike Parry and Alan Brazil were also there on a promotion night. A friend and I were approached by a good-looking hostess who invited us to the VIP section to join them – if we paid £30 for the privilege. I declined, giving the reason that, "There's a chance I might strangle Mike Parry if I get to close to him and he chooses to speak". The offer then went down to £15 (no joke) but we still didn't take it. However, we ended up watching a TV screen that was situated right next to the TalkSPORT VIP section where Mike Parry and Alan Brazil were hosting this promotion night. There were TV screens all over the bar but that didn't hold the interest of Parry or Brazil who make a living out of giving their 'expert' opinions on football. They spent the whole first half munching on chicken wings from the buffet and sipping champagne. They certainly were not paying any attention to the night's Champions League action, which would not be a criticism if they didn't then have the audacity to present a show live from the bar at half-time with their 'expert' opinions of the night's football. Mike Parry got the show started by saying, "Going from the first half it's clear that Manchester United are not the same team without Wayne Rooney". Those of us near the VIP section looked at each other with disbelief; our main thought being that how dare this man preach an opinion on something he didn't even bother watching. A friend of mine was so incensed that he got as close as he could to the radio stage and yelled out some advice to Parry which was along the lines of: "Why don't you shut the fuck up you prick!" To his credit, Mike Parry didn't take the comment too badly and jokingly waved his fist towards my friend. Unfortunately the bouncers did take it badly and the night ended early!

Radio phone-in shows have certainly not been without entertaining moments. My favourite ever call was from a Chelsea fan on TalkSPORT who complained that, "It's all very well having all these posh Herberts at Chelsea these days. But what about the likes of me who like to organise a fight before a football match!" Another call I remember fondly was after Arsenal beat Spurs 3-0 in a North London derby. Gary Newbon was the presenter that day and it went something along these lines:

Caller – Terrible day today mate. Totally outplayed by the Gooners. I hate to admit it but Arsenal are in a different league to us at the moment.

Newbon – Bad day for Tottenham.

Caller – I blame my old man for taking me down White Hart Lane all them years ago and making me a Tottenham fan. As a result of that my life's been a misery. Nothing but hurt.

Newbon – Well thanks for the call. And maybe things will get better for Spurs.

Caller – Oh one last thing Gary. Tottenham are mugs. I'm really a Gooner…Aaahhhaaa…3-0… (loud cheers from people in the background).

Caller hangs up.

Newbon – Well that's very clever. I'm sure you're very proud of yourself. Can we have some serious calls please.

So in principle the phone-in show is a good idea that does have its moments. This should really be on the list of positives, and with a better range of callers and fewer obnoxious hosts, it could be.

_____

Lack of free speech

"I disapprove of what you say, but I will defend to the death your right to say it."

Voltaire

Footballer interviews are now as interesting as John Major discussing car insurance with Andrew Murray. Players seem to have mastered the art of talking at length but not really saying anything. Young players are now even trained by their agents on how to give interviews in the most mundane and robotic-like way. In fact, I wonder if footballers are now so used to speaking in this emotionless manner, that they do so even when not on camera? Perhaps a conversation in their private life would sound a bit like this…

Frank's wife – Frank, you're by far the best lover I've ever had.

Frank Terry – It's not about whether or not I performed well, what's important is that it was a team effort and we both got a satisfying outcome. Hopefully that should leave us full of confidence for the next love-making session.

It must be weird living with these guys. However, at least it would mean the average footballer could stay mentally strong, even in the face of a crisis…

Frank's wife – (starts to sob). It's so unfair that you had to lose an arm in that car accident.

Frank Terry – Well it's never easy to lose an arm, but hopefully another one will bounce back shortly. I'm certainly not panicking and nor is the doctor. It's important that we stay mentally strong in this sort of situation.

I'd recommend therapy for these guys, but I'm not sure how successful it would be…

Psychotherapist – Frank, you have been diagnosed with a condition that represses charisma and prevents an individual from expressing his true feelings. How does that make you feel?

Frank Terry – Well there are no easy conditions to be diagnosed with. Obviously it's not the outcome I would have wanted, however I'm positive that by this time next week I will have turned it around. We've just got to take each session as it comes.

Can we start allowing these guys to talk from the heart please? Not that there is an official rule in football banning people from speaking openly. But to quote a lyric from a Clash song *'You have the right to free speech. Just don't be dumb enough to actually try it'.* The culprits in this case are certain sections of the media who can twist people's words, and the governing bodies who can hand out fines for what they perceive as improper conduct. In 2004, Arsene Wenger was fined under the FA Rule E3 for improper conduct after saying: "We know how Ruud van Nistelrooy behaves. He can only cheat people – we know him very well." Okay, that was not very flattering towards Ruud van Nistelrooy. But those were Wenger's feelings at the time, and he probably had at least some justification for saying those words. He honestly thought that Van Nistelrooy was a cheat. Of course the FA would rather Wenger's comments were along the lines of:

"Well I think Ruud went down a bit easy. There didn't appear to be any contact. Obviously we're very disappointed with the outcome." BORING! And not only is it boring, it is also dishonest. That is not what we as football supporters want to hear.

The FA and Premier League seem to be terrified of anything that doesn't fit in with their safe and conformist image of football. They view disagreement and conflict as a bad advert for the game, which couldn't be further from reality. Arsene Wenger and Alex Ferguson have both been brought to answer to the FA for having a so-called 'war of words', even though this sort of rivalry is what the supporters and media enjoy as part of the entertainment of the game. During his time in English football, Jose Mourinho was a breath of fresh air, because he's a man who lets you know what he thinks – not what other people want him to say. Nowadays, if a manager criticises a referee in a post-match interview, he then opens himself up to possible disciplinary action. I don't like to see managers blame the referee for a defeat when it's usually their own players' bad performance that is to blame. But surely they have the right to voice an honest opinion without having to answer to the FA.

Football television coverage is now censored and certain clips are even banned from being broadcast. For example, FIFA have actually gone so far as to ban the footage of Zinedine Zidane head-butting Marco Materazzi in the chest in the 2006 World Cup Final. In England the authorities have banned the infamous clip of when Eric Cantona karate kicked a Crystal Palace fan in 1995.

Again, these incidents are censored because they send out a 'negative' image of football. This is ridiculous because those incidents were dramatic, and drama is the basis of a sport like football. Nobody got killed or even seriously hurt, and if a lot of people are honest, then that karate kick from Cantona to that gobby Palace fan was, at the very least, intriguing television. During that same week, TV presenter and Stoke City fan Nick

Hancock was asked his opinion on the Cantona incident – *"I thought it was disgraceful, I thought it was shameful, I thought it was disgusting, but most of all, I thought it was very very funny! Easily the best thing to have happened all season."*

These moments of controversy should be put into some sort of perspective. When you consider that at one time, thousands of people attended spectator sports in which lions ripped human beings to shreds, and gladiators slew one another, one isolated karate kick from a poetic Frenchman was hardly going to destroy the fabric of a game like football. I admit to being a hypocrite when it comes to the morals of the game. On the one hand I love to see football played with good sportsmanship and by gentlemen with integrity. But on the other hand, I also love the side of the game that brings up bad behaviour and heated rivalry. But all these things, whether moral or immoral, are what makes sport so interesting and makes us love it. Not everyone wants to live in the superficial world that the FA, Premier League and FIFA like to promote. Maybe football's men in suits have been taking some image advice from the politicians? For example, they spent years trying to ban Brian Haw, who died in 2011, from staging an anti war protest outside Parliament, because they believed it gave a bad impression of Britain to tourists. Quite the opposite, the freedom to stage a protest directly outside the most influential building in the country gave tourists a great impression of our country and its liberties.

Whether it's words or symbols, what is being repressed is a simple freedom of expression. At the Emirates Stadium for the first few seasons, national flags were banned in the stands, for fear of causing offence. As an Arsenal fan, why on earth would I have been offended by, for example, a Nigerian flag that read *Lagos Arsenal Supporters Club*. This all supposedly came about because of a dispute between London based Greek and Turkish Cypriots. Some Greek Cypriots were upset because some Turkish Cypriots had brought their flag into the Emirates, which is a flag that is not recognised by the UN. Some of the London Greek Cypriots who complained to the club were actually Spurs fans who I knew personally. How dare they have an influence over The Arsenal! Because of this dispute, Arsenal thought it best to ban everyone from bringing a national flag into the stadium, which, it could be argued, showed disregard for the other 99.9% of Arsenal fans who have nothing to do with these differences. Greek Cypriots are understandably very passionate over the illegal occupation of a region of their country. But let's look at this from another angle. How would it go down at the football club Apollen Limassol, if all Cypriot national flags were banned from their stadium, because Northern Irish Catholics were unhappy about the flag of Ulster being displayed in the stands?

The attack on free speech has even gone beyond what the football authorities see fit to deal with. In 2005, Aussie midfielder Harry Kewell took Gary Lineker to the High Court in a lawsuit about remarks Lineker had made in the *Daily Telegraph.* His case was no deeper than the fact that Lineker had said Kewell's transfer to Liverpool had made him "ashamed" of football. This was hardly a controversial opinion, as Harry Kewell's transfer to Liverpool showed us how much money certain elements in the game (i.e. agents) make out of player transfers. Harry Kewell joined Liverpool from Leeds for £5 million in 2003. Of the £5 million transfer fee, £2 million went to the company Max-sport which is run by Kewell's personal manager Bernie Madic. The transfer, although legally sound, deserved to be more than just questioned, and I'm being careful with my words just in case Mr Kewell and his personnel are in a litigation mood. His transfer to Liverpool showed fans that their hard earned money goes out of football and into the pockets of people who have too much influence in the way the game is run. Of course his transfer to Liverpool was shameful – end of story. What would Kewell rather Lineker have said? *"The £2 million that went out of the game and into Max-sport's bank account was a true credit to football. It just makes me feel ashamed that it didn't happen when I was playing."* In the end, the judge in the case came to no conclusion so neither side won a victory. If Kewell had won this case, then it would have not just been damaging to what people in football can say, but also damaging to the opinions expressed by those outside the law of football. Could a journalist get sued every time he or she referred to a player's performance as lazy or poor?

Oh by the way, speaking of those certain elements in football who make so much money out of the game...

Player agents

"The major problem is not bungs – my major problem is paying agents full stop. They work on behalf of the player and I don't understand why the club has to pay them as well."

Mike Newell

During the 1980s and 1990s two words helped give agents a negative image within the game:

1. Eric
2. Hall

Yes Eric Hall, remember that guy? The cigar chomping celebrity agent with an 'endearing lisp'. Eric once said that what makes America a better country than Britain is that: "When Americans see you in a Rolls Royce they say 'Hey that guy's a winner'. When the Brits see you in a Rolls Royce they want to scratch it." You're wrong Eric; there is a simple explanation for why this happens. If you've found that people want to scratch your Rolls Royce or stick two fingers up, you have to take into consideration the fact that you happen to be inside it.

Another thing Eric Hall once said on the Saint and Greavsie talk show in 1995 was "What's wrong with managers taking bungs? I don't see the problem." The problem is simple. If an agent offers a manager a backhander to sign a player then that signing can have no credibility. Everyone will see that signing not as a vital addition to the team, but simply as someone brought in by the manager for his own financial gain. In January 2006 former Luton Town manager Mike Newell said that he had been offered bungs and that he was prepared to name names of corrupt agents. He was backed up by Ian Holloway who also claimed to have been offered a bung. After these allegations the general consensus from commentators, former managers and players is that agent bungs are commonplace within football and have been for a number of years. Former football agent Steven Noel Hill has even claimed that if his experience is anything to go by "80% of deals have bungs attached to them". In September 2006 the BBC aired an undercover documentary that aimed to expose this type of corruption within the game. Sam Allardyce was at the centre of the allegations and it was claimed that he received illegal payments from agents via his son, who was one of three hundred licensed football agents in England. The programme itself was considered by many as over-hyped, lacking in substance and a damp squib. Yet one thing it highlighted very clearly was how easy it was to do a bung deal and get away with it. This is because any illegal money transfers would either be made in cash, or paid into a Swiss bank account making them untraceable.

Anyone who is corrupt would have learnt a lesson off George Graham who was found guilty of taking a bung in 1995. Graham accepted a payment of £425,000 from agent Rune Hauge for the signing of Pal Lydersen in 1992. Graham was investigated when the Inland Revenue started to ask questions about the £425,000 that went into his bank account undeclared. George Graham claimed in his defence that the money was given to him as a gift and a thank you (in other words a bung!). But what was interesting was that Lydersen made no impact at Arsenal and played very few games. This scandal cost Graham his job at Arsenal and he was banned from football for two years.

The BBC documentary was shortly followed by a report from Lord Stevens that looked into agent corruption in football. After all these allegations focusing on bungs, agents were understandably on the defensive, with the main line of defence being *There are a few bad apples, but most agents do a good job for their clients*. Agents can get away with claiming that they do a good job for their clients, but one thing you'll never hear an agent have the audacity to claim is "I do a good job for football". Bung scandals and corruption are no doubt damaging for football, but it's what agents are allowed to get away with legally which is the real scandal. When we as fans purchase a football ticket, or buy a team shirt, a significant percentage of that money will go to players' agents. In November 2009, the Premier League declared the amount that its twenty clubs had paid agents from September 2008 to October 2009. These figures, released for the first time, were staggering. In just one year £70 million had been paid to agents, with Manchester City leading the way having spent a whopping £12.9 million. Forget about bungs, £70 million in just one year should wake every fan up as to one of the reasons why we now pay such a high price to follow the game we love.

If there's one thing that brings both the fans and clubs together, it's the shared loathing of player agents. It could be argued, that those of us who dislike player agents, would probably be represented by one if we were footballers. Like them or loathe them, they're the ones with the power to get their clients the best possible wage deal. Well that's the perception, but there are arguments and evidence to the contrary. Robbie Fowler became one of Britain's wealthiest footballers by using a financial adviser as opposed to an agent. Gary Neville is one of very few players to have spoken out against player agents: "They [footballers] think they need them [agents] but it's not the case. They need good advice and good accountants. Not people who are going to take hundreds of thousands of pounds off them."

Agents are most likely to make their main income from a commission, based on a percentage of their client's earnings. Rio Ferdinand famously had a pay dispute with Manchester United before the 2005-06 season. It was reported that he felt his wages should rise from £100,000 a week to £120,000 a week. It was alleged that the extra £20,000 a week would then pay his agent's commission. If the commission Rio Ferdinand's agent earns per week is indeed £20,000, then that's more than many people earn in a year of hard graft, and surely even more reason for fans to withdraw their custom.

Media Sensationalism

Journalism is a fine and noble profession and a free media is essential to living in a free society. Great journalism can be responsible for giving us knowledge, raising awareness, exposing corruption and even saving lives. So to put all the media in the same category is very unfair. Richard Littlejohn and John Pilger both work in the media, but they couldn't be further apart in manners, intellect, charm and talent. It would also be unfair to put brilliant sports journalists like Patrick Barclay, Henry Winter, Oliver Holt and David Conn in the same boat with the more vindictive and condescending columnists. The tabloids themselves have some excellent writers and great journalism is still alive and well.

Sensationalist sports' reporting is certainly not a new thing that has sprung up in the recent years of the Premiership, but reporting in certain sections of the media has become even more ridiculous, vicious and over the top.

With footballers being such highly paid media stars, they now appear in newspapers and magazines on a regular basis in tedious gossip and scandal stories; all part of a culture that has made household names of the non-personalities that take advantage of some footballers' fame. Having an affair with the right footballer has become enough to earn millions as a result and become better known to the public than the Magna Carta. No doubt that the 'World Exclusives' we're provided with also cause plenty of controversy and debate in places like Sudan, Paraguay and Fiji.

In summer 2006, seventeen-year-old Theo Walcott was chosen to be in England's World Cup squad for Germany. Before this he was unknown outside of football, but his surprise inclusion in the England squad put him on the front pages and he was soon hailed by the press as the new Wayne Rooney. The very next day, his sixteen-year-old girlfriend was on the front pages of the tabloids and by the following weekend one newspaper was already running 'World Exclusives' about her sex life. Within one day of being 'famous', some people in the media were saying that she could be worth millions. A sixteen-year-old, who nobody had heard of, who nobody had heard speak, who nobody knew as having any talent, can be worth millions just for being blonde and dating a moderately famous footballer. I know they say that it's too easy to be famous these days but this is nuts. Time to bring in the men in white coats (and check out their wags for any hidden talents, they might be worth millions for having blood and the ability to breathe air).

The wives and girlfriends' hysteria hit boiling point in the 2006 World Cup, as certain papers carried fascinating stories of how they went out of the hotel and did some shopping. Women with lots of money going shopping – what a shocker.

During this period, the *Sun* columnist and professional loudmouth John Gaunt even had the audacity to criticise *The Independent* newspaper for devoting an 'entire' front page to the problem of 4x4 cars and the threat to the environment they carry. Of course John Gaunt is spot on as ever. The issue of the environment is totally trivial compared to the wags' shopping habits, and these muesli-eating tree huggers at *The Independent* should copy the example shown by the *Sun* and start devoting their front page to more worthy news stories.

Many believe that football has become too high pressured and demanding. In the back pages of newspapers, manager and player quotes are now as heavily scrutinised as those of politicians. There is certainly no shortage of media spin, plus a misrepresentation of quotes that are all too common in political coverage. The *Sun* in particular offers a very aggressive confrontational style to its sports reporting. They decide what someone has said to fit the story they want to sell. For example they once had a back page with a picture of Arsene Wenger along with the headline:

YOU MUGS:
WENGER SLAMS OVERSPENDING CHELSEA

One important thing was missing from this headline: quotation marks either side of the words 'you mugs'. No doubt the reason these quotation marks were not there was because Wenger didn't actually use these words (unless this was the Arsene Wenger that starred in *Football Factory* and *The Firm*). The *Sun* newspaper were the ones calling Chelsea 'mugs', but the way they presented the story made Arsene Wenger look like the aggressor. Wenger's actual words were along the lines of: "Chelsea spend over the odds for players". Hardly an outrageous accusation. If anything Wenger was being very polite in explaining why it's so hard to compete with Chelsea and yet he's made to sound disrespectful.

One of countless other misrepresentations like this one had another back page picture of Arsene Wenger along with the headline: **WE DON'T FEAR CHELSEA.** Again no quotation marks, yet the paper manipulates the reader into thinking that these are Wenger's words. In reading the article it's clear that Wenger did not even mention Chelsea. When looking for the quotation marks his actual words were along the lines of: "I still think that Manchester United are the main threat to us this season."

In bold I've put an example of the kind of headlines that feature on the back pages of tabloid newspapers. Below the headline is an example of what the player or manager is more likely to have said.

I'LL SAVE CITY FROM THE DROP

"We've got nine games to avoid relegation. I'll do all I can to help City get maximum points in those nine games."

YOU'RE A BUNCH OF LOSERS

"United have lost a lot of games this season which proves they're beatable."

I'D RATHER LYON WIN THE CHAMPIONS LEAGUE THAN CHELSEA.

"I've got great respect for the Lyon manager from my time working with him. For this reason I hope they can go all the way and win the Champions League."

WE'LL SMASH THE HAMMERS

"We're confident we can go to West Ham and get three points."

I'LL SHOOT US TO WORLD CUP GLORY

"I think we stand a good chance of doing well in the World Cup."

YOU SLAGS! WE'RE GOING TO BURN DOWN YOUR HOUSES, RAPE ALL YOUR WOMEN, EAT YOUR CHILDREN AND THEN PISS ON YOUR GRAVES. LET'S 'AVE IT

"We're looking forward to going up there and getting stuck in."

Okay, so football interviews are boring and the media are looking for more bite to create interest in a headline. But that's still no excuse to misrepresent what someone has actually said. Some people in the media claim that footballers should act as positive role models for children. Fair enough, even though a hospital visit from a footballer to sick patients will not find a place in the back pages of the newspapers, and footballers do this sort of thing more than people think. Before a friend of mine's baby girl died in hospital, the ward got a visit from none other than Thierry Henry, Robert Pires and Patrick Vieira. This kind of gesture means a lot to people and because it doesn't create any headlines proves that those who make these visits do so for honourable reasons. Footballers and other stars are expected to be good role models because they hold such a high profile. But newspapers also hold a high profile in society – why are they not expected to act as role models as well? Every day millions of people read these papers, including children. Surely then journalists have as much responsibility as anyone else in public life to show integrity and pride in their profession. However, it does seem that the example some of them send out to kids is this:

Betrayal is fine. It's okay to pay someone for a kiss and tell story.

1. It's okay to tell lies about people and misrepresent the facts.
2. Character assassination is okay in order to make money.
3. It's okay to be rude, biased and subjective.
4. Racial stereotyping of other nations is acceptable.
5. It's also acceptable to then run headlines of shock and disgust when the same racial stereotyping is displayed by English football fans whilst in other countries.
6. It's right to condemn a celebrity for paying a hooker for sex. But by all means pay the same hooker a five figure sum for that 'World Exclusive'.
7. We must make people feel bad about their bodies through over-fussy and obscene scrutiny – and that it's moral to show a young woman in a bikini under the headline 'Cellulite Church' (Charlotte Church).
8. It's okay to kick people when they're down. Show no mercy. When someone's going through a painful time make the pain even worse and stick that boot in, bosh.

The excuse that hacks always give is that they are simply giving the public what they want. That's debatable; you could also say that people just accept what they're given. Are the masses really demanding to know the latest on Kerry Katona's fascinating existence? There is certainly an argument that some aspects of the media have actually created a culture of triviality and ignorance rather than supposedly giving us 'what we want'. But let's say that they are giving us what we want – wouldn't that be the worst and most shameful line of defence that any self-respecting journalist can give? Is that what they went to university for; cheap pandering to the lowest common denominator? Unfortunately this sort of journalist doesn't seem to be accountable to anyone. If a footballer brings his profession into disrepute then he will be fined and banned by the football authorities.

Maybe journalists should be given a three-month ban from reporting, or even a fine for every time they tell a porky? Some newspapers will happily tolerate a journalist who lies, just so long as those lies are selling more papers. Even if a lie means the newspaper gets sued, there's still a good chance they would have made more money from sales as a result of the lie and subsequent publicity. So when a newspaper pays a 'slapper' to tell all about a one-night stand she had with a footballer, ask yourself one important question: who is really setting the nation a bad example?

FIFA Rankings

June 2010: England get knocked out as early as the second round, in officially their worst ever World Cup performance. Worse even than in 1958, after essential members of the England team had been killed or badly injured in the Munich air disaster during the same year.

July 2010: to the nation's horror, England moves up in FIFA world rankings to seventh place!

June 2006: Italy are ranked outside of the top ten while according to Sepp Blatter and his pals at FIFA, USA are officially the fifth best team in the world.

July 2006: Italy wins the World Cup, while the USA players are a couple of weeks into their vacations after finishing last in the group stages.

These rankings are meaningless mainly because they're based on a country's performance over a period of time and not how good a team currently is.

For example, a team could be rated highly in 2012 partly because they performed well in 2011. But even if the rankings were based on more recent form, who's to say that the Czech Republic are better than Germany, or that Brazil are better than Argentina? For a realistic and more accurate pointer to the best teams in the world, I would suggest looking at the bookmakers betting odds before a major tournament.

And as for England...

Following England

"The Premier League has taken over the importance, prestige and kudos of the game. Therefore these players are superstars regardless of whether they play well for England or not. If England go out in the first round they will go back to their clubs, earn their money and everybody in England will be telling them 'you're great'."

John Barnes, Evening Standard – June 2010

Following England in recent years has become a bit like supporting the international equivalent of Newcastle United. Let's look at some bullet points to back that up:

*Won bugger all in decades.
*Huge expectation based on little or no evidence.
*Huge fan-base, loyal and brilliant almost to a fault.
*High profile status within the game despite lack of success on the football field.
*A never ending road of disappointment and misery.

It never used to be this bad, because it never used to be this desperate. I first started to follow England during the Bobby Robson era which came to an end at Italia 1990. When we got knocked out in the semi-final of that competition, it had only been twenty-four years since we'd been World Champions. At the time of writing it's been forty-five years and the country is as desperate for a trophy as …well, a Geordie of course.

This desperation is leading to false hopes of great teams and Messiahs. Before the 2010 World Cup I felt that the England squad, who were labelled the 'Golden Generation', were our weakest side in years and stood no chance of winning the tournament. It was virtually the same group of players that were average in World Cup 2006 and weren't even good enough to qualify for Euro 2008. My hope however, was that this team might play some good football, and that if we were lucky we'd get to the quarter finals. Turned out that my hope was too much to ask for, but my pre-tournament expectations weren't high enough for me to be devastated about elimination. I've been through that feeling on too many occasions, it's time to be realistic and to learn from experience.

We should always aim high and strive to be the best. Don't misunderstand me – I am longing to see England win a trophy. But as a country we need to lower our expectations and this starts with the media, some of whom manage to ruin every single World Cup and European Championship without fail. The intense coverage that goes with the England team is just unbearable, to the point where it's almost a relief when England does get knocked out. We're either going to win the World Cup, or we're shit, no middle ground. Over hyped expectation is always followed by fickle damnation when the team doesn't perform to the level that the public are deceived into expecting. I consider myself to be a true patriot, but even I can't hold down the cringe worthy jingoism that is now part of the culture of tournament coverage; players wrapped in the St. George flag alongside Churchill quotes, as if they're brave mighty warriors, instead of overrated and pampered multi-millionaires.

Incredibly, the *Daily Star* is the third most popular daily 'newspaper in the country. Here's their front page headline after England drew their opening 2010 World Cup match with the

242

USA: 'DON'T PANIC, OUR BOYS ARE STILL GONNA BRING THE CUP HOME' No pressure there then! No desperation either. The headline should have been accompanied by the message AND IF YOU DON'T WIN IT YOU'RE SHIT. Considering the fact that most people who watch England in the World Cup know very little about football, it's a rather cruel trick to play isn't it? England tournament coverage usually goes in this order:

Pre-tournament: Wave of optimism. We're bringing the trophy home. This is our best chance of glory since 1966.

First two group games: England struggle through undefeated, but get criticism for not performing well. Press are now fickle – You're letting us all down.

Third group game: England improves and plays well. We're now back on track to win it, what was all the panic about. Hysteria meter now measured at 'Very High'.

Second round: England beat a half decent team and progress. World Cup's in the bag, all other nations are below us. Bring out the open top bus, hire out Trafalgar Square, we're World Champions. Belittling of our Quarter Final opposition begins; war references required if applicable.

Quarter Final: Out on penalties to top quality opposition. Inquest begins. England Manager and players are now biggest enemies to our shores since the Nazis.

Post-disaster focus: Murray to make up for football disappointment by winning Wimbledon.

Here's a headline you'll never see in certain papers before an England World Cup game: GOOD LUCK ENGLAND. Indeed, the desperation for England to do well in football now mirrors that to see a British Wimbledon champion. We don't enjoy these tournaments anymore because we're so obsessed with outright victory and anything less is a heartbreaker and disaster. Tim

Henman was shit because he didn't win Wimbledon – no he wasn't, he was a good player, the best we had, he just wasn't as good as greats such as Pete Sampras. Commentators like Clive Tyldesley will introduce England games by saying things like *'I hope you're all prepared for this latest white knuckle ride'*. Surely the better option is for us to get away from this fear and just get back to enjoying supporting our country.

The documentary feature *One Night in Turin* was released just before the 2010 World Cup; a film that focussed on Bobby Robson's England team in Italia 1990. What the film portrayed, I felt, was a group of players who enjoyed the adventure of the World Cup and who had the same passion as the supporters. They had been slaughtered by the media in the build up to the tournament, but that inspired them and they were even filmed ripping up newspapers in front of the TV cameras. Those players were like we were: we really cared about those guys as people.

Along with my low expectations, another reason that I wasn't devastated when England got knocked out of South Africa 2010 was that I simply didn't care about the players. They just seemed to represent the typical modern day footballers: obscenely overpaid, dull personalities, pampered and totally distant from the people who support them. During the national anthem line-ups they looked as uninspired as the football they would go on to play. What a contrast to the patriotic nature from the likes of Terry Butcher, Stuart Pearce, Tony Adams, Ian Wright, Paul Ince, Alan Shearer, and Gazza to name just a few. In the last ten years it's hard to think of any England players that the fans care for in the same way, with the possible exception of David Beckham. Okay Beckham's pampered and overpaid, but no fan would ever doubt his pride and commitment to England, along with his respect for the fans and actually having a small degree of personality. When someone like Ashley Cole is quoted as saying, "I hate England and all the people", it hardly makes you wish to see him victorious on an open top bus and being paraded as a national hero.

In the past, the biggest obstacle in the way of a successful England team has been the upper crust snobs at the FA. To give just one example, back in the 1970s they dismissed Brian Clough's application to be England manager because he wasn't the 'yes man' they wanted. To this day, fans still wonder about what might have been had Cloughie been given that chance. The old boys at the FA are still a major hindrance, but the monster's grown another head – the Premier League. A league that does nothing to help out the England manager, whether it's having a winter break during a World Cup season, to ensuring that youth academies are predominantly for English players. When the ethos of the national game for the past twenty years has been short-term thinking for financial gain, it's no great surprise that the long-term development of English players has been a failure. Craig Johnston, the Aussie midfielder who played for Liverpool in the 1980s (and the inventor of the Adidas Predator football boot) created a database of the technical skills of young players aged from eleven to thirteen in youth academies. He compared the skills of the English players to those of their foreign counterparts and presented the findings to the Premier League. Johnston claims that the results were so 'staggeringly bad' that he wasn't allowed to go public with them. In a scathing attack on the FA just after England failed to qualify for Euro 2008 Johnston ranted *"They're self regulating, they're self governing. The government needs to wake up. An independent body needs to look at these clowns and understand that the national self esteem is too important to have in the hands of these idiots that have destroyed your national game. Mate, you should be really upset with these people."*

Unless the FA and supporters demand that the Premier League starts to make some concessions, then our self esteem is likely to stay low for a long time. In truth, the old Football League did nothing to help out the England team either. Here's a quote from the League's Secretary Alan Hardaker in 1973 before England failed to qualify for the 1974 World Cup: "This is football, not a war. If England do lose, the country won't die. It will be a big thing for six weeks, then everybody will forget about it." So I guess that things were just the same back then, apart from a lot more honesty from the League's ruthless bosses. But the difference here is that when the Premier League was founded for financial reasons, we were sold the lie that it would be beneficial to the England team. In the Premier League years nothing's been achieved to back that up; the England team seems to get worse with each passing year.

On the positive side of things, the England football team does bring the country together in a way that it never used to in the past. During tournaments, people hang out flags from their houses and cars, in a culture that has finally taken the England flag away from the bigots who have degraded it over the years. People from Asian and Afro-Caribbean backgrounds now tend to get behind their country, wear England tops and associate themselves with the St. George's Cross. If the national team does ever win a trophy then the jubilation and unity on the streets of our towns and cities all over the country would be spectacular and dramatic. However, the Italia 1990 team proved that we don't have to win outright in order to bring pride back to our national sport. All we should ask for is a group of players who we care about, who can take on the world with equal skill, and compete to be the best with unrivalled passion for their country. At this moment, I have to admit, that does seem like a rather high expectation.

Chapter 11
Missed opportunities for 'real football'

"Football should be affordable to everybody whatever the economic climate, and we thought we were in a good position to make the demographics of the city work for us. We thought people would want to be involved as long as the price was right, and we have been proved correct."

David Baldwin, Bradford City Board Member

A very common viewpoint is that good atmosphere and 'real football' is still found in the lower divisions. Forget the overpriced and up-tight attitude of the Premiership, for an enjoyable time and great value for money, go to a game in the un-fashionable Football League. The Football League has actually seen an increase in crowd numbers in recent seasons. By 2009 attendance figures were the highest they had been for fifty years, though a couple of years on and clubs are now really struggling to fill up the seats, due to the wider economic recession. A factor behind the 2009 rise could very well be disillusioned fans of Premier League clubs. Given this, perhaps the last thing that lower division clubs should be doing is trying too hard to emulate the bland commercial culture of the top division.

I've been to many games in the lower divisions. A recent one that I attended was in the 2009-10 season, when Darlington visited Dagenham & Redbridge in League 2 (former Division 4, former Division 3, and future Starbucks Premiership Minus 3

Super League). It was typical of the experience of many games that I've been to in the lower divisions. Firstly, it wasn't cheap for a game of this standard: £20 for away fans. Away fans who had already paid a lot of money to travel all the way down from the other end of the country. Furthermore, a section of terracing for the away fans had by this point been replaced by a brand new all-seater stand that looked to have been designed by Legoland (teams in Leagues 1 and 2 are not obliged to have all-seater stadiums). Gone was the freedom of a terrace. We now had the option of sitting down and doing what we're told. Which takes us back on to our good friends in bright orange bibs. If stewards are a pain in the arse in the Premiership, at lower division clubs they can be even worse; because there's so few of you in the stadium it means they can focus their attention on you even more. In the Legoland away end at Dagenham, a few of us were stood up at the back row of the stand. The *back row* as in the *nobody behind us to ruin the view row*. This shouldn't have been a problem but it attracted the attention of the Dagenham stewards who felt the need to clamp down on us unruly rebels:

'Can you take your seat.'

'But there's nobody behind us.'

'It doesn't matter, you have to take your seat.'

'Why is it a problem?'

'Safety. If you have a seat you have to sit in it by law.'

'So by standing up, there's a chance the stand might collapse?'

'You can either sit down or be ejected.'

The ejection offer was tempting – I just didn't want to give the buggers the satisfaction. Who do they think pays for their traffic cone jackets? This incident is by no means exclusive to Dagenham and is just one example of countless times that this has happened. Whereas at grounds like the Emirates and Old Trafford, disillusioned fans are easily replaced, the same cannot be said for teams in the lower divisions. It's so important for clubs to have a greater understanding of their loyal followers – not risk driving them away with high ticket pricing, over-enforced stewarding and un-called for destruction of terraced ends. Here's an example of how not to treat a football supporter on whose money you rely upon: when leaving the Dagenham stadium (twenty minutes before the end of the game), one Darlington fan had dropped his wallet, probably in the away end. When trying to gain access to the stadium to look for it, the officials refused to allow him back in. Rules are rules and that is it, you're not allowed in mate, goodbye, better luck next time. With that sort of respect shown to him, maybe that fan will indeed decide not to go in again – ever.

Equally as counterproductive is to discourage the support of the next generation. Now, I am sure that Dagenham & Redbridge does try hard to attract young supporters to the club. Many lower league clubs make great strides to reach out to young supporters through low ticket pricing for under-sixteen year olds. But that's just one half of it. The other half is to have an environment where young people can have fun, without feeling under the watch of the headmaster. During the Darlington game, a nearby group of twenty Dagenham fans (looked to be aged between ten and fifteen) engaged in chanting and banter with the away fans. One of the young Dagenham fans was particularly vocal, and was full of fists flying in the air and un-complimentary gestures towards the Darlo fans. It was nothing vicious or to take seriously, if anything it was more entertaining than the game. However, the police and stewards took exception to the kid and he was handcuffed and dragged out of the stadium. The Darlington fans laughed and cheered in support of what the police and stewards were doing, which was equally as depressing. A friend turned to me and said, "He didn't actually do anything wrong". Maybe the kid would have attracted less attention from the police had he instead gone to certain housing estates in this country and harassed a vulnerable family.

Like most Football League clubs, Dagenham & Redbridge will have well-meaning people at the heart of it, from the boardroom to the tea room. But they are potentially holding themselves back, by aspiring to be miniature versions of Premier League clubs. At least Premier League clubs have world class players as a selling point.

Like the Premiership, many teams in the Football League have huge financial problems which are self inflicted. The best example is Notts County who by 2010 were spending 350% of their turnover on player wages. These financial problems are used as the justification for high admission pricing for adults: if the small clubs don't charge these prices, they could go under. But the other side of the argument is that if clubs charged less, they could boost their attendance by half. Millwall for example, have a very big fan base, but in recent years have had relatively small crowds for a lot of their home games. Ticket prices have to be a factor here. I'm not a Millwall fan, just a fair-weather follower who very occasionally goes to the odd game. I would go to more games if it were cheaper; therefore I've no doubt that proper Millwall fans would also do the same. With a bigger crowd, the club will make more money on food, merchandise and advertising revenue.

For proof that cheaper admission could boost attendance by as much as half, look no further than Bradford City who at the time of writing are in League 2. In 2007, the club announced an interesting proposal: they would sell season tickets for £138, on the condition that 12,000 people signed up to it. 12,000 did sign up to it, and in the following seasons Bradford City has had the highest average attendance in League 2, by a massive margin. They average 12,700 a game which is around 70% better than their average gate before the scheme was introduced. Because of the cheaper prices Bradford are no better off financially than they were before. But the overall match-day experience is more enjoyable for the fans and for the players. It's better to be poor and have 12,000 followers, than to be poor and have 5,000 followers. It's also a principle that prioritises long term thinking. By making the club affordable to kids and young adults they are creating a new generation of Bradford City fans that actually go to games, instead of following Manchester United or Liverpool from the TV.

The surprising thing about the success of this scheme is that it hasn't caught on. Instead of reaching out to a bigger demographic, most clubs below the Premier League still burden their small band of regulars with the cost of keeping the club going. In 2009, millionaire Crystal Palace Chairman Simon Jordan criticised Eagles fans for the club's poor attendance figures – during the height of a recession. This Hooray Henry had a point: who the hell are these Palace fans to put their priority on gas bills and council tax payments? By 2010, attendances in the Football League began to suffer due to the recession. Clubs now have no choice but to lower ticket prices. In January 2011 Dagenham & Redbridge reduced ticket prices to just 99p for a home game against the MK Dons. They doubled their attendance, which proves that more people would go to watch them if money was not an issue. No-one can expect the Daggers to charge 99p for every game because the club would go bust. But there has to be some sort of compromise between that price and the £20 that they charged me when I went there.

In 2010 some Arsenal supporters set up a group called the Black Scarf Movement; arguing that the club they support has lost its true meaning. On their website there is a guest blog by a fan of Stockport County, who argues that his club has also lost its soul in recent years. The feeling of disillusionment with football is clearly not just exclusive to fans of the big boys. The saddest example of a lower league club losing its soul by trying to emulate the Premier League model, is my dear old second team Darlington FC. In 2010 the Quakers were relegated out of the Football League which is such a contrast to the hopes and dreams of the fantasist who took over the club in 1999. Convicted criminal George Reynolds's plan was to take Darlington to the Premiership by 2003. Darlington's highest attendance of all time was just over 20,000 way back in the 1960s. Around the era when Reynolds took control, Darlington's average attendance would be around the 5,000 mark – during a good season. But bearing in mind Darlington very rarely have good seasons their attendance was usually somewhere around the 4,000 figure and that's being very generous. Their stadium, Feethams, was right next to the train station and the capacity was around the 8,000 mark. The population of Darlington itself is only 98,000. Despite these figures, Reynolds decided that instead of investment in new players, what the club really needed was to go into debt by building a brand new 25,000 out-of-town all-seater stadium in the middle of bloody nowhere – population two sheep, three cows and a scarecrow. Stadiums such as this in Italy are described by the ultras as una cattedrale nel deserto (a cathedral in the desert).

He then named the stadium the Reynolds Arena (no ego trip there). When friends of mine who support Darlington told me about these stadium plans I thought they were just testing me to see how gullible I was. Darlington have never filled this stadium, apart from the time when Elton John played there. They never will, unless they draw Newcastle United or Manchester United in the FA Cup (or Real Madrid in the Champions League) and rely on the support of the away fans and neutrals. The biggest flaw with this whole plan was that even if Darlington were a Premiership team, they still wouldn't fill the stadium. By the 2009-10 season the club were averaging gates of below 2,000. Friends of mine don't bother going any more; it just isn't what they bought into when they became Darlo fans. I've only been once and it was demoralising sitting in a stadium that big, with such a small crowd. The whole project was about as sensible, practical and necessary as women shaving off their eyebrows and then drawing a thin black line as a replacement. As a result of this crazy location move, Darlo went into administration and George Reynolds left the club. The stadium is now named the Northern Echo Arena, and Darlo fans can now boast of having the biggest ground in non-league football. A ground which, by the way, looks incredibly similar to the Riverside Stadium in Middlesbrough. When I emailed a friend who supports Darlington, asking him to sum up his feelings on the situation, his reply was one that the owners of lower division clubs should take careful consideration of: *"It's rubbish. They've ripped the soul out of the club by moving. I live in Darlo and have only been to about four or five home games this year. In the three and a half years since the move I haven't been once and really enjoyed it. Sitting down, no atmosphere, miles from the pitch, empty ground, no character, £18 for 4th division footy, fans with drums. I'd rather go down the pub and watch the scores come in on the vidiprinter."*

Without wanting to sound patronising, the best thing about lower division football is the supporters. Fans of Football League clubs seem to have respect for one another, as they recognise that they are all in the same boat. Teams that do well are usually met with good will, and for the most part bitterness towards other clubs seems only to be reserved for local and traditional rivals. No fans are there for trend or glory, just pure loyalty and pride in their team. It's a great human characteristic and the world needs people who stick up for the underdog. When Fulham were three divisions below the Premier League in 1996, they were averaging home gates of around 4,000. Not pretty, but you'd never question the loyalty of those die-hard Fulham supporters.

Quick related story: during the 2009-10 season I met a chap who claimed to be a Fulham fan (funnily enough around the same time that Fulham had just qualified for the UEFA Cup Final). The next day his mate told me that he was actually a Liverpool fan who was too ashamed to admit who he supported because the Reds were not having a good season. Glory boys like this just don't exist in lower division football, and it's what makes the Football League a great place to be – on occasions!

With the amount of fans turning their backs on the Premiership, there is a market out there for real football and real community which can be exploited even more than it is already. Bradford City have set an example and proved that fortune can favour those with principles.

Chapter 12
The model

"By the turn of the millennium, West Ham United will have won twenty league championships and at least ten major European honours."

Nostradamus on his deathbed – 1566

As far as ethics go, the German Bundesliga has been a model that many English fans will look towards in envy. The fans have overall control of the clubs, the games are affordable to everyone, there's the freedom of open terracing, and the league works with the Deutschland FA to help the national team bring pride to German football. All of which is in total contrast to the *money only* culture of the Premiership.

But there is a glaring drawback with the German league and it's one they share with the other top leagues in Europe. That is the lack of competition on the field. Bayern Munich are Germany's richest club, and have dominated the Bundesliga for much of the past two decades. Between 1990 and 2010 they won eleven league championships.

In Europe, the teams who spend the most win the most – case closed. The dominance of a select few surely can't be good for sport, as excitement in a game like football doesn't just come through fancy footwork or even a high scoring game. A low scoring game can be thrilling simply because of the tension and the competitiveness of the occasion.

For a model of a major world sporting league that truly is competitive the National Football League (NFL) in America is most certainly one to take notice of.

No team ever dominates the NFL and every year different teams compete in the Superbowl final. Between 1990 and 2010 thirteen different teams won the NFL Superbowl and twenty-three different teams competed in the final. No team won the Superbowl more than three times in this twenty year period. The NFL is not quite the perfect model because the league itself is saturated, as there is no relegation, and no teams to get promoted from a lower division. But within the top league itself there is a very high level of competition.

The culture of American football is very different to British football. The career span of an American footballer can be very short. So the fresh players that come out from the college teams are very important. In the NFL, the teams that finish in the bottom half of the league get first pick of the best young rookies; a very socialist concept for such a capitalist society. Other American sports also employ the same college draft system. Some might say that this is an incentive for teams to finish lower down in the table during a bad season. Some will also argue that it's a policy which rewards failure and penalises the teams who perform the best. Well that's very true, which is why this particular draft system from the NFL is not the exact answer.

Let's be clear: the NFL style draft system would not work in football. The suggestion isn't that we give the likes of Stoke City the pick of Oxford University's best players. Football (soccer) clubs have their own youth schemes and scout for their own players from the grass roots of the game. If certain clubs have good scouts and good youth academies then that's commendable, and not a factor in making the league uncompetitive. In fact smaller clubs tend to have a better record of developing the best players, before they're sold off to bigger clubs. What should be copied from the NFL is the basic principle of giving more teams a fairer chance of competing. This could be achieved by regulating the transfer market, which is dominated by a handful of the wealthiest clubs in Europe. Here's an example of just how big the gap is: in 2010, the 20th most prosperous club in football was Newcastle United, who declared annual revenue of €101 million. In 2009, Real Madrid spent just €6 million less than that on the signing of one player. International superstars can waste away on the subs bench because the big teams have enough resources to buy so many top players. Take the example of Rocky Santa Cruz's transfer from Blackburn Rovers to Manchester City in 2009. He'd been brilliant for Blackburn and was in demand from the top clubs. His transfer coincided with City signing a handful of other top quality strikers, meaning that Santa Cruz spent most of the 2009-10 season on the subs bench. As a result, the squads at the richest clubs are stronger but the league as a whole becomes far weaker. For football to be more unpredictable then something has to be done to combat this dominance.

There is a very easy and effective way to make the overall distribution of players fairer. How about a limit to how much one club can spend in the transfer market? A simple way to achieve this would be if UEFA imposed a spending limit of €20 million in one season for each club. If a club were to pay €20 million for a player then that's their shopping over with for that season. Some might say that this proposal would be unrealistic, but it's no more radical than UEFA's current transfer window law that prevents clubs from buying players throughout the majority of the season. In recent years, a team like Real Madrid have been able to outbid anyone at any time, but a European spending limit would inevitably bring down transfer fees meaning the less affluent clubs could compete more in the market.

There can be no doubt that the ethos within the NFL makes the league more unpredictable and as a result more exciting. Let's compare the number of different Superbowl winners (thirteen in twenty years) to the list of winners from the three supposed top leagues of European football over the same twenty year period.

English Premiership winners between 1990 and 2010

2010 Chelsea
2009 Manchester United
2008 Manchester United
2007 Manchester United
2006 Chelsea
2005 Chelsea
2004 Arsenal
2003 Manchester United
2002 Arsenal
2001 Manchester United
2000 Manchester United
1999 Manchester United
1998 Arsenal
1997 Manchester United
1996 Manchester United
1995 Blackburn Rovers
1994 Manchester United
1993 Manchester United
1992 Leeds United
1991 Arsenal
1990 Liverpool

That's just six different winners in a twenty year period and only three different winners since 1995. Of the six winners in this time, Blackburn, Liverpool and Leeds have only one title win, compared to Manchester United with eleven and Arsenal and Chelsea with a combined seven. Hey I'm not that upset about this! As an Arsenal fan it's not my problem because I've seen my team win league championships. Why should I want the likes of Villa

258

or Everton stepping on the toes of those of us at the top? Let them carry on with their annual fight for a European place. I would never get bored with my team winning the title every single year. But from a wider perspective, it makes for a rather boring league for everyone else. Even the FA Cup has been dominated by a select few teams in this modern era. From 1984 to the time of writing, there have only been two FA Cup Finals that haven't involved at least one of these teams: Manchester United, Arsenal, Liverpool, Chelsea, Spurs. One of those two finals was in 2011 and involved Manchester City – not a team struggling to get by on a tight budget. The last team to win the FA Cup for the first time in their club's history was Wimbledon in 1988. The second last was Coventry City in 1987, the third last Ipswich in 1978, and the fourth last Southampton in 1976. So in a twelve year period we had four clubs win the FA Cup for the first time. Since 1988 no-one else has achieved this.

In recent years the relegation battle has been the saviour for top flight football in England, in terms of entertainment based on competitiveness. To give just one example: the 2004-05 season was a one-horse race as Chelsea had unlimited funds and effectively bought the league championship. But on the last day of the 2004-05 season not that many of us were watching Chelsea as they lifted the Premiership trophy. All eyes were on the relegation battle where any three of the bottom four teams would be relegated. WBA, Norwich, Crystal Palace and Southampton all had a chance of avoiding relegation, but by the end of that day only one of them would survive. It was great drama for the neutral fan, and was only settled in the last minute as WBA stayed up despite being the bookies' favourite to go down. If the same competitiveness were at the other half of the table, then that really would be something to watch.

Midway into the 2010-11 season, the Premier League was being proclaimed as the most unpredictable and competitive it had been in years; because the top teams were dropping more points than they normally do. In fairness, it was more interesting than it had been recent years, but the top four teams on the eve of 2011 were Manchester United, Manchester City, Arsenal and Chelsea. Those are the teams that everyone would have predicted to be in the top four places halfway through the season and indeed at the end of the season. If teams like Sunderland and Everton were also in there genuinely challenging for the title, then we really would be on the verge of something exciting. The level of competition in Europe's other top leagues follows a similar pattern.

Spanish La Liga winners between 1990 and 2010

2010 Barcelona
2009 Barcelona
2008 Real Madrid
2007 Real Madrid
2006 Barcelona
2005 Barcelona
2004 Valencia
2003 Real Madrid
2002 Valencia
2001 Real Madrid
2000 Deportivo La Coruna
1999 Barcelona
1998 Barcelona
1997 Real Madrid
1996 Atletico Madrid
1995 Real Madrid
1994 Barcelona
1993 Barcelona
1992 Barcelona
1991 Barcelona
1990 Real Madrid

Even less competitive than the English Premiership. Just five winners in twenty years with Barcelona and Real Madrid winning the title a whopping sixteen times between them. This sort of thing just makes life too easy for bookmakers. In the whole history of La Liga there have only been eight different league winners. The others before 1990 being Atletico Bilbao, Seville and Betis. Since the formation of the Spanish league in 1929, Barcelona and Real Madrid between them have won fifty championships out of the first seventy-three seasons. The Italian league doesn't fare too much better.

Italian Serie A winners between 1990 and 2010

2010 Inter Milan
2009 Inter Milan
2008 Inter Milan
2007 Inter Milan
2006 Title stripped from Juventus and awarded to Inter Milan
2005 Void, title stripped from Juventus
2004 A C Milan
2003 Juventus
2002 Juventus
2001 Roma
2000 Lazio
1999 AC Milan
1998 Juventus
1997 Juventus
1996 AC Milan
1995 Juventus
1994 AC Milan
1993 AC Milan
1992 AC Milan
1991 Sampdoria
1990 Napoli

Seven different winners in twenty years. Juventus, Inter Milan and AC Milan totally dominating with sixteen titles between them. In Serie A there have only been twelve different winners since its formation in 1929.

Scottish Premier League Winners between 1990 and 2010

I'll leave this one blank. Just fill in the year in which you think that either Rangers or Celtic won the title.

2010
2009
2008
2007
2006
2005
2004
2003
2002
2001
2000
1999
1998
1997
1996
1995
1994
1993
1992
1991
1990

The Champions League is the only major high profile league in Europe that offers any credible competition. Because of its knockout nature, the winners cannot be decided until the final game at the end of the season. Discounting 1993, which was void (match-fixing), there have been twelve different winners of the nineteen Champions League finals between 1990 and 2010. That's nearly as competitive as the Superbowl during the same period.

It's good that the Champions League has been competitive over the years, and for that reason it usually is the most unpredictable competition in Europe. It also provides a good excuse not to create the European Super League that the top clubs have supposedly been trying to push for years (not to say that they don't also adore the ultra-rich and commercial Champions League). But as good as it is from a competitive point of view, the fact remains that only a handful of top clubs throughout Europe will get the chance to compete. No more than four teams each for the leagues in Spain, Italy and England, with fewer or no places for smaller European leagues.

The less privileged clubs will just have to carry on competing in their predictable domestic leagues. It's because the Champions League is so lucrative for the teams involved that there is such a huge gulf between those at the top and everyone else. When the same teams make so much money from the Champions League, they just continue to pull further away from all the other clubs. Between the twenty year period of 2011 to 2031, it will be very interesting to see if there will be as many as twelve different winners of the Champions League – considering the wealth gap that developed in the previous twenty years.

In England, it will now be considered a major achievement if a team other than Chelsea, Manchester United, Arsenal, Manchester City, Spurs or Liverpool finish in the top five. When Spurs broke into the top four in 2010 you would have thought they'd actually won the Champions League given the jubilation – they finished fourth! This lack of competition we now have in English football is unprecedented. Not so long ago, a phrase such as 'breaking into the top four' as being a benchmark for success would have been laughed at. During the 1980s, it was a fair bet that Liverpool would win the title, but you could never predict who would finish in the next three places (teams like Ipswich Town, Watford and Southampton achieved runners-up status during this decade). The teams who now finish above everyone else are, not surprisingly, also the highest revenue teams in the country. If football reflects one thing in this world most starkly, then it's the wealth gap between rich and poor that grows wider with each year. Football mirrors free market capitalism; more wealth may be generated, but it ends up in the hands of fewer people.

The Premiership will never reach its full potential in terms of entertainment, until a larger percentage of teams start the season with a realistic ambition of finishing number one. At the start of the 2010-11 season, Aston Villa were eighth favourites to win the Premiership but at 200/1.[10] In previous years, the teams who were 200/1 to win the league were the ones expected to be relegated, not regarded as the eighth best team in the country. Even more worrying is that three teams had odds of over 1000/1 and a further eight teams were at 2000/1. That means that more than half the teams in the league are regarded as so bad that they have odds of at least four digits to one. It shows just how uncompetitive the Premier League has become and yet it's marketed as the 'best in the world'.

The English Football League/Premiership is the oldest in the world and dates back to 1888. Overall there have been twenty-three different league winners, which is a good record and shows

---

[10] Odds from William Hill.

a very competitive history.[11] The most recent team to win the title for the first ever time was Nottingham Forest but that was way back in 1978. The season before this, Nottingham Forest were in the old Second Division and had no history of being a big club. Brian Clough managed Forest to promotion and within a season they were the English Division One champions. Six years earlier he achieved a similar success with Derby County who in 1972 became the twenty-second team to win the English league for the first time. This was just three years after they had been promoted from the old Second Division. The chances of any lower league club repeating this success in this day and age are virtually zero. Back in the 1970s, great management was enough to bring success to Derby County and Nottingham Forest. Jose Mourinho is referred to as the 'special one' and has also been described as the new Brian Clough. Like him or not, Mourinho is a brilliant manager whose record speaks for itself. But let's imagine that Mourinho is the manager of a fairly big lower division club that has never won the English league title. For example Southampton FC. Could Mourinho get Southampton promoted and then win the Premiership title the following season on a limited budget? In fact, would he be able to do it in the next ten seasons? The answer has to be no (though Jose would no doubt claim that he could win Southampton the Champions League as well as the Superbowl). No matter how talented a manager may be, he will never win the Premiership with a club that is not in the financial hierarchy.

---

[11] The twenty-three teams who have won the English League Championship are: Preston North End (2), Everton (9), Sunderland (6), Aston Villa (7), Sheffield United (1), Liverpool (18), Sheffield Wednesday (4), Blackburn Rovers (5), Newcastle United (4), Huddersfield Town (3), Arsenal (13), Manchester United (19), WBA (1), Ipswich Town (1), Portsmouth (2), Spurs (2), Chelsea (4), Burnley (1), Wolves (3), Manchester City (2), Leeds United (3), Derby County (2), Nottingham Forest (1).

As we know, football is now all about making money. But if football wants to make even more money, my advice is to try and achieve a more unpredictable league. It certainly doesn't harm the popularity and commercial value of the NFL. There can be no doubt that a more competitive league would result in a massive rise in fan attendance at matches and a huge increase in viewing figures for the TV companies. Then everyone would be happy including both the fans and the money men. Let's hope that one day we will see a club rise from obscurity to become champions of England for the first time in their history. It would be a shame if the number were to stay at twenty-three forever, but at the moment it looks as if it might. Will number twenty-four please come in – your time is well overdue.

Chapter 13
A very non-commercial attitude

In 2006-07, my mate Will became a season ticket holder at the Emirates, at a cost of £895. The following season he didn't renew his season ticket. He found that the club could be unhelpful, and arrogant to deal with over the phone, and even in person. In my time as a regular follower I experienced the same thing. I always felt the reason for this attitude was that they believe they are doing us a favour by taking our money, rather than the other way round. Customers are easily replaceable, and if one disappears then business will not suffer. In 2010, I went to the Arsenal box for the first time in years, to buy a ticket for our away friendly against AFC Wimbledon. Nothing had changed. I felt that the service I got was second rate. As I got to the front of the queue the man behind the counter looked at me as if he had more important things to do than deal with a paying customer. The service that followed wasn't exactly helpful; no tickets for this game were being sold through the club and he didn't know where they were on sale, next please. My overall feeling however was relief – in that I've got virtually nothing more to do with this type of service that is all too common in football.

One night after a few pints too many, Will started to display a lot of dissatisfaction about the way the club treats the fans and made the point: *"I don't think football is that commercial. If it was commercial then it would have better customer service and customer relations. If you ask me, if it is a business then it's a very badly run business."* His point reminded me of Chapter Four

– Customer Satisfaction. I had been a member at Arsenal for over twenty years and not once did they ever ask my opinion on anything. During this time the club had changed its whole identity, from the stadium, to the badge, to the whole corporate image of the club. Now I hate to sound like I'm advocating a world with even more market research, because there is a lot of that going on right now. What tends to happen is that brands will hold focus groups and interview members of the public regarding their opinions on a product or an upcoming advertising campaign. It usually consists of horseshit like: "If this packaging were a human being, what kind of a human being would it be?" Even feature films are sometimes changed because of focus group analysis, which is absurd because films should remain true to those who make them. But I would advocate an element of 'market research' for football, because the fans care so passionately about everything to do with their club. Certainly more so than a member of the public who's been asked to form an opinion on the human characteristics of a Big Mac.

At halftime during a game in 2002, Arsenal had a special treat for the fans. On the big TV screens at Highbury they unveiled, to all our surprise, a newly designed club crest. To our horror, this new badge carried a style which suggested that the designers had been briefed by Noddy and Big Ears. *This is a joke right? That Walt Disney looking cartoon thing can't be our new crest, can it?* I checked the date and to my despair it wasn't April 1st. If it had been it would have been a brilliant joke, but these guys were serious. Our beloved crest, which to us represented the class and style of our club, had been sabotaged by a team of ill-informed 'branding specialists' who told us that, "Over time it will be seen as a much more exciting and dynamic badge than the current one". During this unveiling in 2002, the Highbury crowd generously voiced their focus group analysis, which consisted of feedback such as: "you cunts", "what have you fucking done to our badge?", "what a load of shit" and "that's bollocks". I asked myself, *if the new Arsenal crest were a human being, what kind of a human being would it be*? Answer: someone who works for a branding specialist and has no sense of class, style or history.

We never objected to the principle of change. After all, a tradition of most clubs is to have a re-design of the club crest every now and then (Arsenal for example have had five different club crests). What we objected to was that we had no say in a matter that we really cared about. We're the people who will spend money on the products that display this badge; it just doesn't make sense to impose one on us that we don't like. Football clubs never poll their supporters on their opinions, which I think has always been conclusive proof that they attach no value to those opinions. They expect us to buy into whatever they give us.

In October 2007, *The Guardian* reported that Spurs might move to a new 60,000 capacity stadium in Enfield. The article stated that Spurs chairman Daniel Levy was set to consult shareholders about the possibility of a move. However, there was no mention of Levy consulting the fans on this issue. Surely a football club with any ethics would not plan a move to a new area without having first had approval from the people they hope will fill the stadium. When Spurs applied to move into the Olympic Stadium in Stratford, once again the views of the fans were ignored, probably because the majority of them did not support such a radical re-location. In January 2011, a statement from Spurs made it clear that they would be leaving their current home whether they were awarded the Olympic Stadium or not. I may hate Tottenham, but the fans and the local community deserve more respect than to be brushed aside in such an arrogant manner. The arrogance that reeks more than anything is the underlying message that says: *We're the ones making the decisions, and as followers you're going to buy into it whether you like it or not, because we know best.*

In contrast, fan-owned clubs like AFC Wimbledon do consult the fans on important issues, including things like the design of the team kit. The Wimbledon fans are given the option of a number of different kit designs and the one which gets the most votes becomes the team kit for the following season. Most professional clubs regularly change the team kit and even the team badge, yet never consult their supporters about what they'd like to see. What kind of commercial business has no interest in what its customers think?

In October 2007, whilst working as a bodyguard for the Pet Shop Boys, Arsenal fan Dainton Connell was killed in a car crash during a tour of Russia. Dainton, a terrace legend, had a lively past in the 1980s with the Herd, but by all accounts was a decent and charismatic human being with a good soul. Not one view was heard to the opposite about the man nicknamed *The Bear*. 4,000 people attended his funeral including Ian Wright, Lee Dixon, Frank Bruno, Janet Street Porter, and the bands Pet Shop Boys and Madness. Friends and family had tried to arrange a wake at the Emirates Stadium, but they were quoted a reported £65,000 to hire out some of the facilities, which was a price far higher than expected. However, when the money was raised, Arsenal said that it was against their policy to hold an event the day before a game, and so the wake was held in another part of North London. The club might feel that they were justified in refusing to allow a remembrance at the stadium, but by being so distant they just continue to alienate more and more fans. The very same fans whose money they happily take to enhance the profits of the club. To further alienate us is not a commercially practical thing to do. People were very upset about this, and a common perception has been that the club simply don't care enough about ordinary fans – they only care about appeasing their corporate clients and shareholders. This statement from someone called Shad, is taken from a *Times Online* forum, and it pretty much sums up the feelings that many fans have on this matter, and indeed the game in general: *"It's typical of the way football is heading that the club I love shower themselves in shame in their lack of effort to accommodate the wake of a man who was widely regarded as Arsenal's biggest fan. For £65,000 I'm sure a few cleaners could tidy a room in time for a match the following day. Shame on them. Rest in Peace 'The Bear'."* If a club like Arsenal want to profit from Shad's money, or Will's money, or my money, or the money of Dainton's 4,000 mourners, then they're potentially going down a very unwise and non-commercial route, which could one day bite them on the arse.

An example of a club chairman who has form in treating supporters like valued customers is Niall Quinn, who runs Sunderland.[12] After an away game against Cardiff City in 2007, Quinn had heard that a plane load of Sunderland fans had been stranded at Cardiff airport, and that they would not be able to get back home until the next day. Quinn stepped in and paid for taxis to take the supporters all the way back to Sunderland. How many other club chairmen would bother to do that? Not many.

But by treating the fans in such a good way, Quinn is creating a culture in which he will find it easier to maintain the supporters' loyalty. If the Sunderland fans at Cardiff airport had been stranded overnight, then some of them might have started to question whether or not following their football team away from home was really worth all the hassle. So when a club chairman makes an effort to help them out of a difficult situation, he leaves behind a group of people who will continue to support them in the future.

---

[12] Niall Quinn is applying the same integrity he had as a player into how he runs a football club. He is a man who in 2002 donated all the proceeds made from his testimonial to charity (thought to be over £1 million).

Chapter 14
Banning orders

Q: If Kelly Brook and Megan Fox were to run on to the pitch during an English league game (say, Hartlepool v Macclesfield) wearing only their necklaces and campaigning for world peace, would they:

(a) Get praised by the authorities for a generous display of entertainment in the name of a good cause?

(b) Win an Oscar?

(c) Get awarded the freedom of Hartlepool?

(d) Get arrested, have their names put on the hooligan register, and then banned from every league ground in the country for three years?

Answer: (d)

Okay, so clear that hypothetical incident from your head and let's focus on the subject in hand. For English football to re-brand itself and attract a new type of consumer, it needed to rid itself of the stigma of hooliganism. They have achieved that aim and crowd trouble at domestic football matches has been significantly reduced in recent years. I don't think anyone disputes the fact that some people do deserve to be banned from football grounds, and from travelling abroad to follow England.

But we are also seeing a draconian attitude being directed towards football fans, in which a person can be punished by the law and given a banning order for 'crimes' that the police wouldn't bother responding to in any walk of life other than football. The law now goes way too far in punishing football supporters for petty acts of foolishness in the name of meeting government targets and safeguarding the corporate image of the game.

I watched England get knocked out of the 2006 World Cup by Portugal in a pub in West London. After the game had ended, about twenty to thirty youngsters began to throw a barrage of glass bottles at the Nandos restaurant on the other side of the street. The bottles could have injured diners and staff in the restaurant and they could have killed people who were walking in the streets. They so nearly did, as glass bottles that were thrown at length and at speed narrowly missed the heads of passers-by, including an elderly lady. One chap was trying to encourage people to go across the road and trash the restaurant. He was the main instigator of the trouble, but was so cowardly that he would not go over to Nandos unless more people went with him. I actually tried to reason with him, but it was like talking to a humanoid with the thinking capacity of a wild boar. I, and the people with me, could have tried harder to stop them, but we knew that by challenging those people it would have ended up in a street brawl. Had it done so, then the police, who were on their way, would have turned up at the right (or wrong) time, seen us fighting and that alone would have been enough to result in a banning order for football-related violence (not to mention the fact that anyone who confronts an attacker in this country is then deemed the criminal). I have no confidence in the fairness of the law when it comes to football-related disorder. A lot of the people on the hooligan prevention list are not as dangerous as we are led to believe. A cousin of mine who follows Darlington was considered a category C hooligan and was put on a banning order for two and a half years (his ban came to an end in 2006). I travelled all over Europe with my cousin to watch England in places ranging from the bleakness of Warsaw and Lens, to the sunshine of Marseilles and Athens. Every time we went abroad to watch England there was trouble, from a small scale brawl to a headline making mini-riot. Not once though did I ever see this listed hooligan actually get involved in the trouble, and yet for two and a half years he was considered a major threat, and had to hand his passport over to his local police station before every England International home and away.[13] A lot of people who have been banned have been treated rather harshly, because with football-related offences it's basically one strike and you're out, which is where it differs from regular law and order punishments for minor offences. You could have twenty years of good behaviour at football matches, only to be banned for one petty act of rule breaking.

The 'crimes' that supporters get banned for in England would be seen as laughable in other countries in Europe and South America. A stand-up comedian received a two and a half year banning order for running on to the pitch at White Hart Lane dressed as Osama Bin Laden! Another man from Darlington was given the same punishment for throwing a snowball at a player (couldn't they have just banned him in winter?).

Football is a game of high emotion. Emotion can sometimes lead to people acting out of character. For example a school teacher at Sunderland, who had no previous history of 'disorder',

---

[13] You can read an online account of my cousin's banning order, in his own words, here:
http://my.telegraph.co.uk/jamie/october_2007/football_banning_orders_fair_punishment_or_abuse.htm

was so upset by his team's poor performances that he walked onto the pitch and chucked his season ticket placidly over his shoulder. Result: a fine, a three year banning order, and a fight to save his job. In 2010, nineteen-year-old Arsenal fan Ricky Regan was fined £500 and banned from football for lighting up a flare in the away end at Stamford Bridge. I watched this incident on TV and it brought me and the people I was with to our feet, as we cheered on Ricky who had just reignited our interest in a match where our team were losing 2-0. Only in English football would this kind of punishment be given to a supporter for such an act of non-violent exuberance. What reeked of hypocrisy was that during this same time, Arsenal displayed an O2 billboard advert in the Emirates Stadium, which carried the image of a group of Arsenal fans cheering while a football fan dressed as a soldier waved a flare in the air.

At the same time, more serious troublemakers go unnoticed because the anti-social behaviour they display in this country has not been football-related. Hypothetically, if I had numerous convictions for non-football-related anti-social behaviour offences and was banned from every pub in my local area, then I would not be banned from travelling abroad to watch England. Yet if I encroached the playing area in celebration of a goal, then I would be put on the hooligan register for three years, banned from every professional football club in the country and prevented from travelling abroad during England away games.

This all fits into the wider argument that football in England is now an Orwellian Big Brother environment, in which any act of spontaneous and exuberant behaviour is heavily clamped down upon.

It takes a lot of police time and money to ban just one person from attending football matches. Compare that with the fact that the police don't have time to investigate crimes such as bike theft, bag theft, shoplifting and burglary. Why does the game get this priority; is the worst thing that can happen in our society a fight at a football match? If football wasn't such big business, would there really be such a high police presence for virtually every game played in this country? It's an over-enforced protection for an industry that relies on a safe and clean image to sell to its new consumers. My advice to anyone who feels a concern at the lack of police in their area is simple – just move nearer a football stadium. As for banning orders, I believe that they should be viewed with suspicion from law-abiding football fans for one very simple reason: you don't have to be convicted of a crime to receive one.

Chapter 15
The English Disease

"I hate so many things about our German football, but in relation to English football everything is still alright here, I have to say. But I'm aware of the danger, today my club has a 'supercool new bling bling arena' which is named after a financial corporation...nothing else to say. This is a trend which has come to Germany too early."

Facebook message sent to me from a reader in Germany called Nils Hannover.

Despite the demise of crowd atmosphere in English football, I hold onto the notion that old-school raw passion in stadiums is still common in other countries. That colour, energy and sense of freedom still exists in this world; you just have to travel a bit further to find it. In fact with low cost air travel, it can be cheaper to fly to Milan, hop on a tram, buy a match ticket at Inter or AC, have a Panini, and then fly back home, all in, for the same price as a ticket to a Premier League game.

I remember when I first started reading George Orwell's *Nineteen Eighty-Four*, my hope was that outside of Oceania, most of the world was still sane and not part of such a crazy and controlled system. It was so depressing when further into the book you got the feeling that it probably wasn't the case.

I have been given a couple of causes for concern recently. Firstly the German publisher Trolsen translated *Theatre of Silence*

(*The People's Game? Ein Buch Gegen Den Modernen Fussball*)
on the basis that it's a warning to the way in which German
football is heading. I found this incredible considering the contrast
in ethics between the ways that German clubs are run compared to
ours. But according to my publisher contact Henning, the game
there is under threat from big business who want to revoke the
50+1 rule; the law which means that the fans have overall control
of the clubs. A law which Henning refers to as a "*measure
introduced to keep a critical minority calm but will soon be
ineffective*". This law is about to be challenged in court by
ambitious businessmen and the future of the People's Game in
Germany is going to be put firmly to the test.

Already things have started to change in which fan power has
diminished. German clubs are member-led sports institutions that
also run basketball teams, volleyball teams etc. What some of
them have already done is outsource the 'professional football
branch' meaning that the football decisions are made mostly by
limited companies, not the fans. Well, I guess that at least the
supporters still get the chance to make important decisions on
swimming and table tennis issues!

Henning also complained that a new breed of affluent fans
are changing the culture of German football, in a way similar to
what has happened in England. A more middle-class crowd now
goes to be entertained and is far more demanding than the
traditional supporter. Henning told me that: "*These people do not
come because of friendship, of togetherness of the mob and a
feeling of belonging. They come because the new ground has
'atmosphere', because it is 'nice', and because the team is
sometimes successful. Demanding success is at the core of the
problem. As the audience wants their team to be successful, the
directors are forced to invest ever larger sums in 'player
material' to keep the club competitive. To be able to do so, they
have to go ever further to collect money. The percentage of
turnstile turnover in relation to the clubs' overall turnovers is*

decreasing each season, thus making the fans' (money-caused) impact constantly smaller. And the main disaster is that the 'new fans' don't care unless they see the goals they have been paying for."

Shortly after the 2010 World Cup I received a Facebook message from an Italian reader called Stefano, who bought my book while on holiday in London. His message was that *Theatre of Silence* is an "anticipation of what is happening in Italy". He informed me of a new scheme called Tessera del tifoso, which prevents away fans from travelling unless they have a football ID card. From now on you cannot travel to away games without having this ID, and they are refused to anyone whom the police choose to blacklist. Like banning orders in England you do not need a criminal conviction to receive one.

This ID scheme sounds incredibly similar to the one Margaret Thatcher tried to impose on English supporters in the 1980s, and failed to do so. Schemes like these will just put off casual followers and neutrals. With such strict rules overall attendances can only go in one direction – down. For Thatcher that wasn't really a concern because she hated the game and its fans. Though I'm sure that today Thatcher would look at the Premier League with great admiration.

I've been to Italy three times to follow Arsenal in the Champions League. On each occasion fans have had to match the name on their passport with the name on the match ticket. That's even stricter than English restrictions and very repressive for casual followers who just want to attend a game. It's a particular problem for those of us who have no choice but to buy tickets from unofficial sources and therefore have someone else's name on the ticket. Luckily the system can be easily fiddled. At AC Milan I used water to wash the pen written name off the ticket, replacing it with my own. At Roma I crossed the name off with a pen and wrote my name next to it – they didn't question it. At

Juventus we couldn't get into the away end (there were plenty of away tickets still on sale but they had a policy of not selling these to anyone with British passports). So we ended up in the home end where a steward let us through because he couldn't be bothered to debate with us in English. This end of the stadium was next to 15,000 Ultras, which is of course far safer for away fans than selling unsold Arsenal tickets to people with British passports.

Overall, Italian domestic football is still less draconian than English football, because when in the stadium the stewards do not impose themselves heavily on fans, probably because they're too afraid to. That's how it used to be in England because the authorities were afraid of the fans – now it's the other way round (except perhaps at Millwall where the fans still scare the stewards into not taking any liberties). Italy is probably at the point where English football was at the start of the Premier League in the early1990s. The authorities will take advantage of crowd problems to change the whole face of the game, from one extreme to the other. Whether or not fans in Italy allow that to happen is something we shall find out. To quote Stefano again, "I'm afraid Italy is going down the same commercial route, we shall soon live on our memories".

The Premier League is such a massive money generator that it's inevitable that other countries will try to achieve the same results by using similar tactics.

It could be that the overbearing commercial culture of English football may be at the point of no return; it may never reclaim its soul. However, supporters worldwide still have something to fight for. My hands-on experience in other countries, for example Italy, is that despite commercialism, top level football is accessible to a wider range of people, and that you still feel like a supporter, as opposed to an over-controlled consumer.

Years ago the rest of the world learnt to play football better than us. Then they did the same with hooliganism and became even crazier than the original pioneers! What a tragedy it would be if they also caught up with us on how to sell your national game down the river. I call out to the ultras of the world never to allow that to happen. I hope that German football fans can fight off the businessmen who try to break the 50+1 law. I also hope never go to Italy to find Lazio and Roma playing in the Stadio Singapore Airways.

Chapter 16
Non growing pains

Today I watch football with very little emotion. For the most part, I don't feel great joy when we win. Neither do I feel upset when we get beaten, unless it's against certain opposition. When I watch Arsenal in most matches, I want us to win, but I'm fairly relaxed and am happy just to watch a good game. It's a total contrast to when I was younger, the result meant everything. Sometimes I would watch games feeling like a nervous wreck. It was a better way to be involved because joy and disappointment are reasons why we watch the game. In football, success is all the sweeter when you know how much defeat can hurt. This feeling of apathy is cold and I don't like it.

I attribute this change in attitude to the fact that I no longer believe in what I'm watching; one set of multi-millionaires beats another set of multi-millionaires, big deal. Football clubs and players don't care about the fans anymore. We're told that we don't matter, money does; therefore to get emotional about the outcome seems rather undignified.

A friend of mine recently claimed that the reason some of us now feel this way about football is simply because we're getting older – we're mature enough to realise that it's not the be all and end all any more. It's an opinion I've heard from more than one person. It's an interesting view, but I don't agree with it for a couple of reasons. Firstly, I see people far older than me who are still so emotional about the outcome of a match. A bad result can ruin their weekend. Getting older hasn't stopped them from caring. Football crowds today are made up of older people not youngsters. Also, if getting older were the case then it would be the case always and not just for most games. In the 2010-11 season I did something I don't usually do any more, I bought a ticket to watch Arsenal away. This League Cup match against our bitter rivals Spurs was attracting fans who hardly go to games in this era but fancied this one. I wasn't going to be left out of a march down the Seven Sisters Road to White Hart Lane with an army of old school Arsenal. During the game, the crowd in the away end shamed the silent home crowd with tremendous support. Now as a result of this, for the first time in ages I really felt nervous about the outcome of the game; and I loved the fact that I was on edge every time Spurs attacked our end. This was because I had something to believe in, even if it was just for one night. The away end was packed with fans who I could relate to and the team had to get that result in order to do the away support justice. There was no difference in my attitude to watching this North London derby at the age of thirty three, than there was when watching the same fixture twenty years earlier.

I'll give another example as to why I don't think the feeling of apathy is down to growing older. As a young man, just turned twenty, I went to see the band AC/DC. I've loved and believed in this group since I was a teenager and had a great time at this gig. I also went to see them play at Wembley Stadium when in my thirties. My feeling towards them hadn't changed in that time. A feeling of cynicism hadn't built up. No feeling of apathy or *well it was good years ago but it's hard to get excited about it any more.* The feeling was the complete opposite.

Had AC/DC consistently sold out over the years then yes, my feelings towards them would have changed. Had they gone on *X-Factor* to promote their music I would have been mortified. Had they changed their style to try and appeal to a different kind of fan, I most certainly would have lost faith. Had there been digital flashing advertising hoardings by the Wembley stage, distracting my attention from the band, then I would have felt short-changed. Had their CDs cost £40+ I would have thought *well I still like them but I'm not paying that*. Had I watched the gig in an all-seated environment where other fans were telling me to sit down, then I would have been well and truly pissed off. Had Angus Young left the band to join Metallica for a slightly better royalty deal I would have felt very disillusioned.

I don't think that age makes you believe in something less just for the sake of growing older, though it does give you the ability to be more mature and weigh things up more rationally. However, I'll finish with this point: I speak to so many young football fans who truly resent the commercialised game they're presented with.

Chapter 17
Blame the pawns not the prawns

During the process of writing this book, one statistic in particular has bothered me, especially when I rail against the route that football has taken since the formation of the Premier League. It's the statistic that attendances at Premiership grounds have risen by as much as 62% since 1992. Despite a small drop in attendances in recent years, 62% is a figure that can be used strongly in defence of how football has changed. I, and many others, may not like high ticket pricing, corporate priorities, players diving, music being played when a goal is scored, 24/7 fixtures, obscene player wages, overbearing advertising, aggressive stewarding and so on. But as all these things and more became an accepted part of English football, the number of new fans who bought in to the Premier League went up – massively. Bugger!

All I can argue then is that popularity doesn't always make something a better product because more people buy into it. In all aspects of society popularity is not an indication of quality and fulfilment, and in contrast the most popular things can also be the most mundane and sterile. McDonalds is the most popular food chain but I don't think there's much to be said for the quality of food they serve. *EastEnders* is a very popular TV programme watched by millions of people, but some might say that the acting is suspect and the storylines could be created by well educated gorillas. Much better programmes than *EastEnders* and *Hollyoaks* will not attract the same high viewing figures. The *Sun* is the most popular daily newspaper but does it offer a better standard of reporting than *The Independent* or *The Times*? Lady Gaga is popular... *Scary Movie 4* is popular... reality TV is popular... All Bar One is popular... capital punishment is popular... *Heat* magazine is popular... The Chris Moyles' breakfast show is popular... Alan Sugar is popular... wearing trousers low with your arse hanging out is popular... *Glee* is popular... Adolf Hitler was popular (declared 'Man of the Year' by *Time* magazine in 1938 remember!). Okay, point proven, popularity shouldn't impress us one little bit. In fact just to prove it a little bit more, here's a quote from Simon Cowell, a man of great taste: "*I've got to tell you, if I had ten Bob Dylans in the final of American Idol, we would not be getting thirty million viewers a week. I don't believe the Dylans of this world would make American Idol a better show.*"

Attending games is popular, but it doesn't mean that the fans are happy and it certainly doesn't mean that things don't need to change. So whose responsibility is it to look after the interests of supporters? Let's look at the government. At the start of the millennium the Labour government created the Football Task Force which was headed by MPs such as David Mellor and the late Tony Banks. It was set up as a watchdog to protect fans against things like high ticket pricing and commercialism. The whole project faded into oblivion, which was a predictable outcome. Unfortunately it was never going to have any meaningful influence, because football clubs are under no obligation from the government to do things such as lower ticket prices. All that would happen is that David Mellor and co. would suggest to the football clubs that they should make attendance more affordable for all. The club chairman would then nod, try not to laugh and say, "Okay we'll think about it!" – and then go and put up ticket prices. Club owners must have had a good chuckle to themselves at the Football Task Force, as they knew that it was well intended but ultimately powerless. In 2007, Sports Minister Richard Carbon reacted to the *Sun's* campaign to lower ticket pricing by taking the issue to Parliament. He also said that he that he would encourage the club chairmen to make the game more affordable. But with similar powers to the Football Task Force, all any Sports Minister can do is 'encourage' and no more than that. If the government are concerned about fans getting a better deal, then they could prove this by bringing in legislation making terracing legal once again.

But whatever the government does or doesn't do, the fact remains that football supporters have the power to do it for themselves. Realistically they are the only ones who can drag football out of the culture of exploitation.

The current situation that we have is this: thousands of fans all over the country are keenly waiting for that economic downfall in football, whilst continuing to keep the gravy train moving. If they are waiting in hope for the people who run football to gain a conscience then they will be waiting a very long time. Football clubs are run like global corporations and their sole aim is to make as much money as they can legally get away with. They don't understand the concept of 'How much is enough?' No matter how much revenue comes into football, it will never be enough to satisfy the profiteers of the game, and fans of many clubs will never get a better deal in terms of ticket pricing or even ticket availability. Take for example Chelsea, a club who have a billionaire owner and no financial hang-ups. Yet, even with all Roman Abramovich's wealth, the ticket prices at Chelsea went higher, not lower, after he took control of the club. Chelsea maintained their status as one of the most expensive clubs in world football. If advertising money, TV revenue and high admission prices mean that a club can pay a player £60,000 a week, then it won't be long before that player starts to believe he's worth £80,000 a week. Once that player gets his £80,000 a week, he'll then start to believe that he's actually worth £100,000 a week. When that player gets his £100,000 a week, he'll look across the Atlantic to David Beckham who earns £500,000 a week, and then start to really feel like he's underpaid. What we have here is a never ending pursuit of riches by people whose bellies are more than full.

The reality is simple: football will not change while you continue to fund it. So the next option is a form of protest. Peaceful protests such as marches are worthwhile, but don't always lead to change. Violent protest can be counter-productive. The protest with the most effect is an economic protest that hits the pockets of those at the top. Hypothetically, if Britain and America were to invade Iran, then there could be six million people on the streets of London and Washington in protest against an invasion – but it wouldn't change a thing. The only thing that would stop them would be a people's boycott of the big corporations that fund politics. Corporations such as the American supermarket giant Walmart (Asda in Britain). If Asda shoppers, opposed to an invasion, boycotted Asda then Walmart would lose a lot of revenue. Walmart lobbyists then put pressure on the White House and threaten to withdraw financial backing for political campaigning if the invasion goes ahead. It is only at this point that the politicians take notice of the argument against war. The unpopular poll tax that the Tories proposed in the late 1980s got scrapped for two reasons: violent protest and the risk of more civil unrest, but more significantly, the fact that millions of people would have refused to pay it. If people were prepared to refuse to pay their tax, thus getting the law changed, is it that inconceivable that fans could organise themselves to stop paying outrageous prices for football tickets?

Chelsea fan Joe Blogs, upset at ticket pricing, calls for a boycott of games all across the country. A small haystack drifts past him and we hear the sound of the wind in the distance. No-one listened to poor naive Joe and his one man protest didn't have the outcome he was hoping for. If there is ever to be a successful boycott of football then it has to come from an organisation that has some credibility. Off the back of having a protest book out, some people have encouraged me to try and start one. Although the passion of individuals should not be underestimated, hardly anyone knows me, and therefore hardly anyone would listen. If I called for a boycott we'd be lucky if the story was covered by the Haringey Gazette! However, people have heard of the Football Supporters Federation, led by Malcolm Clarke. They stand up for the right issues, such as affordable tickets and safe standing, and they do not mince their words in order to avoid upsetting anyone. The Football Supporters Federation does not favour a boycott, not out of principle, but because they simply do not believe that it will work. My argument is not that a boycott wouldn't fail, of course it could; it very possibly would not work. My argument is this: what's there to lose? If a boycott fails then the clubs will take advantage of fans and know that they can get away with it – sounds a lot like what we have already. Big deal, we'll just go back to carrying on as we are now, it wouldn't be the end of the world. At least then we can say that football is officially fucked, and that we had a go to change it but couldn't pull it off. No regrets, now feel free to make some more money out of us Mr Scudamore.

There is a will for economic boycott but what we don't have is the inspiration to get the ball rolling. Seeing as we live in a world of branding and slogans, a stay-away from football needs a good slogan – Boxing Day Boycott! A clear definitive day on which it will take place and an easy to remember slogan to get the message across. If the Football Supporters Federation were to call for something like a 'Boxing Day Boycott' then it would most certainly be reported on by the national media. Would it catch people's attention? Most certainly it would. Would it have enough momentum to be effective? We don't know until we try. Is it worth giving it a go? Well that's for you to decide.

So many people are adamant that a boycott of football would not work. The same way as not so long ago, the majority of people were totally adamant that we'd never see a black man as the President of America in our lifetime. History does prove to us that anything is possible, yet thirty years of Conservative Thatcherism and New Labour compromise have left us cynical of the power of real change. So the common viewpoint is that the current state of football is irreversible. No different to the way that people dislike the way global corporations dominate the world, but don't feel that there's anything they can do to change things. When the American firm Kraft took over Cadbury and sacked the British workforce, they did so in a manner that suggested that they feared no backlash from the customer because we've been fooled into accepting that *that's just the way it is*. The *Daily Mirror* columnist Brian Reade disagrees with that defeatism and in January 2011 wrote: "*The French or the Germans wouldn't put up with this treatment so why us? Why do we consistently fail to realise that we are in charge here. We could force the likes of Cadbury to reverse their decision in a matter of months. Just by boycotting their calorie packed, obesity-creating bars and switching to someone else's. Imagine them having to crawl back here begging forgiveness for all their lies, their betrayal of a great British workforce and a great British brand... It doesn't have to be this way. We can change things.*"

Tony Benn warned (in the documentary film *Sicko*) that an effective tactic in controlling people is demoralising them – make the masses give up hope which then leads to apathy. That sounds a lot like the modern day football fan, demoralised and beaten into accepting 'reality'.

My suggestion of boycotting matches will be counteracted by the argument that if fans of clubs like Liverpool, Arsenal, Manchester United, Chelsea, Tottenham and Newcastle United boycott games, then thousands of others are lying in wait to take their place. This is hard to argue against, but I will make two points to try and give some credibility to the argument of protest. Firstly, the aim of a mass protest is to make some sort of impact even if all aims are not achieved. The idea that every single club would change for the better is ambitious I must admit. But if a boycott changed the pricing structure of say 50% of football clubs then that's still some achievement. For example, a football club who was part of that 50% would be more affordable to away fans of clubs who were part of the other 50%.

Secondly, a sizable minority can make an impact. If fans of popular clubs did temporarily boycott football then it's true that others would take their place – but not enough to fill a 60,000 capacity stadium week in and week out. A boycott taken by all disillusioned fans might only leave 10,000 empty seats in a 60,000 seater stadium, but that would still be a huge statement. Those 10,000 empty seats would represent the fact that something which was once exclusive no longer is. The mercenaries and trend followers will not want to be part of something that is rejected by thousands of others, and a small gesture is one that can trigger a much bigger one over a period of time.

In recent years Manchester United home games have gone to general sale. For the self-proclaimed 'World's most popular football club' that is simply incredible. By 2010, season tickets even went on general sale – and they still didn't sell out. Empty seats have become a far more common sight at Old Trafford and this is without a major nationwide movement.

In 2010 Manchester United supporters created a green and gold scarf campaign as a protest against the Glazer family's ownership of their club. *Green and gold until sold* was the slogan and the sight of those colours became evocative. What would be both evocative and effective would be thousands more empty seats in place of the thousands of green and gold scarves. United chairman David Gill described the protestors as a 'visible minority'. The 'visible minority' did not scare Gill because the TV viewers around the world would have been blind to it. If you were to replace every fan who wore one with an empty seat, Gill would not be so dismissive of the protesters. "But Matt, if those fans didn't turn up, others would simply take their place," I hear you say. Well not if the protesting fans actually had tickets. It's the fans with tickets who are the ones that could make a designated protest day work better than anyone. No-one can replace a seat that has already been bought. Of course this relies on the fact that fans who have paid good money for admission would then have to make the sacrifice of not going to the game. Although this is a downside, the argument is that the long term benefits could be worth it. I would happily buy a seat at the Emirates in the knowledge that no-one else would be sitting there during a designated protest day.

As an example of someone who has stopped going to matches some might say *what do you care? You don't go to games anymore, butt out*! The point is that the thousands of us who have fallen away don't want to be absent forever. Going to support my team was a major part of my life, and I'm very grateful for so many wonderful memories. I do miss going to games, very much, but I will not go in the current climate. I would only go back once football starts to resemble something that is worth following again and where I can feel dignified in being a paying customer. The thought of football maintaining this rip-off culture for decades to come is not a pleasant one. If empires can crumble then so can anything. Football like everything else is not invincible, and can rise and fall at any time.

Of course the whole concept of a boycott is only relevant depending on whether or not you are happy with the way that football is run. Deep down do fans feel satisfied with the 'product' that is being sold to them, and do they feel dignified being customers in this market?

For the fans who feel at ease with modern football culture, I wish them all the best in what they have. If this is the case for the vast majority of football fans then I'll give all the credit in the world to the people who run the game in bringing such a sense of fulfilment and belonging to so many others. Our country can boast of having the world's most prosperous football league so surely happiness goes hand in hand with that? Well, studies on happiness continually show that being economically superior doesn't make a community any happier if their lives are too focussed on making even more money.

The six most prosperous countries in the world, based on GDP, are USA, Japan, China, Germany, France and Britain. In the numerous polls on happiness within a country, the top ten GDP countries very rarely have credible ratings. Is it because we've come to know the price of everything and the value of nothing? In 2009, the New Economics Foundation's survey on happiness was topped by Costa Rica, a country ranked 86th by the IMF for their GDP. In this happiness survey, China came in at number 31, Germany at 81, Japan at 95, Britain at 108, France at 129, and USA at 150 (Zimbabwe came in last at 178, though I think they can be forgiven for being pissed off at the current state of their lives). There's something wrong in our society if we don't realise just how privileged we are compared to the majority of people who have walked the earth. Our ambition and sense of envy is clouding the reality of our current fortunes. One of the most obscene examples of this self pity was a 2010 chart hit from the American rapper Travie McCoy in which he moans to us that he's not a billionaire. Being a petty millionaire wasn't enough for poor Travie. The song was a big hit because people identified with his 'plight'. Our lives are shit because we're not on the front cover of Forbes Magazine right next to Oprah Winfrey and the Queen. In complete parallel, football in this country can boast of great income, but the people are far from happy. You don't need to do a survey, it's clear as daylight for all to see. Stadiums today are populated by miserable downtrodden people; frustrated that their team's ambitions are not being fulfilled, and so concerned with money and success that they've forgotten their values on what really matters.

I run a small venture, and one thing I'm fully appreciative of is that paying customers have total power over the service provider. Instead of being pawns, fans could realise this power and understand that the future is never cast iron despite modern day cynicism. But for this to happen they first need the inspiration.

Chapter 18
The lost community of football...

Guest chapter by John Lydon

> "I'm not worth a chapter!"
> **John Lydon**

Before moving to Finsbury Park I was brought up on Benwell Road which is directly opposite the Emirates Stadium. Right where the stadium is now, used to be an enormous bomb site after the war and it wasn't cleared up for years. We used to play there as kids, smashing up what was already blown up. The first time I went over The Arsenal was as a six year old with my brother Jimmy in the 1960s. It was against Birmingham City and I remember it well because someone nicked my rattle and my brother's scarf; but we made sure that was never to happen again. Our dad let us go to football because we didn't want to be mollycoddled and I'm very proud that he did. One of my highlights during this era was to see George Best play live when he single-handedly beat us 3-1. His skill and style were so overwhelming that it goes beyond your normal hatred for the opposition. I had many joyous occasions at Highbury; the North Bank was just a fantastic terrace. The warmth involved under that roof if you were Arsenal was quite astounding. It was incredibly family orientated and community based because you'd know everyone in there and they'd know you. Friends, neighbours, relatives, priests – a total community. You'd be watching a game, then turn around to realise that you'd be standing next to one of your school teachers. That was part of the enjoyment and the good thing was that you could always move away to another part of the ground if it was someone you didn't want to be next to. Back then the locals wouldn't put up with any nonsense. If you were up to no good you'd get a smack round your head from someone older telling you that you're out of order. That kind of thing was necessary.

When the ground was overwhelmingly full to capacity there was only one way for kids, or nippers as they called us, to get to the front: we would be physically passed down over people's heads from the back of the crowd, and down to the safer areas along the front. There was simply no other way of getting down there through normal methods. We started off in the school boys' section but you'd always be looking at that North Bank, sometimes more so than the game itself. Terracing is vital to community within football. It was a beautiful and wonderful thing, and to have removed it because of Margaret Thatcher's whim was a total tragedy. It was the police and the steel fences that were at fault for the debacle of Hillsborough, let's get it right. We're not animals to be caged, we're football fans. Steel fences can cause trouble and when you treat people like criminal monkeys then they behave accordingly. A large element of hooliganism was born out of self defence, especially when you'd go up north and there'd be no police protection; though tales from other people surpass anything that I had to put up with.

As goes the game, as goes life. That game was our life. Not the be all and end all, but a major factor, and certainly a very good influence on the youth. Football is an arena of incredible feudalism and pageantry. The power of that live experience can be quite spectacular, overwhelming and both emotionally and physically draining. Sometimes you'd come out of the stadium totally exhausted. Kids today need the experience of that live pageantry. If you get denied access to it then it will kill your desire. It's no use complaining that kids don't kick balls around on the street any more when they don't have the inspiration. Look at the city of Glasgow which has tried to stop kids from playing football in some of the parks. So the kids occupy themselves in other ways, like burning cars. Football is an outlet that in many ways stops violence, it doesn't promote it. After attending a game of high tension, colour and flamboyance, the last thing on your mind would be to throw a brick at someone. There is a new kind of vindictiveness amongst communities that wasn't there before: that mindless stupid destruction for the sake of it. When I was considered a nipper you'd have something to do, somewhere to go, and most importantly something to belong to.

Arsenal was the centre point for the community where I grew up, everything focused around it win, lose or draw. We used to call the area Arsenal Land and it was the glue that kept a community together. The community aspect of football has gone – no question about it. It's been taken away from us, I don't know for what reason other than finance. I feel hugely let down by a great number of things with modern football, but none more so than the lack of community. When the Emirates Stadium was constructed they should have built bars and social clubs for the locals, or let the kids in occasionally to train on the pitch. When I was a kid the players used to come round to the local schools to meet us on a regular basis. You'd be in school and all of a sudden someone like Bob Wilson would walk in and give a speech. It was completely awe-inspiring. It gave you aspirations, you'd want to play for your local team. I remember when the Arsenal talent scouts used to come to the local play-centres on the council estates to hold trials. As a player I thought I was fantastic, even though I was rubbish. I told everyone on the estate that I'd been taken on by Arsenal, and it still remains one of my favourite lies. I just couldn't bear being turned down. Of course no-one believed me, but then again all the other kids were on the same lie. At eleven years of age nothing was more important than that, and to have been taken on would have been the most incredible thing. A club like Arsenal used to have a brilliant youth academy, which has now gone by the way. It was something we were really proud of.

I can't relate to the players of today. Names appear and disappear; play half a game, then never hear from him again. The attitude that some of them show on the pitch can be pathetic: tantrums, hissy fits, diving, handbags, and no idea of team spirit. Where's their blood and guts? I know I've got it, Christ, when I go on stage it's 100% and more every time and I'll do that five to six times a week. Some of this lot can't manage ninety minutes. And the modern footballer wears the worst fucking clothes! Those shirts and jeans with silly fucking squiggly patterns – what a bunch of clowns. It looks the same as gear that gets knocked off down the East End – *yeah we'll get this twat to wear this*. On the pitch they're wearing ballet slippers that I wouldn't mince from the bedroom to the toilet in. Then there's those neckerchief warmers – come on you're grown men, I'd run around in just a nappy for those prices. God help us if we ever have to fight a war with this lot.

Not so long ago it was perfectly normal for players to drink in the pubs with the locals, which I still regard as a beautiful and wonderful thing. The players knew they were safe in that environment. It wasn't about alcoholism: it was about socialisation.

Over the years I've built up some nice contacts with Arsenal players, mainly through charity work; people like Ian Wright, Frank Mclintock, Bob Wilson and Tony Adams who I've got nothing but love and admiration for. As a fan today I haven't got any connection with the current players. I know very little about them other than a soppy contrived TV programme called *Arsenal 360* which consists of set-up scenes involving the players chatting

298

to each other in the locker rooms, or showing us what the new dining rooms look like. It's utterly awful how passionless it is. I simply don't care how smart and elegant the chairman's new board room is, that is of absolutely no interest to us whatsoever.

The last time I socialised with the players was when Bruce Rioch was manager in 1996 and he banned me! I was drinking with the team in the players' lounge and Rioch was having none of it. He quoted a statement similar to that of when the Lord Provost of Scotland applied a ban on the Sex Pistols. It was along the lines of 'There are enough hooligans in Scotland without us importing those from England.' which was a statement that I took as a great compliment. But when the Arsenal manager implied that my influence was leading the players to loutish behaviour and alcoholism the hypocrisy was quite astounding and it really fucking annoyed me. A few expletives were passed his way which got me banned for a bit.

When I was growing up, club merchandise was a very hard thing to hunt down, though I didn't feel the need for a uniform and wouldn't have wanted to stand there like a doughnut in identical outfits. Not that we could have afforded it, which was why my mum knitted me an Arsenal scarf. That scarf had meaning; it wasn't a product or something to manipulate my emotions. That's why I was so furious when someone nicked my brother's one. The most important thing was that you were there in the stadium cheering on your team. Now we have 60,000 people all wearing the same shirt; they feel that without one they're not really part of a thing. Talk about bleating amongst the flock. Might as well get a sheepdog in there (in fact Wenger does look a little bit like a sheepdog!).

How on earth the original supporters are expected to afford the ticket prices today I really don't know. I suppose you can go to a pub to watch games, but what's so great about gawping at a TV screen? Watching football on TV is second best at best. When the admission was reasonable, it was normal to go to neutral grounds when there was nothing better to do on a Saturday. I was always interested to see what the lay of the land was like when it wasn't Arsenal, and me and my brother even went to the odd Spurs game in order to support the away team. We went there to see them get beat. In later years when touring the country with the Pistols I'd sometimes go to games in places like Scouse Land or Leeds – which in those days was as scabrous as you could expect. Elland Road was a couple of sheds plonked here and there haphazardly and a load of bad attitude directed towards anyone from down South.

I look at the background that I had as a football fan and think: how did we go from that, to this. It's so far removed from what I grew up with and loved. I just can't feel wrapped up in this poncification. I'm most furious about the new cannon on the re-designed Arsenal club crest. For a start, the cannon's facing the wrong way. The crest looks like a child's squeezy bottle in the bathroom that you keep shampoo in. We're not the Gunners no more, not with that. It's cheap, tacky and it inspires underachievement. You can't rally round something as mediocre as that, because you just feel silly. I went to Africa a couple of years back do to some filming and it was fascinating because all the kids had bootleg Arsenal shirts with cannon designs that were far better than the official tiddlywinks one. I collected about ten of them.

I also did some filming outside the Emirates Stadium a few years ago, but they wouldn't allow us inside which I felt was bang out of order. Once every two weeks they play host to every wannabe and celebrity, but a story of a local boy made good is not one that they have any interest in being attached to. The first time I went there its appearance struck me as an oversized Dagenham bus depot filled with cinema seats. My immediate reaction was 'fucking hell, needs torching', and I still think that's a reasonable opinion. It's such a cold, alien environment and I don't see anything to draw me in there.

The modern football fan never had to earn their wings or go through the rough years. It's all been ready made for them. What you have at a club like Arsenal now is 60,000 Range Rover owners, who look more like tennis followers. Fans telling other fans to 'sit down' because they're spoiling the view. That is so outrageous – what an absolute liberty. The people making demands on others not to enjoy themselves at a sporting event are the ones who should be removed by the stewards. Let's put the shoe on the other foot, get it right. To tell a football supporter to sit down is a crime in itself, let's start treating it as one. Once you take the passion and enthusiasm away from the crowd then it becomes as boring as golf. It's a really weird bunch that goes over there now; a mass gathering of bankers, accountants, and tourists who don't seem to have any interest in communicating with the people around them and don't respect the environment that the stadium comes from. Most important of all is that they have no understanding of what the people who built a club like Arsenal are truly about. They don't grasp the history and appreciate or understand what it means for a team like Arsenal to have sustained what we have done for so long. Instead it's all about where can they park their SUVs, getting a designer lunch, catching a bit of the game and then leaving the ground in enough time to beat the rush. There's a total lack of commitment in it. I turn the volume on the TV off these days, because the roar of the crowd is not the roar that I come from. It's not from the heart. It seems that there's an impassioned orchestrated singing section, which is such a load of bollocks, especially as no-one's yet to find out where in the ground this section is. In theory you should be able to hear them. How many locals are in that singing section? At least our away fans seem to have a bit more passion when they travel to certain games. Look different, sound different, are different, thank goodness.

I try desperately to still feel that emotion of either joy or pain when we win or lose. I can't help it, it's in my blood. But when I'm in the country I won't go to the ground, because I know I'll be surrounded by a load of moos I don't feel comfortable with and who wouldn't defend me or back me up. I'll watch the games in the pub with people I know, though it does seem like a bit of a sad attempt to imitate something from years ago. I own a couple of season tickets at the Emirates which I give to my brother's kids. It's important that people of my social class and breed can still be represented over there and we can't have a situation where there are no Lydons over The Arsenal. To be honest, it was a sham that I was able to obtain these season tickets. If I hadn't known the right accountant I wouldn't have been able to get them. Matt asked me if I would prefer it if this wasn't mentioned in the book, but I'd rather it be known. It's an appalling state of affairs in that this was the way I was able to obtain tickets; that contacts in higher places enabled me to do this.

Once again, as goes the game, as goes life. Football's cultural downfall is the way England has gone. Everybody just sat back and said why bother – well you should bother a lot. Community matters. People don't know their neighbours any more and don't seem to have any obligation towards each other. Not only does the modern fan not want to know one another, but they find one another a nuisance. Which is appalling because the whole idea of going was that you loved that sense of community.

The Americanisation of the universe has played a part in this, and don't you dare start using the word soccer. The Superbowl is all about commercialism first, and sport second. They've cut that game into many pieces just so there'll be advertisements on the TV; meanwhile the players hang around the pitch waiting for the TV companies to dictate the pace. If you like your beer watered down, better get used to it – because here it comes. I live in America now, and it's a hell of a lot different to the place when the Mayflower bunch first arrived. Everything here is about selling you something, even on your death bed. The hospitals here are full of insurance brokers. And they don't seem to notice that as being a problem. Money and profit are in every walk of life here, which is such a shame because generally speaking, deep down, the American people don't want it. It doesn't make for a better world, it makes for a worse one. But like a cat who hears a noise it doesn't like, it just shuts its ears down. But is that really the kind of condition that a British society can adopt and feel happy with? The first indication I noticed that we could go down such a route, was when that crazy American preacher Billy Graham came over to London with his Crusade tour, and sold out Wembley Stadium night after night. I never thought that British people would go for such Americanised wacky evangelism, but they did lock, stock and barrel.

People who think that they're following a business model are leading us down a path of doom and destruction. If you don't take the practical reality of community and culture as your first prerequisite then everything else is pie in the sky and temporary, like dodgy furniture. Within a short period of time things start collapsing.

There are parallels with the music business as football is now pre-ordained by accountants. But the very wealthy are a fickle bunch, and they'll drop you in it when you least expect; and on a whim because they have no emotional backbone. Lord Snooty and co can show off their corporate boxes, but when that malarkey wears off it will be a different kettle of piranha. In a weird way, I hope that the top eight teams in the Premiership get demoted at some point, because it might knock some sense back into them. They might have to go back to the locals, cap in hand, and beg them to start paying some attention to the club once again. Then they'll realise who the founding stones in this game really are. Clubs have lost the love of the locals and they should be really worried about it. It does not bode well for the future.

Fans of clubs like FC United of Manchester seem to be taking the game back to the community. Their supporters are splendid, hands up in the air and praises be. They're showing us something and making the game exciting again. Their team might be a bit crud, so what? They're an absolute clue in to the old type of warmth and pageantry that football crowds once had. That's the original football vibe, they're not a throwback, they're a throw forward.

Chapter 19
The light that never goes out

"It's never been just about the football, it's about the people you watch it with. In the endless pursuit of money, football has managed to lose its soul. And we are that soul."

My mate Kelvin 'Singer' Meadows 2010

In 2005, American tycoon Malcolm Glazer took control of Manchester United. Many of the United fans were very upset, about this, mainly because Glazer had to borrow the money in order to become the overall shareholder. Their argument was that this would put the club into massive debt (which it did) and would inevitably lead to rises in ticket pricing (which it did). As a result of this take-over, fans from Manchester once again had a club which they could truly feel part of. It is a club where the fans have genuine power and a say, and where the owners' priority is community and not financial profit. FC United of Manchester aka FCUM, are a new football club founded in the year 2005, who play their home games at the stadium of Bury FC. After the Glazer takeover, a strong group of disillusioned Manchester United fans didn't go along with the belief that *if you can't beat them, join them*. FCUM's first ever season was in the North West Counties Football League Division 2, which they got promoted from in 2005-06. A season later in 2006-07, they won promotion from the North West Counties Division 1, then the season after that they were promoted to the Northern Premier League. At the time of writing they are three divisions below the Football League and attempting to build their own stadium in Newton Heath; the very same area where Manchester United began in 1878.

When I first heard about the plans of these United fans and their splinter club, I thought that it was nothing more than an over-ambitious project unlikely to enjoy even short-term success.

But it's possible that FCUM could have a longer and more interesting impact on English football than anyone could have imagined.

Just a year after their formation, they had established a fan base of 4,000 supporters who are prepared to watch FCUM in small northern divisions, against teams who can't even pull in 100 fans. By 2009 their average attendance was 5,000. The 5,000 fans they are capable of attracting is already more than nearby established clubs such as Rochdale, Bury and Stockport County. If this amateur team can pull in 5,000 fans in such a low division, then what would happen if FCUM actually made it into the Football League? The thought of them achieving league status in the future is by no means unrealistic. Every time FCUM get promoted to a higher league, more fans will take them seriously, and if they ever reach the division below the Football League then a regular fan base of 10,000 could very well be achievable. By 2010, the club made the most noticeable impact in their short history by beating League 1 side Rochdale, away from home in the FA Cup First Round. People who had never seen FCUM before were able to catch the game live on ESPN and were witness to a fanatical away support.

The culture within FCUM is a reminder of what being a football fan was once like. Their fans stand up throughout the whole game and appear to make more noise than the 75,000 at Old Trafford do at most home games. They have community and the fans seem to know and trust each other. Kids are allowed to run freely and safely around the stands while their parents focus their attention on the game. I don't want to create a false image of football fan utopia here, but when I attended a FCUM home game I felt a sense of trust, enjoyment and terrace humour that is now so lacking elsewhere in football.

At FCUM there is genuine democracy and the supporters have a say on off the field matters, in a similar way that the fans of Barcelona and Real Madrid do. They are an industrial and provident society. This means that they do have shares obtained though membership, but they can be bought for as little as £1, and all members have the same amount of power regardless of how many shares they have. FCUM have a manifesto that includes the following principles:

1. The board will be democratically elected by its members.
2. Decisions taken by the membership will be decided on a one member one vote basis.
3. The club will develop strong links with the community and strive to be accessible to all. Discriminating against no one.
4. The club will endeavour to make admission prices as affordable as possible, to as wide a constituency as possible.
5. The club will encourage young local participation – playing and supporting – whenever possible.
6. The board will strive as much as possible to avoid outright commercialism.
7. The club will be a non-profit organisation.

The owners of FCUM are not empty-headed dreamers with an unrealistic ideology. They come across as intelligent and passionate people who should not be underestimated. What they have achieved so far is more than most people would have predicted when the club was first formed. The seven principles of this manifesto are all ideals that thousands of football fans everywhere will embrace.

Other clubs in England/Wales that are owned by the fans themselves include Brentford FC, Exeter City and Newport County. Arguably the highest profile are AFC Wimbledon, who are a splinter club of the old Wimbledon FC, who became Milton Keynes Dons FC. The old Wimbledon FC were a club that many football fans all over the country had a soft spot for, because they were a small fish surviving in a big pond and they caused a stir along the way. Milton Keynes Dons on the other hand are a club which fans all over the country do not respect, because of the way in which the owners took away a football club from one community and gave it to another. Fans all over England view Milton Keynes Dons as a false club with no history or credibility and they were soon branded 'Franchise FC'.

No one dislikes the fans of Milton Keynes Dons because they're just supporting their team and are no different to the rest of us. The disrespect lies with the directors and owners who in 2003 quite literally took Wimbledon FC about fifty miles away from one city to another. It was all the brainchild of music entrepreneur and promoter of Milton Keynes, Pete Winkelman, who is now the chairman of the Milton Keynes Dons. He was passionate about the idea of Milton Keynes having a high profile football team and had apparently tried and failed to get other struggling clubs such as Barnet, QPR and Luton Town to move to the city. The directors of Wimbledon FC were prepared to make the move, much to the overwhelming disapproval of the fans. In the 1990s the same fans had feared that their club was going to be moved all the way over the Irish Sea to Dublin. Wimbledon were a Premiership team at the time and because of this I'm sure that the 'Dublin Dons' would have attracted massive crowds at Lansdowne Road. It was a novel and exciting idea for football fans in both England and Ireland. As an Arsenal fan I would have loved to have gone to watch my team play a Premiership match in

Ireland. But it didn't happen and that was the right decision. The basic principle as to why the move would have been wrong was that the most important people in the debate were the established fans of Wimbledon FC, who were happy with their club being in South London. The relocation of their club to Milton Keynes was finally confirmed in 2002, a year before the change was actually scheduled to take place. In Wimbledon's last ever season in South London, the fans returned the favour of rejection and boycotted the matches resulting in the club going into administration. Their home fan base had fallen to just triple figures while their away support went no higher than double figures. By 2010, the average attendance of Milton Keynes Dons was around the 8,000 mark. Their dream is that they will one day attract bigger crowds and rival the big city teams in England.

If Pete Winkelman and Milton Keynes were so desperate for a football team, then they should have been made to do what every other professional club had to do at the beginning of their history. That would be to start at the bottom and make their way up to Football League status. In an incredible and brilliant irony AFC Wimbledon have just shown us how that's done. At the time of going to print they've just made it back to Football League status after only nine years of being founded. They are a club with a special spirit, because of course the other irony is that if there was one team in the country who achieved a rise from the bottom to the very top in such a short period of time, then it was the original Wimbledon FC. They went from non-league football to the top division in just ten years. They were the hope and example for all small clubs in the country. Now their memory represents a fear that all small clubs can justifiably have. The fear that a businessman can take a football club away from a town or city by using small crowds as an excuse, and then relocate in another part of the country.

This franchising is another Americanism that we simply don't want in our game. We have no desire to see our football clubs relocated to other cities through the wishes of the owners and not the fans. The city of Los Angeles has been without an NFL team since the LA Raiders became the Oakland Raiders and the LA Rams became the St. Louis Rams. When the team moves to another state it's not considered to be a newly formed club. For example, the Oakland Raiders claim the history of the LA Raiders. In fact they could move to the other side of the country, become the Cape Cod Raiders and still claim the history of the LA Raiders. From 2003 until 2007, Milton Keynes Dons claimed the history of Wimbledon FC. Therefore in the Milton Keynes Dons honours list they credited themselves as FA Cup winners from the year 1988. The famous final when underdogs Wimbledon beat mighty Liverpool 1-0. This claim on another club's history was without merit, and eventually the trophies and medals were sent home to Merton council in South London. AFC Wimbledon unofficially claim the history of Wimbledon FC. On their website they have released the following statement in justification of them doing so: *"The supporters of AFC Wimbledon believe that our club is a continuation of the spirit which formed Wimbledon Old Centrals in 1889 and kept Wimbledon Football Club alive until May 2002. We consider that a football club is not simply the legal entity which controls it, but that is a community formed by the fans and players working towards a common goal. We therefore reproduce the honours won by what we believe was, and always will be, 'our' club, in our community."* There can be no doubt that AFC Wimbledon is the same club as Wimbledon FC. They have the same club colours and symbols, more importantly the same fans, and in case anyone forgot they're called Wimbledon. The franchise team from Milton Keynes was never the same club from its very formation. The team colours and symbols are different, the fans are different and in case anyone forgot, they're called Milton Keynes Dons. The club recognise this which is why they are now officially a new football team that were founded in 2004, and not Wimbledon FC under a different title.

In effect all they did was to take Wimbledon's place in the Football League while the real Wimbledon FC was taken over by the fans, had a slight name change by one letter, and ended up four divisions below the Football League. Now they've returned and at the time of writing they are only one division apart from the Milton Keynes Dons. In the 2010-11 season they came within a whisker of playing each other in the FA Cup. Had Milton Keynes beaten Stevenage Borough in a First Round replay, then AFC would have been waiting for them in the Second Round. A few UN peace envoys might be needed for a game between these two; it's not regular football rivalry and is no joke. When you take something as important as a football club away from a community the feelings run very deep. A Wimbledon director told me that he actually dreads this potential fixture, because he fears losing control of his emotions in the shared directors' enclosure.

I was privileged enough to be invited to do book signings at AFC Wimbledon and FCUM. My experience of being at both clubs went beyond my expectations. It was such a pleasure to be somewhere where both the owners and supporters shared the same principles and trusted each other. The football itself didn't meet my expectations either; it was actually a lot better than I thought it would be. I expected bog clumsy amateurish play, however there was a credible level of skill and I saw very little difference in the overall standard of play compared with most games that I have attended in Leagues 1 and 2.

Of course having principles usually leads to dilemmas. At FCUM a common perception that I encountered was their fear of compromise – involving the very things that they have rebelled against. To give just one example: being told by TV companies what day and what time they have to play their fixtures. In 2007-08, the owners of the club actually went so far as to ask their own fans to boycott a fixture when an internet TV company dictated the time of the kick-off. There is a genuine fear from people within FCUM of the club rising higher, and many would be happy to stay put where they are in the semi-professional leagues.

I found their fear frustrating mainly because the club has such potential and can go further. I also felt it was insular and that they were missing a wider point. Many of us who are not FCUM fans want them to succeed in order to put fear into those whose aim is to take advantage of football supporters. If a group of disillusioned followers can create their own football club and achieve relative success, then that opens up a bargaining point for fans of other clubs whose loyalty and support is abused. The people who have turned football into an industry of obscene greed have much to fear from the principles of a club like FCUM. In contrast, those of us who believe in football as the People's Game have nothing to fear, because that concept has already been crushed.

If a compromise means that they very occasionally have to play a televised game on a Sunday, in order to be able to afford to financially survive without a shirt sponsor, then maybe the rational option is for them to be flexible. They can of course stay where they are and keep every single principle they have 100% of the time – but what a waste when those values go mostly unnoticed.

By 2010 never was FCUM so relevant; nobody was in any doubt that Glazer's takeover was despicable. Manchester United will always be a global super-club and be well supported no matter what FCUM ever achieve. But if FCUM ever do make it to league status, then a sizable minority of Manchester United fans could very well start to support them as well. They would not be abandoning Manchester United, they would simply be rejecting the money driven culture of the Premiership, which is not the same thing.

FCUM fans are still Manchester United supporters; they make no secret of that. They carry Manchester United symbols to the games and they also sing Manchester United songs. A true United fan can feel as at home at FCUM as he or she would inside Old Trafford these days. One fan even admitted to me that he had reluctantly shed a tear of joy when United beat Chelsea to win the 2008 Champions League Final. An emotion he thought that top-level football was incapable of producing from him ever again.

The one thing I assumed that the fans of FCUM dreamed of, in fact happened to be the one thing so many of them dread. That would be to one day play a competitive game against Manchester United. After all, having been in conversation with fans of AFC Wimbledon, it is clear that an overwhelming desire of theirs is to play against Milton Keynes Dons.

The possibility of a Manchester United fixture however puts fear in the hearts of many FCUM fans because of the divided loyalty that it would bring. Rejecting Malcolm Glazer and the commercial values of the Premier League is one thing, but to cheer on another team against The Reds, well that's another thing altogether. One fan said to me: "If we ever get drawn against [Manchester] United, that will be the day this whole thing dies".

I understand the dilemma facing FCUM fans. But from an outsider's perspective who admires what they stand for – if that fixture ever does happen, it will be the day that FCUM succeeded beyond all expectations, achieved something truly unique and struck a blow for football's soul.

I've concentrated parts of this book on blaming fans themselves for tolerating the commercialism and greed within the sport. But as a supporter, what have I really done other than stop giving financial backing to the money men of football? Those involved in FCUM and AFC Wimbledon have gone so far as to take positive action and create something that they do believe in, rather than just moan and reject something they don't agree with.

Some may not see the idea of fans turning their back on a club as very positive. But the most negative thing we football fans can do is sit back and do nothing. AFC Wimbledon and FCUM appear to have both integrity and ambition, which puts them a class above those whose only goal is money. They prove that the spirit and soul of football really does live on, and let's hope they can do more than just survive, and that they can achieve that priceless longevity.

Of all the FCUM fans that I encountered, none made more of an impression than Mick, an original 'Cockney Red' from the 1960s. His devotion and love for Manchester United (and now FCUM where he believes that the true spirit of Manchester United now lies) was profound. Since the late 1960s he had followed United all over England by hitchhiking from his home in Hertfordshire; failing to reach his destination on only one occasion in over four decades. During my signing, Mick sussed out a weakness and made me an offer that I was happy to accept. He'd buy my book if he could hitch a lift back down to London with me and a fellow Arsenal supporting friend. No problem, there's room in the back, anything to boost sales mate.

Mick is everything that a Cockney Red should be in terms of credibility. I had no business questioning a fan of his devotion about supporting a team so many miles from the area in which he grew up. With Mick, a strong connection with the area as well as the club was clearly evident. Big deal that he was from London, it didn't matter, he was an honorary Mancunian. His affinity to Manchester went beyond football. Manchester is the home of English working class revolution and that was engrained in his love for the city. Red the colour of revolution, red the colour of United and Red also the name of his son (who thank God is not a Chelsea fan). He had composed terrace chants that mixed working class Mancunian culture with his football team. The most notable one being a song about Manchester United players from the early twentieth century who had gone on strike for the right to join a players' union. Mick had also changed the words of the famous Woody Guthrie song *This land is your land* to *This badge is your badge*, which has become a club anthem for FCUM supporters.

Mick's life is clearly and unashamedly laid out on the line: *No country, no family, just United.* I'm not sure if I envy his wife or son, but when it comes to football Mick is the person you want to stand by in the terraces through thick and thin.

Arsenal lost me as a loyal, passionate and regular follower, but I've never been as devoted as someone like Mick; well I never hitchhiked for my team, put it that way. If Manchester United can lose a fan of this calibre, then that truly speaks volumes about the distance there now is between the club and supporter in the so-called 'best league in the world'.

There is a difference between a supporter and a spectator. A supporter follows their team through good and bad. They go to the game to get behind and support their team. They want their team to play good football and to be successful – but it's not demanded. The only thing demanded is that the players try their hardest and show the same passion that they do. The spectator is there to be entertained; in fact they demand to be entertained. Even if their team wins, if they haven't won in style then the spectator goes home unhappy and phones up *TalkSPORT* to complain about the lack of flair in the team. Top-flight modern football crowds now have too many spectators and not enough supporters. In contrast, at clubs like FCUM and AFC Wimbledon, there are only supporters.

Sources

Quotes from Aime Jacquet, Jorge Valdano, Hugo Sanchez, Diego Maradona and Jimmy Hill are from *History of Football*, DVD – Freemantle Media.

Quotes from Melvin Bragg and Bobby Charlton are from *The Rules of Association Football, 1863*, Bodleian Library.

Quotes from Brian Clough are from *Cloughie: walking on water – my life*. Headline Book Publishing.

Quote from Ashley Cole is from *My defence*. Headline Book Publishing.

Other Sources

Evening Standard, Daily Mail, Daily Mirror, The Daily Telegraph, The Guardian, The Independent, The London Lite, The London Paper, The Metro, The Sun, The Daily Star, The Times and USA Today.
BBC News and Sport.
www.bbc.co.uk
Getty Images
BBC FIVE LIVE
Sky News.
BBC Panorama 2006.
Tax Rate Information Centre.
Wikipedia.
Powerslam (magazine).

Sport (magazine).

Time (magazine).

Times Online.

Deloitte.

www.Statistics.gov.uk

www.Soccerlens.com

Football Fans Census website.

The Football Network.Net.

TalkSPORT

Official websites for Premiership football clubs up to the 2011-12 season.

Official club websites for Millwall FC, Milton Keynes Dons FC, Oakland Raiders, FC United of Manchester and AFC Wimbledon.